Cultural Competency

FOR HEALTH PROFESSIONALS

Shirley A. Wells, MPH, OTR
Roxie M. Black, MS, OTR/L

AOTA® The American
Occupational Therapy
Association, Inc.

AOTA Staff

Joseph C. Isaacs, CAE, Executive Director
Chris Bluhm, CPA, CMA, Associate Executive Director, Business Operations Division
Jennifer J. Jones, Director of Publications

Krishni Patrick, MA, Editor, Books
Barbara Dickson, Editorial Assistant
Carla A. Kieffer, Publications Assistant

Robert A. Sacheli, Manager, Creative Services
Sarah E. Ely, Book Production Coordinator, Cover and Text Design

The American Occupational Therapy Association, Inc.
4720 Montgomery Lane
PO Box 31220
Bethesda, Maryland 20824-1220

Disclaimers
This publication is designed to provide accurate and authoritative information in regard
to the subject matter covered. It is sold or distributed with the understanding that the
publisher is not engaged in rendering legal, accounting, or other professional service.
If legal advice or other expert assistance is required, the services of a competent
professional person should be sought.
—*From the Declaration of Principles jointly adopted by the American Bar Association
and a Committee of Publishers and Associations*

It is the objective of The American Occupational Therapy Association, Inc., to be a
forum for free expression and interchange of ideas. The opinions expressed by the
contributors to this work are their own and not necessarily those of either the editors
or The American Occupational Therapy Association, Inc.

ISBN: 1-56900-105-7

Composition by R. Lynn Rivenbark, Macon, Georgia
Printed by Boyd Printing Company, Albany, New York

We dedicate this book to our mothers,
Sammie L. Polk Wells (who passed away in 1989)
and Faylene N. Perkins, who gave us the courage to
believe in ourselves, the strength to follow our beliefs,
and the wisdom to see the value in all people.

Contents

About the Authors

Shirley A. Wells, MPH, OTR, has been a practicing occupational therapist for over 20 years. From the Navajo Indian Reservation of Arizona, the border cities of Texas and Mexico, the urban areas of Minnesota, to the rural areas of Texas, she has worked with a variety of ethnic and diverse populations. She has presented, nationally and internationally, on topics related to diversity, multiculturalism, and health care. She has authored books, including *Multicultural Education and Resource Guide for Occupational Therapy Educators and Practitioners* (1994) and *A Guide to Reasonable Accommodation for Practitioners with Disabilities: Fieldwork to Employment* (1998), and a video, *Creating a Multicultural Approach and Environment* (1996). She has also served as the manager of the Multicultural Affairs Program of the American Occupational Therapy Association. She is currently in private practice as well as a consultant on diversity and the Americans With Disabilities Act.

Roxie M. Black, MS, OTR/L, is an associate professor and director of the master's in occupational therapy program at Lewiston–Auburn College of the University of Southern Maine. Roxie graduated from Boston University in 1968 and specialized in pediatric practice, beginning in the American Schools in Fuerth, West Germany in 1969–1970. After 14 years of pediatric practice, Roxie became an OT educator—her profession for the last 16 years. For the last 10 years she has been studying about and infusing gender and multicultural content in her classes. She was co-editor of the November 1992 special issue on feminism in *The American Journal of Occupational Therapy.* Her scholarly work has focused on diversity and multicultural issues in occupational therapy curricula, and she is currently working on a PhD in educational studies at Lesley College in Cambridge, Massachusetts, where her research is in multicultural curricula for health professionals.

Foreword

Congratulations! You have taken the first step to becoming culturally competent by picking up this book. Much research and personal revelation lie ahead. Have you ever had an aunt or family friend give you a gift that you did not want or appreciate? Have you ever had them give you that same gift on every gift-giving occasion? Or worse, have you had a significant other call you by a pet name that you did not like or misinterpret almost everything you said? Even in these simple, well meaning acts, the receiver was offended and perhaps even hurt in the process. If something this simple can be offensive and hurtful within culture, what about weeks of well-meaning therapy or health services by someone who has little knowledge or appreciation for the nuances of language and the meaning of dress, customs, and other cultural norms? This book provides a guide to recognizing the importance of cultural awareness and gives useful exercises and explanations for moving beyond the obvious. As twenty-first century health professionals, it is unethical and unacceptable to trample on and ignore culture as being essential to effective human health care intervention.

Cultural competence is a lifelong process of taking on another person's perspective. Cultural competence is about responding to cues, developing an attitude of openness, and developing an ability to listen without interpretation. Further, it is about learning to respect and appreciate the core values, central to the lives and well-being of our clients. Becoming culturally competent is the key to providing effective and meaningful solutions to human dilemmas rather than simply applying generic solutions that may fit some people and may have worked in the past. A lack of cultural sensitivity signals to the client that he or she is a statistic and that you cannot relate, and whatever he or she feels as a person is not important to the intervention process. In a "client-centered" health profession, we should find it strange that our best researched solutions often do not work and are not worshipped or held in such high regard by our clients. Have you ever thought it strange when clients continue to arrive to treatment late, or when they focus on how soon the treatment would be over rather than eagerly engage in the treatment process? Whatever happened to that expensive piece of equipment that you worked so hard to get to send home with the client? What a waste and what a sad excuse for expensive health care solutions when we, as well meaning health care providers, miss the value of culture in providing quality health care.

People who are committed to making a difference in the lives of those they serve will continue to reach beyond the scientific borders of professional disciplines and make a meaningful connection with the individual behind the service need. In our quest for answers to human suffering, illness, injury, and disease, we must not only focus on discovering the best theory, research method, or using the latest technology, but we must develop best practices that seek to understand the effect of culture on health and wellness.

The authors of this text give the reader a conceptual framework for understanding cultural competence as a twenty-first century health care provider. The well-researched information provided, with practical activities and explanations, guides the reader through perspective-taking exercises and solutions that develop one's cultural understanding. The varied teaching-learning styles used in the book gives one a practical appreciation for the effect of culture on practice. Beliefs, attitudes, values, customs, and lifestyle choices shape our destiny toward health and wellness. As health care providers, the choice of knowing how to provide meaningful intervention may well be found in the pages of this book.

SHIRLEY J. JACKSON, MS, OTR/L, FAOTA
Howard University

 *Preface*

The issue of cultural diversity, multiculturalism, and inclusion has a long and often tortured history in the United States, going back to the first encounters with Native Americans. It was at the heart of what was a major crisis in this nation—the Civil War. It was behind the evacuation, incarceration, and resettlement of Japanese Americans during World War II. And most recently, it was the goal of the Americans With Disabilities Act of 1990 (ADA, Public Law 101-336). Some say that diversity, multiculturalism, and inclusion are a subtext of all American history, whether one talks about the notion of the "melting pot" or the post–World War II efforts in the area of civil rights, the desegregation of public schools, and mainstreaming people with disabilities.

Issues of cultural diversity, multiculturalism, inclusion, and cultural competency are not trivial or ephemeral matters. They are a reality. They are transforming cities, a number of states, and the world. The voices of America, particularly those voices that have been excluded or muted or silenced, are stepping up to the podium and demanding to be included. They are demanding that their realities be given credence, their needs be addressed, and that their approaches be added to the pool of acceptable alternatives. Persons from culturally diverse groups are seeking an America expansive enough to accommodate the culture of their disparate roots while they simultaneously adopt norms of mainstream culture.

The concept of cultural competence promotes a society of pluralism and multiculturalism. It promotes a society that welcomes differences and will not force people to change their beliefs and values to be accepted. As more and more differences in language and culture are present in the health care system, the need for cultural competency becomes imperative. Being unskillful in interacting with people of different cultures can lead to erroneous assumptions, interpretations, and judgments. If we as health care providers are going to respond appropriately to clients with varying identities, cultures, backgrounds, lifestyles, and needs, we must become culturally competent in our approaches and interactions. To effectively serve our clients, diversity and inclusion must be more than a human resource initiative. They must become a fundamental competency.

In becoming culturally competent there are several principles to heed. One principle is: *the culture and lifestyle of people do matter*. These characteristics along with gender, age, education, religion, class, sexual orientation, geographic location, disabilities, life experiences, and a host of others, shape the individual and his or her responses. They can create emotions of serenity, expectations, and doubts; questioning of beliefs; and direct confrontations for the practitioner as well as the client. To overlook or ignore their influence and importance is to deny the individuality of people.

What is culture? *Culture* is a complex and multifaceted social phenomenon that has powerful influences on all aspects of modern life. It is a boundary that conditions people into a reasonable cohesive system for viewing themselves and their work. It is the shared ways that people make sense of reality, a collective sense of members of social groups. It is the rules by which *civilized* life will be played (Seelye & Wasilewski, 1996). Culture includes a broad range of social factors that lead people to think and act in very unique ways. There are regional cultures that influence member's behaviors; there are culture groups based on ethnic, racial, and religious commonalties; and there are cultural behaviors exerted by biological gender. People of different ages, educational and socioeconomic levels, occupations, and sexual orientation belong to their own cultural group. Persons who share certain health conditions—such as being blind, deaf, or diabetic; or suffering from cancer, AIDS, a spinal cord injury, or a terminal illness—have their own cultural orientation. Even in the area of health, therapists have a culture different from other health care providers, such as physicians and nurses (Kreps & Kunimoto, 1994).

As multicultural beings, every individual is composed of a unique combination of different cultural orientations and influences. Each person belongs to many different cultural groups. It is important that we recognize the influences of many cultures on our lives. On the basis of his or her own heritage and life experiences, every individual develops a personal idiosyncratic multicultural identity. When working with clients and families, having the ability to cross or bridge these cultural boundaries ensures the provision of holistic, sensitive, individualized, and effective intervention and care.

Another principle is: *be aware of discriminatory intent versus discriminatory effect*. As health care providers, no one intentionally sets out to discriminate against or alienate clients. *Not* acknowledging the client's ethnicity or cultural background, adhering to the client's cultural norms and behaviors, or integrating the client's perceptions can, unintentionally, give the effect of discrimination. Many clinical procedures and approaches that appear unbiased may, in fact, limit, prevent, or eliminate participation of some groups of individuals. We must view the world from the perspective of the client, family, and caregiver.

This book looks at the *why* and *how* of cultural competency in the health care field. Section I focuses on the *why* of cultural competency for health care providers. It outlines the reality of the demographic changes that are occurring in this country—a declining birth rate, a *graying* of America, a growing ethnic population, and so forth. It looks at the ways that culture influences and shapes a person's sense of being and identity. This section describes the health disparities and equalities based on race, ethnicity, gender, and socioeconomic status. Ethnic minorities tend to have higher mortality rates and lower life expectancies. Motor vehicles and traffic injuries account for about 60% of all injury deaths for Native Americans. The rate of tuberculosis is five times higher for Asian Americans and Pacific Islanders than the general population.

Section I looks at the effect of culture on access to care and utilization of services. Barriers to care extend beyond the issues of underinsured and uninsured. Location, inconvenient hours, long waits, transportation, attitudes, and acculturation level are but a few barriers. This section also examines the limited, inconsistent, and lack of health statistical data from most national sources by socioeconomic status, gender, race, and ethnicity. Issues surrounding the increasing difficulties in respecting cultural differences and ethical decisions in the delivery of health services as well as the lack of cultural research are presented. As health care providers do we have a moral obligation to ensure access to health care to all people? Is it unethical to deny practices or treatment that are clearly unacceptable by Western standards? Do we blindly accept all and any research on race, ethnicity, and gender as truth? Lastly, Section I introduces a global perspective of acceptance of differences.

Section II of the book investigates the dynamics of power, language, and privileges as they shape cultural interaction. The distribution of power between cultural groups as well as the therapeutic relationship and its effect on our interactions are discussed. The privileges of being a member of a dominant group (White Americans), or being male, or possessing other characteristics of power are often invisible to those who have them. Those who do not enjoy these privileges are very aware of the differences and the ways they are exhibited. Two elements that help determine and maintain positions of power, whether individual, organizational, or structural, are prejudice and discrimination. This section also examines the relationship between language and power in the health field. Is health jargon used to separate providers from consumers? Does a person's linguistic style affect his or her social status?

Section II takes an extraordinary look at what it means to be a White American in today's society. It explores the power, privileges, perceptions, guilt, emotions, and a host of other adjectives used to describe or not describe this racial group. The authors offer thoughts on being a White American clinician who works with diverse clients. The section "Can a White Teacher Teach about Diversity?" (in chapter 8) lays the foundation for becoming a culturally competent person.

Sections III and IV focus on the *how to* of becoming culturally competent health care providers. Section III presents the framework for developing competency. Based on the premise of multicultural education and three sociological perspectives, the Cultural Competency Education Model offers a framework for developing and acquiring the knowledge and skills needed to be culturally competent. This model is designed to foster understanding, acceptance, knowledge, and constructive relations between individuals of various cultures and differences.

By addressing three areas—self-exploration and awareness, knowledge, and skills—health care providers can develop a lifelong plan for becoming culturally competent. The model can be used to structure teaching and learning strategies.

Using the Cultural Competency Education Model, Section IV presents specific ways of integrating culture into the day-to-day operation of clinical practice and educational experiences. A step-by-step plan is provided to assist the health care professional to design his or her course for becoming culturally competent. Case studies and suggested activities are used to further the learning process. Lastly, Section V shares two personal life stories, journeys, and appeals for pursuing cultural competency.

The twenty-first century will bring a diverse environment not only for the United States but also the world. Health care professionals must *go beyond* being aware of and sensitive to differences to a level of mastery of strategies and skills in cross-cultural communication and interaction. New models, skills, partnerships, and perspectives are needed if we are to address and improve the health status of all Americans. Success in this new millennium favors culturally competent practitioners.

Clearly, we stand at a critical crossroad in which the future of health care seems to be linked with a rare opportunity for historical choice and change. Equally clear, cultural diversity, multiculturalism, inclusion, and cultural competency cannot be viewed as passing fads. For in the United States what is explicitly emerging is a new reality. So, whatever the future may or may not hold, it will be culturally diverse.

References

Kreps, G. L., & Kunimoto, E. N. (1994). *Effective communication in multicultural health care settings*. Thousand Oaks, CA: Sage.

Seelye, H. N., & Wasilewski, J. H. (1996). *Between cultures: Developing a self-identity in a world of diversity*. Lincolnwood, IL: NTC Publishing Group.

 *Acknowledgments*

We wish to thank our friends and colleagues who encouraged us to write this book, the occupational therapy practitioners from diverse backgrounds who shared their insights and stories, and the students who read parts of the manuscript and offered their advice and feedback.

We want to give special thanks to Shirley Jackson, Program Director of the Occupational Therapy Program at Howard University, for all of her support, encouragement, and advice regarding the development of this book.

Explanation of Terminology

The terminology used to described racial and ethnic populations in the United States has changed over time. The self-reporting of ethnicity and race have also been found to change from year to year. In this book a variety of descriptors are used. To help you understand why certain terms are used over others, the following rules apply:

- For research and statistical reports, the racial and ethnicity categories defined by the Office of Management and Budget (OMB) Directive No. 15 will be used (see chapter 4);

- For research and statistical studies, the actual terminology or descriptors appearing in the study will be used; and

- For general content, the following terms will be used: Native Americans, African Americans, Asian Americans and Pacific Islanders, White Americans, and Hispanics.

Scope of Diversity

I

"To be free—to walk the good American earth as equal citizens, to live without fear, to enjoy the fruits of our toil, to give our children every opportunity in life—that dream which we have held so long in our hearts is today the destiny that we hold in our hands."

—Paul Robeson

Objectives

The information in this section is intended to help the reader

- understand the social realities of a changing world, the influence of culture and ethnicity on human growth and development, and the challenges of providing effective and quality health care to all people;

- understand how race, ethnicity, class, gender, and culture influence health status, access to care, and scope and quality of health care;

- realize the effect of culture on ethical and moral decision making in delivering health care;

- recognize barriers to effective cultural research and their effects on health care policies and delivery; and

- appreciate the need for a global perspective of diversity.

CHAPTER ONE

The Need for Cultural Competence

Key Points

- Change is inevitable.

- The diversification of the United States is a result of several demographic trends:

  – A declining birth rate

  – An increasing aging population

  – An increasing immigrant and refugee rate

  – An increasing ethnic population

  – An increasing death rate

  – An entering workforce of persons of color, women, and immigrants

- The political, social, and economic forces and events of society, both historically and currently, affect not only the lives of individuals but also institutions and health systems.

- Ethnicity and culture are influential variables that shape an individual's identity and behaviors throughout the human growth and development process.

- Some elements of culture can be modified or changed over time and with experience, but the core remains the foundation of a person's sense of being and identity throughout his or her life.

- Western medicine is grounded in mainstream America and expounds a system in which individualization and independence are highly valued, yet it has evolved into one that emphasizes individuals as the focal point of problems and intervention.

- Cultural competency is a primary key to providing quality and effective health care to all people.

The new century will find our societies in uncharted waters. It will be multiracial, multicultural, and multilingual. It may best be known as the years of *cultural imperative* in the United States. Never before have the issues of race, ethnicity, and cultural differences had such saliency for so many Americans. The whole notion of cultural competence, cultural diversity, multiculturalism, inclusiveness, cultural pluralism, and a host of other such terms will dominate every aspect of our lives—business, education, health care, and policies.

The notion of cultural competence will have critical and far-reaching implications for all institutions designed to provide medical assistance, health care services, and rehabilitation to the people of this nation. These shifts will challenge health care providers to perform evaluations and develop treatment plans and programs with consumers who may not share a common language with them; who may have differing beliefs, values, attitudes, and behaviors; and who may have a different understanding of the nature of work, leisure, and self-care. Concepts of cultural competence have even more urgency as the racial, socioeconomic, and gender disparities in health status increase. Changes in health care delivery models and reimbursement are also driving practitioners towards cultural competent systems of care. By understanding and acknowledging others' customs, beliefs, and values, health care providers have a better chance of evaluating and producing effective outcomes.

Cultural competence should be a constant pursuit of a health care provider for three reasons: the social realities of a changing world, the influence of culture and ethnicity on human growth and development, and the challenge of providing effective and quality health care to all people. These reasons explain not only the need for cultural competency, but also the knowledge and skills necessary to communicate and interact with persons of any culture. Each reason plays an important and unique role in establishing the justifications, parameters, and directions for cultural competence.

Social Realities

Diversity is part of us, our neighborhoods, our schools, and our community. The United States is extremely culturally pluralistic, socially stratified, and racially divided. Diversity of race, culture, ethnicity, social class, religion, language, and national origin are fundamental features of interpersonal interactions and community structures. In the past, societies have operated primarily within a monocultural and monolingual perspective. Persons were expected to give up the values, norms, and beliefs of the society they were emigrating from in favor of new opportunities (Parrillo, 1997).

Immigrants today are unwilling to passively and submissively assimilate the way that they may have in generations past. Many different persons and groups have stopped trying to deny their ethnicity for the sake of being accepted unconditionally into mainstream society. They now insist that there is no inherent contradiction between allegiance to their own ethnic and cultural heritages and being an American. Instead these dual identities are complementary and should be respected and promoted.

Focus on Culture and Ethnicity

There are many persons who become uneasy with the increasing emphasis on culture and ethnicity in this country. The legacies of racism, oppression, and discrimination are still unacceptable and untenable concepts that most Americans ignore or pretend do not exist. These issues evoke concepts and images that go against the grain of fundamental American values and ideals.

People tend to personalize racism and oppression, and they cannot objectively view society and institutions from such perspectives. There is a natural American tendency to dismiss racial differences or cultural variations as key factors to be addressed by persons or institutions. There are several major precepts of American culture that question the need for cultural competence (Cox and Blake, 1991; "The New Politics of Race," 1991), such as the following:

- The American value system supports the belief that a person can overcome any condition (i.e., the old *pull yourself up by your bootstraps* or *mastery over nature* concepts).

- The Civil Rights movement of the 1960s took care of any and all racial or ethnic problems.

- Cultural diversity is really a form of reverse discrimination.

Demographic Changes

The diversification of the United States is the result of several trends, such as the declining fertility and birth rates, especially among White Americans. The U.S. population has steadily declined since 1960. This trend is explained by an increase in deaths coupled with a decrease in births. From 1990 to 1995, the total U.S. population grew at an aver-age annual rate of 1.9% (U.S. Department of Health and Human Services [HHS], 1997). By 2050, the population is expected to increase by a rate of only 0.2%. Large groups of baby boomers (born between 1946–1961) will start dying off faster than new Americans are born, curbing the net population increase (Census Revelations, 1990).

Between 1990 and 1995, the overall birth rate declined 7% to 65.6 births per 1,000 women 15 to 44 years of age, yielding a national birth rate of 14.9 births per 1,000 population (HHS, 1997; Mattson, 1992). The rate was 14.2 in 1997. According to the 1990 Census, the number of persons 10 to 24 years of age declined because of the delayed births of the late 1960s and early 1970s. Delayed child bearing has been a growing trend in the United States during the past 25 years. The per-centage of women 25 to 29 years of age who had not had at least one live birth increased from 20% in 1965 to 42% in 1985 to 44% in 1995. Among women 30 to 34 years of age, the percentage that had not had a live birth increased from 12% in 1970 to 25% in 1985 to 26% in 1995 (Census Revelations, 1990; Mattson, 1992; HHS, 1997). For White Americans in 1990 the rate was 1.7 children per mother, as opposed to the much higher birth rates for ethnic groups. For African Americans the rate was 2.4 children per mother, for Mexican Americans 2.9, for Viet-namese 3.4, and for Hmongs 11.9 (Sue, 1992).

Over the next 10 years the U.S. population will grow by 42 mil-lion. By the year 2010, the United States will have between 264 and 282 million residents. By 2025, these figures will increase from 262 to 348 million. Racial minorities will make up 17.6% of the population. Population growth will be extreme for African Americans and Hispanics, and it will virtually come to a halt for White Americans by the year 2025. Hispanics will account for 47% of the growth, Blacks 22%, Asians 18%, and Whites 13%. Persons with physical and mental impairments will comprise the single largest minority—approximately 45 million people (Mattson, 1992; Census Revelations, 1992; HHS, 1994).

The aging American population is another trend that has con-tributed to the diversification of the United States. Between 1990 and 2000, the fastest growing segment of the population is 45 to 54 years of age. The oldest baby boomers turned 40 in 1986, ushering that massive generation into midlife. During the 1980s, 11 million people entered their 30s and are now poised to turn 40. In 1989, 21.1% of the population was over 55 years of age. This figure is expected to balloon to 26.5% by 2010. Between 1990 and 1995, the elderly population 75 years of age and over grew at an average annual rate of 2.5% to 14.8 million; and the population 35 to 54 years of age, which includes the baby boomer generation, grew at an average annual rate of 3.3% to 73.5 million. In the first decades of the new century, the fastest growing group will be between 55 to 64 years of age. This will be a *graying* of America (Census Revelations, 1990; HHS, 1997; Jacobs, Siegel, & Quiram, 1996; Mattson, 1992).

Another trend prompting diversification is the rate of immigration. The number of immigrants (documented or undocumented) and refugees are at an all-time high. Current waves of immigration consist of primarily Asian (34%) and Hispanic populations (43%), as well as other visible racial and ethnic groups. Unlike their early European counterparts, these two groups are not necessarily oriented toward joining the melting pot. Instead, they often prefer to retain their cultural heritage. They are bicultural. Overall, the net civilian immigration is expected to level off at approximately 500,000 by the year 2000. Anywhere from one half to three quarters of a million immigrants are expected to make the United States their home each year for the remainder of the twentieth century (Mattson, 1992; U.S. Government, 1995; Jacobs, Siegel, & Quiram, 1996; Sue, 1992).

The implications associated with the dramatic increase of non-White populations are extensive. The bulk of the entering workforce in the 1990s is and will be persons of color, women, and immigrants. They will account for 85% of the net growth of the nation's labor force. By the year 2000, women will constitute 47% of the labor force and 60% of its new entrants. Non-Whites will constitute almost one third of the workforce (Workforce Trends that Could Impact your Career, 1997; Jacobs, Siegel & Quiram, 1996).

These demographic changes mean that

- change is inevitable—the chances of working for a woman boss at some point in a career are greater, baby boomers passing into middle and old age will age the labor force, and career mobility and success will belong to those who work well with people of all backgrounds;

- more and more differences in language and culture will be present in health care systems;

- intercultural experiences and knowledge of other languages will be real assets; and

- cultural competency will be a primary key to success in such a multicultural environment.

These changes have already begun to transform the United States and will continue to affect organizations, health care, government, communities, and society as a whole. They will change those who live and work in America for the rest of the decade and beyond. The increasing demographic changes of the U.S. population make cultural competency for all health care providers imperative.

Sociopolitical Reality

Many persons in the United States still believe that there is a single acceptable way to live, look, and behave as an American and a human being. Standards for determining what is appropriate are embedded in a Eurocentric orientation. Many are taught that European and American cultures, institutions, and lifestyles are superior to those of other groups (Gay, 1994; Jones & Carter, 1996). Any deviation from these standards are scorned, subjected to discrimination, or considered un-American. This leads to "denial of equal access to institutional opportunities, political rights, economic rewards, and respect for human dignity" (Gay, 1994, p. 5).

Persons of color do not operate or control the major institutions of American life (e.g., government, corporations, financial markets, the media, health care institutions), and their thoughts and beliefs do not become public opinion. Their views do not shape the actions of the major institutions, nor can they create and maintain stereotypes about themselves. The struggles of persons from diverse backgrounds in the United States have been primarily for physical and cultural survival (Browser & Hunt, 1996).

Although laws exist to prohibit discrimination based on race, color, gender, age, creed, and disability, U.S. society continues to be plagued by attitudes and behaviors that are derogatory to some and preferential to others. Unofficially, inequality flourishes, manifesting itself in racism, ethnocentrism, prejudices, favoritism, discrimination, cultural appropriation, and cultural hegemony. These inequalities and the power to change them—enlightened or otherwise—belong primarily to Whites, not because they are the majority of the nation's population but because they have the status and associated power to maintain and advance their perceived interests (Bowser & Hunt, 1996).

Worldviews of both the health care provider and client are linked to the historical and modern day experiences of racism and oppression. The practitioner, client, and clinical process are influenced by the state of race relations in the larger society and by the racial and cultural biases of his or her forebears. Health care providers need to recognize that treatment does not occur in isolation from larger events in our society. The political, social, and economic forces and events of society affect not only the lives of individuals but also institutions.

Cultural competency is a potential way for correcting these distortions and inequities. It is a way of helping persons perceive the cultural diversity of the U.S. citizenry so that they may develop pride in their own cultural legacy, awaken to ideas embodied in the cultures of their neighbors, and develop an appreciation for the common humanity shared by all persons on earth.

Human Development

Culture influences and shapes our total way of living—including values, beliefs, linguistic expression, patterns of thinking, behaviors, and attitudes. Human behaviors result from a process of socialization. Socialization occurs within a specific cultural and ethnic environment and is passed on from generation to generation. Hence, humans are social beings that carry within them their individual biological and psychological traits as well as legacies of their ethnic group's historical background, collective heritage, and cultural experiences.

The influence of culture and ethnicity is established early and thoroughly in the process of human growth and development, and it prevails thereafter for the remainder of one's life. Some elements of culture can be modified over time and with experience, but the core features continue to be the mainstay of a person's sense of being and identity throughout life (Gay, 1994; Devore & Schileslinger, 1981). The stages of the life cycle are acted out in as many variations as there are groups. Major life events—birth, childhood, adulthood, marriage, parenting, late life—are perceived and carried out according to norms of the group and culture. The movement to each stage of life may entail varying degrees of stress if the expected task cannot be filled in a way that meets the standards of the individual or the group. For example, at the celebration of baptism the Hispanic child becomes a member of the church. At the same time, *campadres* of the parents present themselves as caretakers, assuming responsibility with the parents for continuity in the faith as well as in the group. The giving of gifts celebrates entry into the social or cultural group. This ritual symbolizes its importance.

The marking of a Jewish boy through circumcision is a *sign of union,* a permanent mark that incorporates him into the social group.

The gifts given represent acceptance and continuity. Hispanic and European infant girls are marked by the ceremony of ear piercing. This act identifies the baby as a girl, one of us, and in need of protection. Whether children are viewed as small replicas of adults or treated matter-of-factly is often a matter of culture and class perception. Viewing adolescence as the preparatory period for the tasks of adulthood, as opposed to viewing it as the beginning of adulthood, is a matter of historical and group perspective (Devore & Schileslinger, 1981).

Ethnic and diverse groups do not all perceive gender roles in the same way. Some encourage gender equality, and some do not. Unequal gender treatment begins early in life. Parents instill differences in subtle ways, including what they pack in children's lunch boxes. In Ecuador, a girl between 16 and 20 years of age does not go out unaccompanied. Going out without a chaperone would ruin her reputation. The stage of development not only gives us a clue as to the expected universal tasks, but it is also an indication of the ethnic dispositions that are imposed upon those tasks (Dresser, 1996).

Life cycle, stage, universal task, ethnic disposition, and social class are all essential considerations for understanding the cultural perception and development of people. When people claim that they treat everyone the same, as human beings, regardless of ethnic identity, cultural backgrounds, or economic status, they are creating an antilogy. "A person's humanity cannot be isolated or divorced from his or her culture and ethnicity. One cannot be human without culture and ethnicity, and one cannot have culture and ethnicity without being human" (Gay, 1994, p. 7).

To make responsible health care decisions, providers must be conscious of how culture shapes not only their own but also their clients' attitudes, values, behaviors, and beliefs. Understanding that we are all products of our own culture and live within given values and beliefs frees us from the effects of prejudiced interpretations. Being knowledgeable of the influence of culture on human development ensures that each person is an individual with his or her own identity, culture, background, and lifestyle.

Health Care

Western medicine is grounded in mainstream American cultural concepts. In matters of institutional policies, practices, and power, Anglo-centric and middle-class cultural values predominate (Gostin, 1995; Wilson, 1998). This is illustrated in the policies that govern access to parts of the health care system on the basis of one's ability to pay. The ability to pay is often based on one's occupation and insurance coverage, which in turn is based on one's cultural background. Another illustration of the predominance of Anglocentric, middle-class culture is that the major power positions tend to be held by persons from this cultural background. Health care programs and systems are developed to meet a conglomerate of needs identified by concerned emissaries of the dominant society and culture. The negative implication of monoculturalism is that the White American culture is such a dominant norm that it acts as an invisible veil, preventing health care providers from seeing health services as potentially biased systems.

America's health care traditionally expounds a system in which individualization and independence are highly valued. In reality, it has evolved into a system that acknowledges and emphasizes individuals as the locus of problems and intervention (Gostin, 1995; Kavanagh & Kennedy, 1992; Wilson, 1998). It involves an intricate web of evaluation, diagnosis, and intervention. This approach assumes that people are composed of parts to be examined for problems, diagnosed, treated, and released. The role of the person seeking health services is to submit to the authority of the health care provider and follow their advice (Reed & Sanderson, 1992). Health care providers assume that disease prevention is a matter of biological intervention without consideration for the individual, environment, economic, social, or spiritual factors. One example would be to provide training in the use of a variety of adaptive equipment and devices without considering the client's needs, culture, home environment, financial resources, and the lifestyle changes the equipment will induce.

The challenge is to provide appropriate care to increasingly diverse consumer populations. There is an even greater need to eliminate practices and policies that require consumers to adapt and conform to a limited set of norms and values in order to use resources. The influence of patterned culture characteristics, the symbolism and meaning attached to those characteristics, and the effects of those and other population-level factors have not been consistently incorporated into health care providers' knowledge bases (Kavanagh & Kennedy, 1992; Krep & Kunimoto, 1994).

Summary

Cultural diversity is a normative description of U.S. society. Ethnicity and culture are influential variables in shaping individual identity and behavior. They shape human behavior, values, and beliefs. Cultural socialization is ingrained early and deeply in the human personality and persists thereafter. Because most persons in the United States live in ethnic and cultural enclaves, they have only tangential interactions with and superficial knowledge of persons who are culturally different from them. Regardless of whether the differences are rooted in age, culture, health status and condition, experience, gender, ethnicity, sexual orientation, or race, they all affect the health system.

Cultural competency would allow the consumer to receive treatments reflective of both the dominant culture of the health care system and the individual. Multiculturalism is a form of holistic practice that interweaves the cultures of the consumer, health care system, provider, and traditional health practices.

Because change is so very frightening and difficult, it has been far easier to ignore cultural and ethnic diversity rather than confront it. It is at the front door again and more pressing and urgent than ever. For various reasons, American society is at a point where it can no longer ignore the issues and hope that the issues of cultural competence will disappear. There are many forces shaping the present focus on ethnicity and culture that require the nation to face the cultural imperative if it expects to maintain a leadership position in the 21st century.

These are all reasons for becoming culturally competent. Being knowledgeable of the influence of culture on human development ensures that each client is an individual with his or her own identity, culture, background, and lifestyle. Being knowledgeable of our own attitudes, values, behaviors, and beliefs and their effects on others frees us of prejudiced interpretations.

References

Browser, B. P., & Hunt, R. G. (1996). *Impacts of racism on white Americans.* Newbury Park, CA: Sage.

Census revelations. (1990). *American Demographics* (pp. 22–30).

Cox, T. H., & Blake, S. (1991). Managing cultural diversity: Implications for organizational competitiveness. *Academy of Management Executives, 5*(3), 45–54.

Devore, W., & Schileslinger, E. (1981). *Ethnic-sensitive social work practice.* St. Louis: C. V. Mosby Company.

Dresser, N. (1996). *Multicultural manners: New rules of etiquette for a changing society.* New York: Wiley.

Gay, G. (1994). A synthesis of scholarship in multicultural education. *Urban Education Monograph Series*. Oak Brook, IL: North Central Regional Educational Laboratory.

Gostin, L. O. (1995). Informed consent, cultural sensitivity and respect for persons. *Journal of the American Medical Association, 274*(1), 844–845.

Jacobs, N. R., Siegel, M. A., & Quiram, J. (1996). *Profile of the nation*. Wylie, TX: Information Plus.

Jones, J. M., & Carter, R. T. (1996). Racism and White racial identity: Merging realities. In B. P. Browser & R. G. Hunt (Eds.), *Impacts of racism on white Americans* (2nd ed., pp. 1–23). Newbury Park, CA: Sage.

Kavanagh, K. H., & Kennedy, P. H. (1992). *Promoting cultural diversity: Strategies for health care professionals*. Newbury Park, CA: Sage.

Kreps, G. L., & Kunimoto, E. N. (1994). *Effective communication in multicultural health care settings*. Newbury Park, CA: Sage.

Mattson, M. (1992). *Atlas of the 1990 census*. New York: MacMillan.

The new politics of race. (1991, May 6). *Newsweek*, pp. 22–31.

Parrillo, V. N. (1997). *Strangers to these shores: Race and ethnic relations in the United States* (5th ed.). Boston: Allyn & Bacon.

Reed, L., & Sanderson, S. N. (1992). *Concepts of occupational therapy* (3rd ed.). Baltimore: Williams & Wilkins.

Sue, D. W. (1992). The challenge of multiculturalism. *The American Counselor* (pp. 6–14).

U.S. Government. (1995). *U.S. population estimates by age, sex, race, and hispanic origin: 1990 to 1994*. Washington, DC: Bureau of the Census.

U.S. Department of Health and Human Services. (1997). *Health United States 1996–1997 and injury chartbook*. Hyattsville, MD: Centers for Disease Control and Prevention, National Center for Health Statistics.

U.S. Department of Health and Human Services. (1994). *U.S. Public Health Service: Improving minority health statistics*. Washington, DC: Public Health Service, Office of Minority Health.

Wilson, G. (1998). Medical ethics and culture: Whose ethics should we follow? *Contemporary issues* [online]. The Cleveland Clinic Foundation, Department of Bioethics. Retrieved from: http://www.ccf.org/education/bioethic/ biocon.

Workforce trends that could impact your career. (1997). *Dimension in diversity* (pp. 5–6). Lincoln, NE: Southeast Community College.

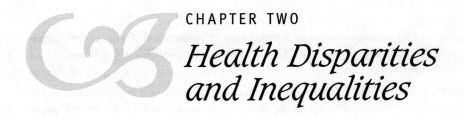

CHAPTER TWO

Health Disparities and Inequalities

Key Points

- Closing the gap on health disparities and inequalities among different racial and ethnic groups, the genders, and socioeconomic levels will lead to better health for all Americans and is a responsibility of all health care providers.

- Comprehensive health data by race, ethnicity, gender, or socioeconomic status are limited, inconsistent, unreliable, or totally missing from most national statistical data sources. Ethnic minorities tend to suffer more from certain diseases, have higher mortality rates, and lower life expectancies.

- Data on a socioeconomic status should be routinely analyzed as risk factors for poor health status or adverse health outcome.

- Gender makes a difference in health—teenage pregnancies, rape, domestic violence, pulmonary disease, heart diseases, breast cancer, obesity, and depression—throughout the life span.

- Individual health cannot be assessed without considering one's economic capacity, accessibility of health care services, the availability of culturally compatible services, or gender and genetic makeup.

- Race, ethnicity, gender, and socioeconomic levels are powerful factors that affect health status, access to health care services, and the scope and quality of health care.

The next time you go to the movie theater where the audience is about half African American and half White American, take a look around. Everyone may look equally healthy. But chances are, more of the African Americans in that theater will eventually need a heart transplant than the White Americans—because heart disease affects African Americans more than it does White Americans. The same is true for cancer and many other diseases. Going right down the list of some of our major killers, the story is the same.

We have been—and remain—two nations: one majority and one minority, separated by the quality of our health. Ethnicity, race, gender, and socioeconomic status are powerful factors that affect health status, access to health care, and the scope and quality of health care. Many studies have documented racial and ethnic disparities in the United States health care system. Ethnic minorities suffer from certain diseases at up to 5 times the rate of White Americans. Several studies have shown that the highest rates of poverty are concentrated among the same U.S. subgroups of non-White persons affected by a disproportionately worse health status. Greater deprivations in health strike those who are poor and non-White.

To fully understand the causes of disparities in health, it is essential to consider the effect of socioeconomic and cultural factors, such as income, education, health behavior, nativity, and recent immigration, all of which affect health status and access to care. This chapter will explore some of these factors, as well as the challenges of eliminating these inequalities. Reducing the health disparities among different racial and ethnic groups, genders, and socioeconomic levels will lead to better health for all Americans.

Health Status

Since 1993, key indicators have shown that the nation's overall health has greatly improved. Childhood immunizations are at an all-time high, infant mortality is at a record low, and HIV and AIDS rates are falling. More women are having regular mammograms and clinical breast exams, and Medicare will now pay for mammograms for women 40 years of age and older (Brooks, 1998; U.S. Department of Health and Human Services [HHS], 1998b; Shalala, 1998). Despite these improvements, the gap between Whites and non-Whites, poor and nonpoor that existed for many diseases have remained about the same. The health status differences between poor and nonpoor, Whites and persons of color, and adults and children can be linked to differences in available services, the nature and quality of those services, and the ways persons are helped to make use of them.

Problems with accessing the health care system result in lower health care usage and contribute to worse health outcomes, especially for the poor and other disadvantaged groups. Ethnic minorities and the poor have higher rates of disability, disease, and death for a wide range of health conditions. Ethnic populations and the poor suffer from many adverse health conditions, which may not necessarily result in death, but do result in a lower quality of life (Geiger, 1996; Pinn, 1998; Shalala, 1998; Smith, 1998; U.S. Public Health Service (USPHS), 1994). The link between poverty and living conditions, health, and early death are real for millions of Americans.

Health Data

To evaluate and understand the causes of racial, socioeconomic, and gender disparities in health status and to develop approaches to overcome them, health data are essential. Monitoring and reporting on the changing health status and the emerging risks to health and service delivery have been major contributions of setting national disease prevention and health promotion objectives, such as Healthy People. Healthy People 2000/2010 are national initiatives and objectives used to achieve improved health for all Americans. Through a national process, people from across the country help define and are pursuing a prevention agenda for the nation. *Health status data* describe the well-being or ill health of the population so that interventions for preventing and controlling diseases can be determined and implemented and the effect of these interventions evaluated. Health status data include a variety of measures—including the nature and extent of mortality, morbidity, and disability in persons and populations. It also includes measures of their knowledge, attitudes, and behaviors concerning health and health care.

Health data encompass all major areas of health statistics, including population and health status, health resources, health care usage, and health care expenditures, as well as program management data. In support of its mission to protect the health of the nation's population, the Public Health Service (PHS) relies on a wide variety of timely and reliable data. Epidemiological and statistical information is needed on a periodic basis. To meet these needs, PHS uses a variety of data collection, analysis, and dissemination activities. Available health data come from a variety of sources. The National Center for Health Statistics (NCHS) is one component of the Centers for Disease Control that serves as the federal government's designated agency for general-purpose health statistics. The NCHS obtains information on the health of the U.S. population through several mechanisms, such as the National Vital Registration System, National Health Interview Survey, National Health and Nutrition Examination Survey. The NCHS also uses record-based surveys of health care providers, including hospitals, physicians' offices, and nursing homes. Some of the information is collected annually, whereas some is obtained more frequently.

In addition to the NCHS, other centers and agencies collect data from surveys that include items on race and ethnicity. They include the Center for Chronic Disease and Health Promotion, Alcohol, Drug Abuse, and Mental Health Administration; National Institute on Drug Abuse; National Institute on Mental Health; Agency for Health Care Policy and Research; and others, such as the Indian Health Service, National Institutes of Health, and Health Resources and Services Administration. Although improvements have been made, data on the health status of racial and ethnic minority populations in the United States still have a number of gaps.

Getting information on the U.S. ethnic and gender health is not easy. There are no clearinghouse statistics that list comprehensive data by race, ethnicity, gender, or socioeconomic status. In terms of race and ethnicity, a wide variety of health data are available for White and African American populations, but considerably less national data are available for other ethnic populations. Some sources site figures for Whites and Blacks; others list African Americans, Hispanics (who may be Black or White), and Whites; and yet others list African Americans, American Indians (or Native Americans), Asian American and Pacific Islanders (AAPI), Hispanics, and Whites. Few tables list any further breakdown by ethnicity. Very limited data are available on the Asian and Pacific Islander population in the United States. National data tend to mask the diversity among Chinese, Japanese, Korean, and most recent immigrants from Southeast Asia. Similarly, national data on the total American Indian population are limited. Nor is there such information available according to tribal affiliation.

To complicate matters further, the definition of race and ethnicity has changed over time, and self-reported ethnicity has been found to change from year-to-year (see chapter 4, "Culture and Research"). With this in mind, the data presented here have been gathered from a variety of sources and years. All groups may not be represented.

Racial and Ethnic Populations

Life Expectancy

Life expectancy reached an all-time high of 76.1 years for the nation in 1996. Record life expectancies were reached for White and Black men (73.8 and 66.1 years, respectively), and for Black women (74.2 years). The gap in life expectancy between Blacks and Whites has narrowed from 6.9 years to 6.5 years after several years of increasing (HHS, 1998c). Between 1970 to 1992, the life expectancy for Hispanics was 74 years for men and 79.2 for women (U.S. Ethnic Health Data, 1998). The life expectancy for AAPIs, 80.3 years, is higher than that for the total population. Among AAPIs, Japanese have the highest life expectancy, 82.1 years; Native Hawaiians have the lowest, 68.3 years (Healthy People 2000, 1997; Table 1).

Mortality Rate

Health status is often described in terms of statistics on deaths. The death rates for racial and ethnic minorities are often higher than for White Americans. For 1996, the overall mortality rate for African Americans continues to be about 60% higher than for White Americans; for Asian Americans the rate is 37% lower than for White Americans; and the rate for Native Americans under 55 years of age (60% for men and 85% for women) are higher than for White Americans. The mortality rate for American Indians, 1 to 4 years of age, is almost double than for White American children. For Hispanic Americans, the overall mortality rate is 20% lower than for non-Hispanic White Americans, except for men 15 to 44 years of age. The death rate for this group is 53% higher than for non-Hispanic White men (HHS, 1997; Fastats, 2000).

Table 1. Life Expectancy at Birth

All Americans	76.5 yrs.	All Males	73.6 yrs.
African Americans	70.2 yrs.	All Females	79.4 yrs.
Hispanic Americans	74.0 yrs.		
Asian Americans & Pacific Islanders	80.3 yrs.		
American Indians & Alaskan Natives	73.0 yrs.		

Note. The data in this table originate from several useful resources: Healthy People 2000 (1997, September 13), *Asian Americans and Pacific Islanders progress review*, Washington, DC: U.S. Department of Health and Human Services, Public Health Service; U.S. Department of Health and Human Services (1998c, March), Race, ethnicity, class, and culture, *Closing the gap: Office of Minority Health Newsletter*, p. 5, Washington, DC: Author; and U.S. Ethnic Health Data (1998), Life expectancy, *FWFS-ethnic health data*, retrieved from http://www.fwfs.com/healthdata/htm.
Table by Shirley A. Wells

Table 2. Mortality Rate

Age-Adjusted Death Rates per 100,000 in 1997:
African Americans	738.3
American Indians	455.5
Hispanic Americans	325.3
Asian Americans & Pacific Islanders	277.4

Leading Causes of Death:
Heart Diseases
Cancer
HIV/AIDS
Youths and Young Adults—Homicide, Motor Vehicle Accidents,
  Firearms, Suicide
Elderly—Unintentional Injuries, Suicide, Homicide

Note. The data in this table originate from several useful resources: Fastats (2000), Fastats, A to Z, retrieved from: http://www.cdc.gov/nchswww/fastats/hstatus.htm; U.S. Department of Health and Human Services (1997d), *Health United States 1996–97 and injury chartbook,* Hyattsville, MD: Centers for Disease Control and Prevention, National Center for Health Statistics; and U.S. Department of Health and Human Services (1998b, March), Minority health in the U.S.: An overview, *Closing the gap: Office of Minority Health Newsletter,* p. 5, Washington, DC: Author.
Table by Shirley A. Wells

In 1996, infant mortality reached its lowest rate for the nation (7.2 deaths per 1,000 live births). Rates for Blacks declined 6% (from 15.1 to 14.2), whereas the rate for Whites declined 5%—reducing the gap in infant mortality between Blacks and Whites for the first time in several years (HHS, 1998b; Fastats, 2000). The rate is still nearly 2 1/2 times higher for African Americans—and 1 1/2 times higher for Native Americans—than for Whites. These discrepancies are thought to be due largely to prematurity and low birth weight (Fastats, 2000; Healthy People 2000 Progress Review for AAPI & HA, 1997; Shalala, 1998; U.S. Ethnic Health Data, 1998; Table 2).

Disease-Based Mortality Rate

For most of the 12 leading causes of death in the United States, mortality is higher for African Americans than for other racial and ethnic groups. Heart disease is the number one cause of death for all groups in the United States, followed by cancer. Compared with White Americans, heart disease mortality was 41% lower for Asian Americans and 49% higher for African Americans in 1995. Stroke was the only leading cause of death for which mortality is higher for Asian Americans (18% higher) than for White Americans (HHS, 1997d). In 1995, the death rate for HIV infection for Black women was 9 times the rate for White women. The death rate for HIV infection for Black men was 4 times that of White men. The homicide rate for young Black men was 12 times the rate for young White men (HHS, 1997d). The homicide rate for Hispanics, American Indians, and Asians was 5, 3, and 1.5 times the rate for White American youths (HHS, 1997d; Healthy People 2000 Progress Review for HA, 1997).

Among teenagers and young adults, the unintentional injury death (mostly motor vehicle, traffic, and firearm injuries) accounted for about 60% of all injury deaths for Native Americans, about 64% for Asians and Hispanics, and 29% for African Americans (HHS, 1997d). The suicide rate for this same age group was about 1.5 times higher for American Indians, Hispanics, and Blacks than for Whites (HHS, 1997d; Healthy People 2000 Progress Review for AI/AN, 1995; Healthy People 2000 Progress Review for AAPI, 1997). Among the elderly in 1995, unintentional injury death accounted for 85% of the deaths in each racial and ethnic group except for the Hispanic elderly. The suicide rate for the elderly was highest among White Americans—1.3 times higher than Asians, 2.4 times higher than Hispanics, and 3.7 times higher than Blacks (HHS, 1997d). Asian American women have the highest suicide rate among women 65 years of age and over (Healthy People 2000 Progress Review for AAPI, 1997). The homicide rate, on the other hand, was highest for the Black elderly population, about 5 times higher than the White elderly (HHS, 1997d).

Health Diseases

Hypertension is exceptionally high for African Americans. It is the leading health concern for Black Americans. Between 1988 and 1994, the prevalence of hypertension for non-Hispanic Black men was about 40% greater than for non-Hispanic White or Mexican American men. The rate was also substantially greater for Black women (34%) than White women (19%) or Mexican American women (22%) (HHS, 1997d). African Americans with hypertension are 5 times more likely to develop chronic heart failure and 10 times more likely to suffer from kidney failure than the general population (U.S. Ethnic Health Data, 1998).

The number of African Americans and Native Americans with diabetes is 3 times the national average. The prevalence of diabetes among American Indians and Alaska Natives—70 per 1,000 versus 30 per 1,000 for total population—exemplifies the seriousness of this health problem in this population (Healthy People 2000 Progress Review for AI/AN, 1997). Native Hawaiians have 2 times the rate of Koreans and Filipinos living in the state, and 3 times the rate of Chinese in Hawaii. Asian Indians and Samoans have shown rapidly increasing rates of diabetes after immigrating to the United States as compared to other AAPI (Shalala, 1998; U.S. Ethnic Health Data, 1998). The prevalence of diabetes among Mexican Americans increased from 54 to 66 cases per 1,000 between 1986 to 1994 (Healthy People 2000 Progress Review for HA, 1997).

      The increase of AIDS cases during the past five years has been greater for minorities than Whites. Over half of the cases occur in Blacks and Hispanics, although these groups comprise less than one fourth of the total U.S. population (Healthy People 2000 Progress Review for HA, 1997; U.S. Ethnic Health Data, 1998). These figures are even more alarming for women and children. Three quarters of the cases among women and children are among minorities. Seventy-five percent of AIDS cases in women are Black and Hispanic women, and 80% of the cases among children are Blacks and Hispanics (HHS, 1996a; HHS, 1998b; Horwitz, 1998; U.S. Ethnic Health Data, 1998).

      Asthma, the leading chronic disease among children, is also more common among racial and ethnic minorities. More than one fifth of African American children living in older homes have elevated blood lead levels. The number of Hepatitis B cases among Asian American children is 2 to 3 times higher than for all children. Hepatitis rates have increased for American Indians, although they have decreased for the total U.S. population. Tuberculosis rates have increased for AAPI and Hispanics, but they have decreased for Whites. Tuberculosis incidence rates for AAPI are five times higher than the rates for the total population. African Americans are affected 3 times and Hispanics 2 times as hard with tuberculosis. Infectious diseases, such as tuberculosis and hepatitis, are more common among immigrants (HHS, 1998b; HHS, 1997b; HHS, 1996c; Healthy People 2000 Progress Report for AAPI, 1997; Healthy People 2000 Progress Report for HA, 1997).

      Vietnamese women are 5 times more likely to face cervical cancer than White women. Hispanics suffer from stomach cancer at 2 to 3 times the rate of Whites. Chinese Americans are 4 to 5 times more likely to be victims of liver cancer. Asian American women are among those at high risk for osteoporosis. And about 800 to 1,000 migrant and seasonal farm workers (the majority of which are Mexicans, followed by Puerto Ricans, Caribbean Blacks, and African Americans) die each year as a direct consequence of pesticide exposure (HHS, 1998b; HHS, 1997b; HHS, 1996b; Healthy People 2000 Progress Report for AAPI, 1997; Shalala, 1998). Research also shows that racial and ethnic

Table 3. Major Health Diseases

African Americans	Heart diseases; cancer; cerebral vascular accident; diabetes; hypertension; cirrhosis; anemia; AIDS/HIV; asthma
Asian Americans and Pacific Islanders	Heart diseases; cancer, such as cervical and liver; cerebral vascular accident; diabetes; pneumonia; influenza; suicide; depression; infectious diseases, such as hepatitis, tuberculosis; osteoporosis
Hispanic Americans	Heart diseases; cancer, such as stomach cancer; cerebral vascular accident; cirrhosis; hypertension; diabetes; AIDS/HIV; pesticide exposure
American Indians	Heart diseases; cancer; cerebral vascular accident; diabetes; alcohol-related diseases; unintentional injuries; homicide; suicide; substance abuse; pneumonia

Note. The data in this table originate from several useful resources: Fastats (2000), Fastats, A to Z, retrieved from: http://www.cdc.gov/nchswww/fastats/hstatus.htm; U.S. Department of Health and Human Services (1997d), *Health United States 1996–97 and injury chartbook,* Hyattsville, MD: Centers for Disease Control and Prevention, National Center for Health Statistics; U.S. Department of Health and Human Services (1998b, March), Minority health in the U.S.: An overview, *Closing the gap: Office of Minority Health Newsletter,* p. 5, Washington, DC: Author; and U.S. Ethnic Health Data (1998), Life expectancy, *FWFS-ethinc health data,* retrieved from: http://www.fwfs.com/healthdata/htm. Table by Shirley A. Wells

minorities less frequently receive immunizations, screenings for cancer, or regular care.

Data on health status are developed from a variety of sources, and issues of data availability and data gaps vary considerably depending on the source. Data are needed to help determine why important health disparities persist. The identification of risk is important to elucidate possible etiologic factors for a disease and to plan and develop appropriate prevention measures or educational intervention (USPHS, 1994; Pappas, 1994; Shalala, 1998). Race and ethnicity are important variables in the generation of hypotheses to determine risk. When differences in health status are observed, the differences may represent the contribution of a number of factors—culture, income level, education, occupation, acculturation, and stress or discrimination—that affect health status in a positive or negative way (Table 3).

Socioeconomic Status

Socioeconomic level plays an important role in the maintenance of health, perception of illness, and the pattern of treatment sought by a person. It is one of the major factors influencing ethnic minorities and gender health status. Poverty has been shown to have a high correlation with adverse health, primarily because it serves to limit or preclude access to needed health services (Smith, 1998). Poverty rates are based on a set of money income that varies by family size and composition. Families or persons with incomes below their appropriate level are classified as below poverty.

Poverty Rate

According to the U.S. Census Bureau, in 1998, 13.7% of the population lived below the poverty level. This meant that 34.5 million people lived in poverty, including 13.5 million children. The southern United States was the most impoverished region; about 14% of poor Americans lived in the West. The South achieved an all-time low with a poverty rate of 13.7%. The Northeast had a rate of 14.0 % and the Midwest 10.3%. Twenty-seven percent of the poor lived in metropolitan areas while 8 million (14%) lived outside the metropolitan areas. By race and ethnicity, the poverty rate was 26.1% Blacks, 12.5% Asian and Pacific Islanders, and 25.6% Hispanics. Even though the poverty rates for Whites (10.5%) and non-Hispanic Whites (8.2%) were lower than those for the other racial and ethnic groups, the majority of poor people in 1998 were White. Among the poor, 68% were White, and 46% were non-Hispanic White (U.S. Census Bureau, 1999).

In 1998 the number of poor and the poverty rate for children under 18 years of age had declined to 18.9%, but it still remains disproportionately high. The number of poor children is down to 13.5 million. Children make up less than 26% of the U.S. population, but close to 40% of the poor. The poverty rate for Mexican American children was 39%, Black children 42%, Puerto Rican children 53%, and only 16% of White children (U.S. Census Bureau, 1999).

> Poor children are more likely than nonpoor children to be
> born too soon or too small, to die in the first year of life or
> during early childhood; to experience acute illness, injuries,
> lead poisoning, or child abuse or neglect; and to suffer from
> nutrition-related problems and chronic illnesses, and hand-
> icapping conditions. . . . Certainly a large part of the prob-
> lem is economic (Klerman, 1991, p. 3).

The total number of families living below the poverty level in 1998 was 10%. However, the rate remained disproportionately high for Black (26.1%) and Hispanic (22.7%) families. It was 12.7% for AAPI families. More women-headed households (29.9%) lived below the poverty level than married-couple (5.3%) families. Even though married couples had the lowest poverty rate, they comprised 40% of the share of poor families as compared to female head householders (53%). Among the women-headed households, the racial and ethnic breakdown was 27.2% White, 43.7% Black, and 50.9% Hispanic (U.S. Census Bureau, 1999).

Relationship to Health

According to the HHS (1997d), health status and family income are strongly associated. In 1994 the age-adjusted percentage of persons with a low family income (less than $14,000) who reported fair or poor health was 5 times higher than for persons with an income of $50,000 or more (20% and 4%). Similarly, the age-adjusted percentage of low-income persons affected by limitation of activity due to chronic health conditions was almost 3 times the level for high-income persons (26% and 9%). The disproportionate number of African Americans living on the economic margins is almost certainly one of the reasons they are more frequent victims of serious health problems.

Relationship to Race and Culture

Racial and ethnic populations in the United States differ widely in social and cultural characteristics as well as in economic status. However race is often used as a proxy for social class, and ethnic minorities are often disproportionately represented among the economically disadvantaged in the United States. Analyses sometimes focus on race differences alone, when we know that poor education, lower income, and lower occupation standing of ethnic populations have important effects on the health survival of both adults and children (Otten, Teutsch, Williamson, & Marks, 1990; Haan & Kaplan, 1985; Kleinman, 1990). Racial disparities are often reduced when these factors are taken into account. Similarly, racial disparities in health care are reduced when individual health behavior is considered (USPHS, 1994).

The complex ways in which social and economic class and race and ethnicity create disadvantages and produce disparities in health are not clearly understood. Studies have shown that when social factors, such as occupational status, income and education are used to understand the distribution of health risks, disparities in health status decrease for ethnic minorities and low-income populations (Cromptom, 1993; Williams, 1990). In a study of a national sample of deaths, Rogers (1992) demonstrated that the racial differences between Blacks and Whites in death rates were eliminated after an adjustment for income, martial status, and household size. When socioeconomic factors are controlled in cause-specific mortality, he found that Blacks are at a lower risk than Whites for death from respiratory diseases, accidents, and suicide; they are equally at risk for cancer and circulatory diseases; and Blacks are at higher risk for infectious diseases, homicide, and diabetes. Waitzman & Smith (1994) found that a declining occupational status and low occupational status were associated with an increased incidence of hypertension for both Black and White men.

When ethnic and cultural patterns of health beliefs are considered along with socioeconomic status, the social distribution of risk behaviors may be a factor in explaining the growth of health disparities among racial and ethnic populations. Perez-Stable et al. (1994) demonstrated differences between Latinos and White non-Latinos in behavioral risk factors. When age, gender, education, and employment were adjusted, Latinos were less likely to drink alcohol or to smoke and were more likely to be sedentary. Latino women were less likely to have ever had a Pap test or clinical breast examination than non-Latino White women. The authors suggest that health-promotion campaigns must address the audience's ethnicity.

Data on socioeconomic status are not routinely analyzed as risk factors for poor health status or adverse health outcome. Public health research has only begun to look at the relationship between social disadvantages, race, and culture to understand increasing disparities in health status. Comparing racial health differences to social classes is a first step. Applying the understanding of the dynamics of race and class to improve access to health care, change behaviors through health promotion, and reform the health system is more important (Pappas, 1994; Shalala, 1998). Closing the gap between racial, ethnic, and class groups will require altering the socioeconomic conditions of the disadvantaged in the United States. The fight against poverty must be a part of any overall strategy for eliminating health disparities.

Gender Issues

The issue of gender is emerging as one of the most complex and public issues of the 1990s. As women demand an integrated, multidisciplinary approach to disease prevention and health maintenance throughout the life span, the number of teenage pregnancies rises, and the effects of poverty on single families are questioned, the effect of gender needs to be more closely examined.

Gender makes a difference in the social and political activities in this country. Rape, assault, and domestic violence are public health problems affected by one's gender. According to "Assessing and Improving Women's Health" (WREI, 1994), an estimated four million women are severely assaulted by their male partners every year. Twenty-five percent of women in college have been victims of rape or attempted rape. Regardless of the type of violence (e.g., rape, other sexual assaults, robbery, or assault), the rate of women's victimization has increased 30% since 1990. The victimization rate decreased with increasing household income. Women with lower incomes ($10,000 or less) experience higher rates of violence perpetrated on them than women with higher incomes ($50,000 or more). Women of all races and ethnicity are about equally likely to report violence by a husband, ex-husband, boyfriend, or ex-boyfriend (HHS, 1997d).

Gender makes a difference in health throughout the life span. A teen mother starts one out of three families with a woman head of the household. In 1996, the teen birth rate had decreased to 12% from a rate of 62% in 1991. The largest decline (23%) was among Black teens. Hispanic teens now have the highest teen birth rates in the country (Brooks, 1998; HHS, 1997d). In 1995, more women (17%) than men (14%) reported being in fair or poor health. The chronic obstructive pulmonary diseases rate nearly doubled for women, although it remained stable for men between 1990 to 1995. During the same time period, the death rate for lung cancer decreased for men (9%), whereas it increased for women (5%). Lung cancer continued to rise among older women (26%) and fell for younger women (15%) (HHS, 1997d).

The leading cause of death among women is coronary heart disease; they are more likely than men to die after a heart attack or to have a second attack (HHS, 1996c; HHS, 1997d). One of every eight women can expect to be diagnosed with breast cancer in her lifetime. Breast cancer is the second leading cause of death among women. Between 1989 and 1992, there was a decrease in mortality rates of more than 5% for White women, but there was a 3% increase for African American women (HHS, 1995). Women are at high risk for osteoporosis largely because they have less bone mass and lose bone faster than men, particularly with the onset of menopause. It is estimated that 50% of women 45 years of age and over, and 90% of women 70 years of age and over, have some degree of osteoporosis. White and Asian women have the disease more often than African American and Hispanic women (HHS, 1996b).

Being overweight or obese poses a major health challenge. According to the National Heart, Lung, and Blood Institute, 97 million American adults, or 55% of the population, are overweight or obese. Thirty-six percent of all women are overweight or obese. It is a serious health problem for women of color—affecting 48.2% Mexican Americans, 40.2% Puerto Ricans, and 50% African Americans. The highest prevalence of obesity is among Native Hawaiian (63%) and American Samoan (66%) women. Obesity among Native Americans varies by tribal affiliation—61% Yaqui Indians, 60% Seminoles, 63% Navajos, and 75% of American Indians from Oklahoma nations. Asian women, in general, have the lowest rates of obesity. It is reported that 26% of Filipino Americans, 18% of Japanese, and 13% of Chinese women are obese (Urgo, 1998; U.S. Ethnic Health Data, 1998). Being overweight or obese is also more common among women with lower incomes and less education. Fifty percent of African American and 31% of White women living in poverty were obese in 1991, compared to 37% of African American and 21% of White women with incomes 3 times the poverty level (HHS, 1998a; Urgo, 1998).

Studies have consistently found depression to be 2 or 3 times more prevalent among women than men. Elderly Asian American women suffer from very high rates of depression and suicide. At 45 years of age the rate for Chinese women begins to rise, and the rate for Japanese women 75 years of age and over is higher than that of White women in the same age group (Oxendine, 1998). Low self-esteem has been found to be a common characteristic of teenage girls. Girls are at 10 times greater risk than boys for anorexia and other eating disorders (Thiers, 1994).

Being homosexual also results in major health care challenges. Most people are familiar with the increasing research and literature on HIV and AIDS and its high occurrence among male homosexuals in the United States. But many people may not be aware that lesbian women may be at higher risk for breast, ovarian, and uterine cancer, and for heart disease and stroke than heterosexual women. Traditionally, little research has been done with this group, but the results of a survey presented at the National Lesbian and Gay Health Conference by Dr. Ann Pollinger Hass (1997) suggests that lifestyle differences may account for the increase. Lesbians who reported on the survey tended to weigh more than heterosexual women, exercised less, had an increased history of drug or alcohol problems, and were less likely to have children or breast-feed, all of which might increase their risk for disease.

Aging produces a triple risk for lesbian women. Deevey (1990) argues that the exclusion of research on elder lesbians may result from a triple minority status for older lesbians combining age, gender, and sexual orientation. Our society is beginning to increase health research on elders, but we tend not to look at the sexuality of older women and men. "Societal attitudes toward aging and towards homosexuality play an important role [in the diminished research on this group]" (Quam & Whitford, 1992).

A more current report (Health Central, 1999) from the Institute of Medicine, entitled "Lesbian Health: Current Assessment and Directions for the Future," indicates that there are still not enough research dollars allocated to study the health risks of all lesbian women. Dr. Jocelyn White, editor of the *Journal of the Gay and Lesbian Medical Association,* notes that "within the medical arena, lesbians have been an overlooked and understudied population."

If the disparities in health statues and health outcomes for women are to be eradicated, then the knowledge about why these disparities exist is essential. It is imperative that we expand the science base that underpins medicine by increasing the medical community's understanding of gender differences and the interplay of race and culture in illness. Research is needed to provide the scientific foundation for changes and improvements in health practice and health care policies. Study populations must include women and minorities so that these contributing factors can be identified and studied. Only by ensuring the inclusion of women of all backgrounds and circumstances in clinical studies can we develop appropriate preventive and treatment interventions to improve the health and longevity of all women in the United States (Table 4).

Access to Health Services

As discussions occur about managed care, reduced federal influence, and expanded role of the states in providing care, access to services is a major problem for ethnic minorities and poor populations. Many never see a physician; they are locked out of the health care system by an inability to pay. Complex eligibility requirements for federal programs—Medicaid and Medicare—leave many poor families uninsured. The United States is one of two major industrialized nations that lack universal entitlement to basic medical care (Waitzkin, 1991). Access to routine medical services has been identified as a major factor in the increasing

Table 4. Examples of Gender Differences in Health

Women	Increased risk for rape, assault and domestic violence
	Higher risk for osteoporosis, obesity, anorexia and eating disorders, high blood pressure, coronary heart disease, breast cancer, chronic obstructive pulmonary diseases, lung cancer, diabetes and HIV/AIDS
	More likely to be the head of the household
	Suffer more from depression and low self-esteem
	Have a greater proportion of admissions for mental health services
Men	More at risk for homicide and suicide
	More likely to survive a heart attack
	Suffer more from amputations, head injuries, spinal cord injuries, burns and liver cirrhosis

Note. The author created this table referencing four useful cultural competency resources: U.S. Department of Health and Human Services (1997d), *Health United States 1996–97 and injury chartbook,* Hyattsville, MD: Centers for Disease Control and Prevention, National Center for Health Statistics; U.S. Department of Health and Human Services (1998a, June/July), Obesity: Facts and figures, *Closing the gap: Office of Minority Health Newsletter,* p. 6, Washington, DC: Author; U.S. Ethnic Health Data (1998), Life expectancy, *FWFS-ethnic health data,* retrieved from: http://www.fwfs.com/healthdata.htm; and Women's Research and Education Institute (1994), *Assessing and improving women's health: A report,* Washington, DC: Author. Table by Shirley A. Wells

health disparities among racial and ethnic populations, the poor, and women (HHS, 1998c; HHS, 1995; Geiger, 1996; USPHS, 1994; Shalala, 1998; Young, 1994).

Barriers to quality care extend well beyond the issues of under-insured and uninsured. Expense, distance, inconvenient hours, long waits, and the prospect of unfriendly treatment construct a formidable barrier to care (Young, 1994). Facing an unpleasant and bewildering set of circumstances, many persons abandon their quest for care. In addition to economic status and health knowledge, attitudes and behaviors are factors related to race and ethnicity, which may pose barriers to access and health care use. Immigration status, acculturation, language, organizational and other cultural factors also affect access to care, patterns of health care use, and outcomes (Clarissa, 1992; HHS, 1995; Friedman, 1994; USPHS, 1994).

Health Care Usage Data

Health care usage data describe the uses of health services and resources. It measures both the volume of use and the persons who use the services. National data are collected and categorized into three modes of medical care: (1) ambulatory care, (2) inpatient care, and (3) extended care. The examination of usage data allows an understanding of which parts of the health care system are used, to what extent, by whom, for what, and why. Current health care usage data are limited in terms of completeness and comprehensiveness. General provider-based surveys do not encompass the full range of provider types or settings, nor do they contain sufficient sample sizes to permit the development of estimates for ethnic populations. Furthermore, many of these provider-based surveys rely on medical records, which often do not contain sufficient information on the race and ethnicity of the client (USPHS, 1994).

Most available national health care data are limited to the White and Black populations. Increasingly, data for the Hispanic population are becoming available. Health care usage data for American Indians and Alaska Natives are limited to data developed by the Indian Health Service on its own user population (USPHS, 1994). Comprehensive usage data are needed to evaluate and monitor access to care among the ethnic minority population, relate health status to health care use, understand and overcome barriers to usage, and allocate health resources equitably.

Health Care Use

There are differences in the ways the various racial groups view medical care. The need for regular routine medical care through a primary physician is evidenced by the misuse of emergency rooms. The use of emergency rooms was 62% higher for Blacks than for Whites in 1992. In 1995, about half of low-income Blacks and Hispanics did not visit a physician during that year, compared with one third of Whites. The use of physicians' offices was 16% lower for Blacks than Whites. Disparities in health care use appeared to be both race-specific and geographic; in the Northeast, 47% of Blacks and Hispanics had not visited a doctor in the past year, compared to 35% of Whites. According to *The Nation's Health,* in the South 53% of Blacks and Hispanics had not visited a doctor in the past year, compared to 41% of Whites ("Study Confirms," 1995).

Between 1993 and 1995 women with a family income below the poverty level had 28% fewer visits with a physician than women above the poverty line. And poor men had fewer visits (16%) than nonpoor men. In 1995, physician offices and hospital outpatient departments were used more often by women than men, whereas women and men used the emergency departments at about the same rate. The usage of inpatient short-stay hospital care is greater for persons with a low family income than for persons with a high family income. In 1994, the days of care reported by low-income persons were 3 times the rate for high-income persons (HHS, 1997d).

From 1991 to 1994, more AAPI had a regular source of primary care—70% and 78%, respectively. However, these percentages are still lower than that for the total population (84%). For many AAPI, language and cultural differences are likely barriers (Healthy People 2,000 Progress Review for AAPIs, 1997; NCHS, 1998). Among Hispanics, Mexican Americans are least likely to have a regular source of primary care. The 1994 data indicated that 71% of Hispanic adults had a regular source of primary care—still lower than the 81% for the total population (Healthy People 2000 Progress Review for Hispanic Americans, 1997). During this same time period, 78% Blacks, 70% American Indians and Alaska Natives, and 71% low-income people had a regular source of primary care (Healthy People 2000 Midcourse Review, 1995).

Geography and lack of transportation can result in the under-use of health services. The lack of physicians and locations of available health services compromises access. The growing number of hospital closings, as a result of ongoing structural and political changes in health care, raises the issues of lack of access to hospital and physician care. Hospitals that historically served ethnic communities have either closed, relocated to predominately White communities, or privatized (Butts, 1992). When a hospital closes in an area, rural or urban, often physicians leave the area. The remaining physicians have extremely heavy workloads (Friedman, 1994; Randall, 1994; Smith, 1993). If no providers are available, whether or not a person has insurance is irrelevant. Clients who are housebound, who lack private transportation, or who face other transportation difficulties are increasingly vulnerable as available providers become distant (Friedman, 1994).

Racial and ethnic stereotypes also play a role in the under-use of health services. Health care professionals, like Americans in general, tend to treat Asians, Pacific Islanders, and Hispanics as homogenous groups, when each is a highly diversified ethnic group with differing health statuses, health needs, and cultures (Lin-Fu, 1988). This stereotyping of clients may be one of the reasons why African Americans are less satisfied than Whites with their health care providers' behavior toward them (Randall, 1994; Wolf, 1992).

Homosexual women also underuse health services. Societal stigma may limit lesbian women's access to health care out of fear of discrimination and rejection. As a result, lesbians are diagnosed late in the course of a disease, and many do not receive optimal health care (Carroll, 1999). Carroll expresses concern that because they perceive themselves at low risk for cervical cancer, many lesbian women do not visit their gynecologist regularly, nor do they get routine Pap smear exams, increasing their risk for breast, uterine, and ovarian cancer.

Health Care Coverage

Access to regular care is contingent upon the possession of health insurance, private or public, which is directly connected to one's employment or lack thereof. This connection leaves a large number of persons without access to care. Health care costs account for an increasing share of the U.S. economy; and they place a rising burden on federal, state, and local governments and private employers. Because of these costs, a rising proportion of the population lacks health insurance coverage. *The Nation's Health* reported that the need for universal health coverage has not gone away ("Study Confirms," 1995). Low-income families spend a larger share of income for health care services—up to 11% of household income compared to 2% for upper-income families, and higher numbers of uninsured Blacks and Hispanics are found in the South and West ("Study Confirms," 1995).

In 1993 the percentage of Americans who were uninsured was 35% for those with a family income less than $14,000, compared to only 5% for those with a family income of $50,000 or more (HHS, 1995). Young adults 15 to 44 years of age are most likely to be uninsured. In 1993, 63% of this age group did not have health insurance. Among the elderly under 65 years of age, 77% White, 17% Black, and 20% Hispanic were uninsured. Black and Hispanic elderly are more than twice as likely as White elderly to have only Medicare (USPHS, 1994).

Blacks and Hispanics are disproportionately uninsured. They are twice as likely to have no coverage as White persons are. In 1993, low-income Whites were more likely to have private health coverage whereas Blacks were more likely to have public coverage. The racial disparities in service access are far worse for the uninsured than they are for anyone covered by Medicaid. Medicaid has greatly reduced the disparities in insurance coverage, especially among low-income persons. The racial disparities are greater among high-income populations for health coverage (USPHS, 1994).

In 1995 more than 13% of White children, 15% of African American children, and almost 27% of Hispanic children did not have health insurance. Consequently, the U.S. Congress expanded the Earned Tax Credit and passed the Kassebaum-Kennedy legislation to improve the availability of health insurance for working families and their children (Shalala, 1998). The problem is that the delivery of health insurance alone does not ensure equality of access or care. Other factors are also important in equalizing access to health care, such as disparities in the availability of services in different neighborhoods and the possibility of discriminatory policies and practices.

Scope and Quality of Care

Health policies and delivery systems targeting ethnic minorities and the poor population have historically employed two opposing but similar approaches. In one approach the importance of race and economic status are downplayed or negated in health analysis. The other approach claims that these groups experience poor health and premature death because of pathological behaviors, such as smoking, drinking, consuming the wrong food, engaging in unprotected sex and violent behavior, and leading sedentary lifestyles (Smith, 1998; Dula, 1994; Geiger, 1996). There are assumptions that individuals alone can control their health destiny without consideration of their economic capacity to do so, the accessibility of health care services, the availability of culturally compatible services, or their gender and genetic makeup.

A growing body of literature suggests that being a member of an ethnic minority group can, in and of itself, constitute a barrier. The medical literature reports that Blacks are less likely than Whites to receive certain surgical or other therapies for similar ailments, even when differences in income and severity of diseases are taken into account (AMA Council on Ethical and Judicial Affairs, 1990). Geiger (1996) said that the most striking result of a multitude of studies, in a recent literature search covering a 10-year period (1984 to 1994) on racial and ethnic disparities in health care, was the consistency of the findings—"race is the overriding determinant of [ethnic] disparities in care" (p. 816). Even when a variety of variables—age, gender, Medicare and other insurance status, income, disease severity, concomitant morbid conditions, and underlying incidence and prevalence rates—are controlled for race-influenced clinical decisions.

Latinos are less likely than non-Hispanic Whites to receive pain medication in at least one California trauma center (Todd, Lee, & Hoffman, 1994). In Los Angeles county, non-Latino Whites are more likely than ethnic minorities with the same diagnosis to undergo invasive cardiac procedures, even after adjustment for insurance: although increased income moderated the difference, especially for Asian Americans, it remained important for Latinos and Blacks (Carlise, Leake, & Shapiro, 1993).

Diabetes and high blood pressure, both of which are major chronic diseases among adults, are greater burdens for racial and ethnic groups, as their higher rates of amputations and kidney disease show. Despite being disproportionately represented on waiting lists for kidney transplants, Blacks are half as likely than Whites to receive them and wait longer for them (Gaston, Ayres, Dooley, & Diethelm, 1993). Blacks are less likely to receive renal transplant, hip or total knee replacement, and gastrointestinal endoscopy, among other procedures, but they are more likely to undergo hysterectomy and amputation of the lower extremity (Gormick et al., 1996). African Americans are also less likely to receive potentially sight-saving treatment for glaucoma than Whites (Javitt, 1991; Seddon, 1991).

Race also operates as a determinant of the quality and scope of care without regard for insurance status and income level. African American women receive less appropriate hospital care than White women for breast cancer, and they are less likely to receive rehabilitation and client education after a mastectomy (Diehr, 1989). African Americans are accepted less frequently for psychotherapy, assigned more often to less experienced therapists, and seen with less intensity and for shorter periods (Council on Ethical and Judicial Affairs, 1990). White clients in the Department of Veterans Affairs hospitals are more likely than Blacks to undergo invasive cardiac procedures (Whittle, Conigliaro, Good, & Lofgren, 1993). Racial differences in treatment of Medicare beneficiaries are found in a variety of services. Black Medicare beneficiaries are less likely to receive 25 services, including cardiac care, cerebrovascular care, some gastrointestinal procedures, cataract extraction, and mammography; Whites are less likely to receive seven services, including barium enemas and computed tomographic head scans (Escare, Epstein, Colby, & Schwartz, 1993).

In one multihospital study, Kahn, Pearson, and Harrison (1994) found deficiencies in the most basic components of clinical care for Blacks and poor clients as compared to White and affluent clients, although all were Medicare beneficiaries. Other studies have shown that Blacks are much less likely to undergo angiography, angioplasty, coronary-artery bypass grafting, or cardiac catherization, even if they are enrolled in Medicare or free-care systems (Geiger, 1996; Goldberg, Hatz, Jacobson, Krakauer, & Rimm, 1992; Hannan, Kilburn, O'Donnell, Lukacik, &

Shields, 1991; Peterson et al., 1994). Gormick et al. (1996) found that Blacks with high incomes had only a modified—but never an equalizing—effect on Black to White ratios for visits to physicians for ambulatory care, mammography rates, and immunizations against influenza. Even a high-income level did not alter the higher risks among Blacks for amputation of all or part of the lower limb and bilateral orchiectomy.

These studies raise troubling questions about inequalities in the health care system. The evidence indicates that color can be a barrier to quality health care, regardless of the client's insurance status. Racism is an organizing principle in the United States. The health care delivery system is no different than all other components of the U.S. social structure in terms of its reactions to race and class. In this structure, racism and inequality are institutionalized. In health care, it does not end with unpleasant personal encounters, but creeps into treatment decisions (AMA Council on Ethical and Judicial Affairs, 1990; Carlisle et al., 1995; Ford & Cooper, 1995; Geiger, 1996). If racism is involved, it is unlikely to be overt or even conscious. Racism may influence clinical decisions in ways that health care providers do not even recognize (Escare et al., 1993). Disparities based on race, income, education, socioculture, and failures by the medical profession, according to the American Medical Association's Council on Ethical and Judicial Affairs (1990), "violate fundamental principles of fairness, justice, and medical ethics" (p. 2346; Table 5).

Cultural Consideration

Many factors play into why a person uses or does not use health services, including the ease of accessing services and a willingness to seek help. Culture is at the heart of such factors. For example, in traditional Chinese culture, many diseases are attributed to an imbalance of cosmic forces—yin and yang. So the goal is to restore the balance, and that might be accomplished through exercise or diet and not necessarily through the mainstream health system. Each group—racial, ethnic, gender, and socioeconomic—has its own way of dealing with the health care system. The help-seeking behavior of individuals is closely linked to their culture.

Cultural phenomena can present barriers, such as availability of health services on Sundays for persons who work all week and keep Saturday as a Sabbath. The inability to communicate in English or Spanish is another problem. For the homeless, the confused, and the chronically mentally ill, trying to cope with organized delivery systems and insurance

Table 5. Barriers to Health Care Usage and Care

Location	Ineffective outreach materials
Insurance	Misperception of need for preventive
Inconvenient hours	care or health services
Long waits	Language
Access to child care	Immigration status
Lack of transportation	Acculturation level
History of discrimination	Geography
Cultural differences between providers and clients	Being a member of an ethnic minority group
Inability to take time off from work	Cultural help-seeking behaviors
Scheduling difficulties	Mistrust of health care system
Parents own poor health, family crises	

Note. The author created this table referencing four useful cultural competency resources: Dula, A. (1994), African-American suspicion of the health care system is justified: What do we do about it? *Cambridge Quarterly of Healthcare Ethics,* 3, 347–357; Friedman, E. (1994), Money isn't everything: Nonfinancial barriers to access, *Journal of the American Medical Association, 271*(19), 1535–1538; U.S. Department of Health and Human Services (1997c, September), The help-seeking behavior of minorities, *Closing the Gap: Office of Minority Health Newsletter,* p. 8, Washington, DC: Author; and Young, L. J. (1994), Toward an ethic of care and community in education and medicine, in A. Dula & S. Goering (Eds.) *"It just ain't fair:" The ethics of health care for African Americans,* p. 244, New York: Praeger.
Table by Shirley A. Wells

is a formidable proposition (Friedman, 1994). "Many of the poor don't go the doctor; they go to the institution," says Terry Davis, a Louisiana psychologist.

A history of discrimination tends to obscure any desire to seek or get medical care. Mistrust of the health care system for many African Americans stems from memories of the Tuskegee Syphilis Study (Brooks, 1998). According to Young (1996), elderly Asian Americans harbor a general distrust of Western medicine. Recent immigrants view the system as intimidating and too hard to understand. "Native Americans often have a built-in distrust of the mainstream system, so they won't always seek help," says Thomas (HHS, 1997c). Although low-income groups grapple with the greatest barriers to care, moderate and higher income Hispanics and Blacks also face barriers, such as lack of confidence in the health system ("Study Confirms," 1995).

Other cultural barriers deal with language. Hispanics with limited or no English skills are often very afraid that they cannot communicate well. So they do not seek mainstream health services for fear of being misunderstood (HHS, 1997c). Lack of language translation services or providers who can speak the client's language are often reported by AAPI. Many find they are unable to communicate health needs because of language barriers (Tom, 1992; HHS, 1996c). Differences in the use of language contribute to misunderstanding and distrust. Health care workers may use unfamiliar terms and medical jargon that many African Americans and other ethnic groups are unlikely to understand (Dula, 1994). Language barriers are considered not only a block to health access, but also a source of possible confusion in diagnosis.

Cultural differences between providers and clients can be major blocks when it comes to providing and receiving health services. Many Hispanics are more comfortable with Hispanic health care providers who have an understanding or appreciation of their culture (Brooks, 1998; Hudson & Watts, 1996). According to Julia Mayo, Chief Clinical Studies, Department of Psychiatry, African Americans are usually uncomfortable working with White therapists. They prefer to work with mental health professionals of the same background as themselves (HHS, 1997c). A study by Asbury, Walker, Belgrave, Maholmes, & Green (1994), of African Americans in rehabilitation, found that the most influential predictor of level of participation was whether or not the service provider was of the same of race or ethnicity as the client. Those clients who were of the same ethnic group as the service provider were more likely to participate in rehabilitation on a continuous basis.

Some barriers to care emerge from the failure to develop culturally specific health delivery services. Leaving cultural concerns out of health care only send minorities and disadvantaged persons the message that their culture, belief system, and health care are not valued. Mayeno (1992) advocates for ethnically targeted, comprehensive community-based primary health care services for Asian Americans. She states that comprehensive community-based services have the ability to respond to the changing needs in the community. It is the first line source of preventive health care, outreach, and education, and it focuses on the whole person. This type of holistic service is very important to Asian cultures (Tom, 1992; HHS, 1996c). These centers will provide bilingual, bicultural, and culturally competent services.

The need for inclusive and comprehensive services has also been argued for American Indians. Including the whole realm of self (i.e., mind, body, spirit, and feelings) must be at the core of any health services for American Indians. According to Whiterabbit (HHS, 1995), simply addressing a specific health disease or disorder is not going to be a catalyst for evoking change. In addition to "talking about how to protect both the mind and body from disease, you must go into loss of issues that are specific to the community, like how loss of land and loss of culture affect attitudes about health" (HHS, 1995, p. 4). There is a strong inter-relationship between culture and well-being.

Two of the many barriers faced by migrant workers include a lack of knowledge or understanding about how to access and use services, and a lack of ability to fully participate in the medical interview. There are approximately 300,000 children of migratory farm-workers in the United States. Even though the majority of these children are impoverished and meet one of several criteria for Medicaid enrollment, the transitory nature of their parents' work, language and cultural barriers, and difficulties transporting Medicaid benefits among states pose formidable access barriers to Early and Periodic Screening Diagnosis and Treatment for eligible children (National Conference of State Legislature, 1996).

Families face many obstacles with health services. Among them are problems arranging care for children or other family members, inability to take time off work, family crises, the parent's own poor health, misperception of the child's need for preventive care, a lack of sense of responsibility for the children's health, a child's chronic illness that makes well-child care secondary, outreach materials that are ineffective (including print materials mailed to parents who cannot read or do not read English), scheduling difficulties, and trouble with transportation. Paying for health coverage is not the only factor that families consider in whether or not to use health services (Riportella-Muller, Selby-Harrington, Richardson, Donat, & Luchok, 1993).

The link between culture and health is of key importance in reducing health disparities. Understanding and appreciating life histories, cultural attitudes, behaviors, and language can go a long way to eliminating the distrust of the health care system that is shared by many racial and ethnic populations. At the individual and social levels, overcoming linguistic and cultural barriers are fundamental to providing culturally competent care to all persons. Developing access to services, such as hiring bilingual and bicultural staff members, tailoring interventions through the learning of another culture, modifying services, such as integrating traditional medicine with Western medicine, and developing appropriate cultural service models and specialized programs, are a few steps toward achieving ethnic sensitive health care services.

Increasing the number of trained health care providers from ethnic backgrounds is another strategy that must be pursued (Komaromy, Grumbach, Drake, Vranizan, Lurie, Keane, & Bindman, 1996). They are the ones most like the racial and ethnic communities who need to be targeted because of their disparate health status. Health care professionals must be trained to consider the culture of their clients rather than just their human service needs.

Immigrants

The increasing numbers and diversity of immigrants arriving in this country have compounded the problem of access to health care and presented additional challenges to provide bilingual and bicultural services. In the fragmented U.S. health care system, immigrants face additional institutional, income, and communication barriers to adequate health care. Barriers, such as legal status and program eligibility requirements for medical services, prevent some immigrants from participating in government-sponsored health care programs. A patchwork of public health agencies, community and migrant health centers, and public hospitals usually have inadequate fiscal and human resources service immigrants.

Trends in immigration and health care policy are exacerbating the barriers to adequate health care for a population with important health needs, poor English language skills, and cultural beliefs that often conflict with traditional medical treatment in the United States (National Conference of State Legislatures, 1996).

Summary

How do we explain, let alone justify, the evidence of racial, gender, and class disparity in a health care system committed in principle to providing care to all persons? It is clear that we, in this country, are in a crisis for the delivery of health care for the poor, elderly, immigrants, women, and ethnic populations. Working together, sharing knowledge and research, finding common grounds, and setting common goals can only solve the health disparity in the country.

The United States has made great progress in strengthening the overall health of the nation. Although progress had been made in closing the gap in some key health areas, far too many still remain. It is difficult to determine what it is about some clients that compromises their access and use of health services. Yet, there are great disparities that cannot be solved by just a few programs or the delivery of health insurance. Universal coverage alone does not ensure equality. Restrictive admissions practices, geographic inaccessibility, culture, racial and ethnic stereotypes, gender, socioeconomic level, diagnosis, gender discrimination, and the failure to employ ethnic health care professionals will still create barriers to health care services. The fact is that important nonfinancial barriers exist, and they will not disappear with the delivery of insurance, whether public or private.

The issue of health disparities cannot be ignored or subsumed in such concepts as the underserved, the uninsured, or the poor. A system biased against race, gender, and socioeconomic status presents a barrier to quality care that providers frequently do not recognize their personal role in perpetuating. Providers must attain knowledge and information about diverse communities. They must recognize, understand, and incorporate into treatment regimens the sociopolitical and ethno-racial variations found with these communities. The health problems of women, ethnic minorities, and the poor would be more adequately treated if understood within their respective sociopolitical contexts. Health providers must work in partnership involving mutual understanding and collaboration with not only the client but also the family or caregiver, and the community at-large.

Concepts, such as family, systems, communities, cultures, organizational mission, and societal commitments, must be foremost in the minds of both researchers and practitioners if health practitioners are to change the way health care is practiced by providers and received by women, ethnic minorities, and the poor. When everyone participates, when everyone is accountable, and when the changes are systemic and cultural, the gap of health disparities can start to close.

References

AMA Council on Ethical and Judicial Affairs. (1990). Black-White disparities in health care. *Journal of the American Medical Association, 263*(17), 2344–2346.

Asbury, C. A., Walker, S., Belgrave, F. Z., Maholmes, V., & Green, L. (1994). Psychosocial, cultural, and accessibility factors associated with participation of African Americans in rehabilitation. *Rehabilitation Psychology, 39*(2), 113–121.

Brooks, J. (1998a, December/January). Minority participation in clinical trails: The impact of the Tuskegee syphilis study. *Closing the Gap: Office of Minority Health Newsletter,* p. 3.

Brooks, J. (1998b, June/July). Teen birth rates down in all states. *Closing the Gap: Office of Minority Health Newsletter,* p. 10.

Carlise, D. M., Leake, B. D., & Shapiro, M. F. (1993, June 29). *The role of income and ethnicity in predicting the use of selected cardiovascular proce-*

dures in Los Angeles County. Paper presented at the 10th annual meeting of the Association for Health Services Research, Washington, DC.

Carroll, N. M. (1999, April). Homophobia is a public health problem. *Obstetrics and Gynecology.*

Cromptom, R. (1993). *Class and stratification: An introduction to current debates.* Cambridge, England: Policy Press.

Deevey, S. (1990). Older lesbian women: An invisible minority. *Journal of Gerontological Nursing, 16*(5), 35–39.

Diehr, P. (1989). Treatment modality and quality differences for Black and White breast-cancer patients treated in community hospitals. *Medical Care, 27, 942.*

Dula, A. (1994). The life and death of Miss Mildred: An elderly Black woman. *Clinics in Geriatric Medicine, 10*(3), 419–430.

Dula, A. (1994). African-American suspicion of the health care system is justified: What do we do about it? *Cambridge Quarterly of Healthcare Ethics, 3,* 347–357.

Escare, J. J., Epstein, K. R., Colby, D. C., & Schwartz, J. S. (1993). Racial differences in the elderly's use of medical procedures and diagnostic tests. *American Journal of Public Health, 83,* 948–954.

Fastats, a to z. Health status. (2000). Hyattsville, MD: U.S. Department of Health and Human Services, Centers for Disease Control and Prevention. Retrieved 2000 from: http://www.cdc.gov/nchswww/fastats/hstatus.htm.

Friedman, E. (1994). Money isn't everything: Nonfinancial barriers to access. *Journal of the American Medical Association, 271*(19), 1535–1538.

Gaston, R. S., Ayres, I., Dooley, L.G., & Diethelm, A. G. (1993). Racial equality in renal transplantation. *Journal of the American Medical Association, 270,* 1352–1356.

Geiger, H. J. (1996). Race and health care—An American dilemma. *The New England Journal of Medicine, 335*(11), 815–816.

Goldberg, K. C., Hatz, A. J., Jacobson, S. J., Krakauer, H., & Rimm, A. A. (1992). Racial and community factors influencing coronary artery bypass graft surgery rates for all 1996 Medicare patients. *Journal of the American Medical Association, 267,* 1473–1477.

Gormick, M. E., Eggers, P. W., & Reilly, T. W. (1996). Effects of race and income on mortality and use of services among Medicare beneficiaries. *New England Journal of Medicine, 335,* 791–799.

Haas, A. P. (1997, July). *Survey results on the health status of lesbian women.* Presented at the National Lesbian and Gay Health Conference, Atlanta, GA.

Hannan, E. L., Kilburn, H., O'Donnell, J. F., Lukacik, G., & Shields, E. P. (1991). Interracial access to selected cardiac procedures for patients hospitalized with coronary artery disease in New York State. *Medical Care, 29(5)*, 430–431.

Healthy People 2000 (1995, February 15). *American Indians and Alaska Natives progress review.* Washington, DC: U.S. Department of Health & Human Services, Public Health Service.

Healthy People 2000 (1997, September 13). *Asian Americans and Pacific Islanders progress review.* Washington, DC: U.S. Department of Health & Human Services, Public Health Service.

Healthy People 2000 (1997, April 29). *Hispanic Americans progress review.* Washington, DC: U.S. Department of Health & Human Services, Public Health Service.

Horwitz, S. R. (1998c, June/July). Impact of domestic abuse on HIV prevention in Hispanic women. *Closing the Gap: Office of Minority Health Newsletter,* p. 8.

Hudson, J. C., & Watts, E. (1996). Hispanic preferences for health care providers and health care information. *Health Marketing Quarterly, 14(1),* 67–83.

Javitt, J. C. (1991). Undertreatment of glaucoma among Black Americans. *The New England Journal of Medicine, 325,* 1418.

Kahn, K. L., Pearson, M. L., & Harrison, E. R., (1994). Health care for Blacks and poor hospitalized Medicare patients. *Journal of the American Medical Association, 271,* 1169–1174.

Klerman, L. V. (1991). *Alive and well? A research and policy review of health programs for poor young children.* New York: National Center for Children in Poverty.

Kormaromy, M., Grumbach, K., Drake, M., Vranizan, K., Lurie, N., Keane, D., & Bindman, A. (1996). The role of Blacks and Hispanics physicians in providing health care for underserved population. *The New England Journal of Medicine, 334(20),* 1305–1310.

Lesbian health focus of new report. (1999, January 19). Retrieved 2000 from: http://www.healthcentral.com/news/newsfulltext.cfm?id=id8754& StoryType=ReutersNews.

Lin-Fu, J. D. (1988). Population characteristics and health care needs of Asian Pacific Americans. *Public Health Reports, 103,* 18.

Mayeno, L. (1992). Primary care recommendations for health care system reform. *Partners in Human Service: Shaping Health Care and Civil Rights Policy for Asian and Pacific Islander Americans, Final Report* (pp. 20–23) [Conference proceeding]. Washington, DC: U.S. Department of Health and Human Services.

National Conference of State Legislatures (1996). *State's Legislatures' Role in Multicultural Health: Project Summary.* Washington, DC: Author.

Office of the Federal Register. (1998). *Federal Register, 63*(36), 9235–9238. Washington, DC: Author.

Otten, M. W., Teutsch, S. M., Williamson, D. F., & Marks, J. S. (1990). The effect of known risk factors on the excess mortality of Black adults in the United States. *Journal of the American Medical Association, 263,* 845–850.

Pappas, G. (1994). Elucidating the relationship between race, socioeconomic status and health. *American Journal of Public Health, 84,* 892–893.

Perez-Stable, E. J., Marin, G., & Marin, B. V. (1994). Behavioral risk factors: A comparison of Latinos and non-Latino Whites in San Francisco. *American Journal of Public Health, 84*(6), 971–976.

Peterson, E. D., Wright, S. M., Daley, J., & Thibault, G. E. (1994). Racial variation in cardiac procedure use and survival following acute myocardial infarction in the Department of Veterans Affairs. *Journal of the American Medical Association, 271,* 1170–1180.

Pinn, V. W. (1998d, June/July). Improving the health of minority women: The role of research. *Closing the Gap: Office of Minority Health Newsletter,* p. 3.

Quam, J. K., & Whitford, G. S. (1992). Adaptation and age-related expectations of older gay and lesbian adults. *The Gerontologist, 32*(3), 367–374.

Randall, V. R. (1994). Racist health care reform: Reforming an unjust health care system to meet the needs of African-Americans. *Health Matrix, 3,* 155–156.

Riportella-Muller, R., Selby-Harrington, M. L., Richardson, L. A., Donat, L. N., & Luchok, K. J. (1993, June 29). *Barriers to the use of preventive health care services for children: The case of early and periodic screening, diagnosis, and treatment program.* Paper presented at the 10th annual meeting of the Association for Health Services Research, Washington, DC.

Rogers, R. G. (1992). Living and dying in the U.S.A.: Sociodemographic determinants of death among Blacks and Whites. *Demography, 29,* 287–303.

Seddon, J. M. (1991). The differential burden of blindness in the United States. *The New England Journal of Medicine, 325,* 1440.

Shalala, D. E. (1998, Spring). Eliminating racial and ethnic health disparities. *SACNAS News, 2*(2), 27.

Smith, D. B. (1993). The racial integration of health facilities. *Journal of Health Politics, Policy and Law, 18,* 850.

Smith, M. B. (1998e, March). Race, ethnicity, class, and culture. *Closing the Gap: Office of Minority Health Newsletter*, p. 2.

Study confirms inequalities in routine care, insurance coverage for Black, Hispanic Americans. (1995, October). *The Nation's Health*, p. 11.

Todd, K. H., Lee, T., & Hoffman, J. R. (1994). The effect of ethnicity on physician estimates of pain severity in patients with isolated extremity trauma. *Journal of the American Medical Association, 271,* 925–928.

Tom, C. (1992). Health care reform: Beyond financial barriers to access to care. *Partners in Human Service: Shaping Health Care and Civil Rights Policy for Asian and Pacific Islander Americans, Final Report* (pp. 9–11) [Conference proceeding]. Washington, DC: U.S. Department of Health and Human Services.

Urgo, M. (1998, June/July). New obesity guidelines: Minority women at risk. *Closing the Gap: Office of Minority Health Newsletter*, p. 6–7.

U.S. Census Bureau. (1997). March current population survey.

U.S. Census Bureau. (1999). *Poverty in the United States, 1998: Current Population Reports.* U.S. Government Printing Office, Washington, DC: Author.

U.S. Department of Health and Human Services. (1995, July). Recognizing the link between Indian culture and health. *Closing the Gap: Office of Minority Health Newsletter*, p. 4. Washington, DC: Author.

U.S. Department of Health and Human Services. (1996a, September/October). Studies shed new light on HIV transmission. *Closing the Gap: Office of Minority Health Newsletter*, p. 10. Washington, DC: Author.

U.S. Department of Health and Human Services. (1996b, May/June). Asian among those at high risk for osteoporosis. *Closing the Gap: Office of Minority Health Newsletter*, p. 6. Washington, DC: Author.

U.S. Department of Health and Human Services. (1996c, May/June). An OMH-funded project serves elderly Asian Americans. *Closing the Gap: Office of Minority Health Newsletter*, pp. 1–2. Washington, DC: Author.

U.S. Department of Health and Human Services. (1997a, October). NIAID supports national inner-city asthma study. *Closing the Gap: Office of Minority Health Newsletter*, p. 6. Washington, DC: Author.

U.S. Department of Health and Human Services. (1997b, October). Migrant farm-workers suffer from pesticide exposure. *Closing the Gap: Office of Minority Health Newsletter*, p. 10. Washington, DC: Author.

U.S. Department of Health and Human Services. (1997c, September). The help-seeking behavior of minorities. *Closing the Gap: Office of Minority Health Newsletter*, p. 8. Washington, DC: Author.

U.S. Department of Health and Human Services. (1997d). *Health, United States, 1996–97 and injury chartbook.* Hyattsville, MD: Centers for Disease Control and Prevention, National Center for Health Statistics.

U.S. Department of Health and Human Services. (1998a, June/July). Obesity: Facts and figures. *Closing the Gap: Office of Minority Health Newsletter,* p. 6. Washington, DC: Author.

U.S. Department of Health and Human Services. (1998b, March). Minority health in the U.S. An overview. *Closing the Gap: Office of Minority Health Newsletter,* p. 5. Washington, DC: Author.

U.S. Department of Health and Human Services. (1998c, March). Race, ethnicity, class, and culture. *Closing the Gap: Office of Minority Health Newsletter,* p. 5. Washington, DC: Author.

U.S. Ethnic Health Data. (1998). Life expectancy. *FWFS-ethnic health data.* Retrieved from: www.fwfs.com/healthdata.htm.

U.S. Public Health Service. (1994). *Improving minority health statistics: Report of the public health task force on minority health data.* Washington, DC: U.S. Department of Health and Human Services, Office of Minority Health.

Waitzkin, H. (1991). *The politics of medical encounters: How patients and doctors deal with social problems.* New Haven, CT: Yale University Press.

Waitzman, N. J., & Smith, K. R. (1994). The effects of occupational class transitions on hypertension: racial disparities among working-age men. *American Journal of Public Health, 84,* 945–950.

Whiterabbit, H. (1995). Recognizing the link between Indian culture and health. *Closing the Gap: Office of Minority Health Newsletter,* p. 4. Washington, DC: U.S. Department of Health & Human Services, Office of Minority Health.

Whittle, J., Conigliaro J., Good, C. B., & Lofgren, R. P. (1993). Racial differences in the use of invasive cardiovascular procedures in the Department of Veterans Affairs medical system. *The New England Journal of Medicine, 329,* 621–627.

Williams, D. R. (1990). Socioeconomic differentials in health: A review and redirection. *Social Psychology Quarterly, 53,* 81–99.

Wolf, S. M. (1992). Toward a theory of process. *Law, Medicine & Health Care, 20,* 283.

Women's Research and Education Institute. (1994). *Assessing and improving women's health: A report.* Washington, DC: Author.

Young, L. J. (1994). Toward an ethic of care and community in education and medicine. In A. Dula & S. Goering (Eds.), *"It just ain't fair:" The ethics of health care for African Americans* (p. 244). New York: Praeger.

CHAPTER THREE

Culture and Ethics

Key Points

- Ethics are principles of conduct that help govern human behaviors, determine which acts are right and which are wrong, and are used by society for evaluating the behaviors of individuals and groups.

- All moral and ethical choices involve values and beliefs that are culturally sensitive, contextually defined, and dependent on a network of sociocultural relationships that provide meaning and significance.

- Professional codes of ethics are documents that articulate and reflect the basic principles, conducts, and standards of behaviors relevant to professional practice. These documents cannot make a person ethical; they can only inform and serve as guides for something to aspire to.

- Bioethics deals with the daily moral dilemmas and choices and ethical puzzles in providing health care.

- The principle of autonomy is at the center of most cultural ethical medical decision making or conflicts, especially those dealing with truth telling, advance directives, and informed consent.

- Each health care provider should establish a hierarchy of values and priorities that will define his or her individual and social ethical responsibility not only to individual clients but also to the public as a whole.

- Ethical conflicts based on cultural differences should be mediated with strategies that allow both the client and the provider the opportunity to clarify their values as well as the context in which they are made.

Over the past years, ethical dilemmas have assumed a major importance in health care, as advances in medical technology and the rising cost of health care have forced many providers to deal with difficult ethical choices surrounding life and death, allocation of resources, and provider–client relationships (Ferguson, 1994). Every health care provider is constantly making ethical choices. Sometimes those choices are dramatic, life-and-death decisions, but often the more subtle, less conspicuous choices are the most important.

The multicultural composition of the United States can produce new, often unforeseen, concerns about ethical dilemmas and choices in current practices. Cultural pluralism poses a challenge for health care providers and clients alike who come from diverse backgrounds and yet visit the same hospitals and providers. The moral consequences of respecting differences within a multicultural society are complex and raise difficult questions for ethicists and policymakers as well as researchers and clinicians (Davis & Koening, 1996).

In the presence of cultural differences, health practitioners frequently find themselves confronting choices that depend more on moral and ethical values than on medical knowledge. There are cases in which religious, cultural, and family values greatly influence the clinical decision-making process. For example, many Asian cultures hold a reverent view about persons in positions of authority (e.g., health professionals, therapists). Families from those cultures may be open to discussing their medical condition and treatment options. However, they expect the professional to know what is best and to tell them want to do. In contrast, there are many Native Americans who believe that any negative discussions will negatively influence the treatment outcomes. The latter cultural value system conflicts with the generally accepted medical ethics of the United States of providing clients with information that allows them to make an informed decision about their care. So, the *one size fits all* approach is rarely effective. Whose cultural values and morals should be followed?

It is the intent of this chapter to examine how culture influences the ethics of decision making and health policy. It will also examine questions regarding the ethical responsibilities of practitioners and the rights of the client and family.

Ethics

What is ethics? Ethics is concerned with the study of right and wrong. The term *ethics* comes from the Greek word *ethos,* meaning *cultural custom or habit.* The word *moral,* which is often used interchangeably with the term *ethical,* also means *customs.* The identification of ethics and morality with cultural norms or customs reflects the fact that most adults tend to identify morality with cultural customs (Boss, 1998). Ethics is:

> . . . a system of moral principles: the ethics of a culture; the rules of conduct recognized in respect to a particular class of human actions or particular group, culture, etc.: medical ethics, Christian ethics; moral principles, as of an individual: His ethics forbade betrayal of a confidence; the branch of philosophy dealing with values related to human conduct, with respect to the rightness and wrongness of certain motives and ends of such actions. (*The Random House College Dictionary,* 1988).

Ethics may be thought of as principles of conduct that help govern the behaviors of individuals and groups. It is the study of the values and guidelines by which people live as well as the justification of these values and guidelines. Ethics is used to refer to "a set of standards of right and wrong established by a particular group and imposed on members of that group as a means of regulating and setting limits on their behavior" (Boss, 1998, p. 5). It represents what *ought* to be and helps set standards for human behavior.

Ethics affects all levels of life. *Normative ethics* gives us practical guidelines or norms, such as *do not lie* or *do no harm,* that we can apply to real-life situations. At the basic level it (i.e., *personal ethics*) is concerned with the person cultivating a virtuous character and developing a proper self-esteem. In relationships with others, ethics (i.e., *interpersonal ethics*) deals with the rightness and wrongness of particular actions, the nature of obligations toward others, and obligations to ourselves. At the community level, it (i.e., *social ethics*) focuses on social policies that affect the wider community, the protection of the community, and the treatment of each member of the community. Our moral obligation toward the environment (i.e., *environment ethics*) is becoming increasingly important (Boss, 1998). Ethics and lifestyle are intertwined. What we do or fail to do often affects not only us and those close to us, but also people all over the world.

Theoretical ethics (also called theoretical morality), on the other hand, operates at a more fundamental level. It argues that everyone already knows what is right and wrong. It is the starting point for the most basic insights regarding morality. Morality, synonymous with culture, is different for different people. It can vary from time to time and from person to person. When behavioral standards and moral values are accepted by virtually all societies or when they can be applied to all humans (e.g., human rights), ethics may be referred to as *universalistic*. Ethics can also be particularistic or culture-specific. This is when moral norms are adhered to by a given cultural community but not by others (e.g., ancestor worship). Ethics may be referred to as a situation when a shared universal or cultural standard does not automatically apply but is more a function of the specific circumstances (e.g., telling *white lies*) (Becker, 1995; Boss, 1998; Paige & Martin, 1996; Howell, 1981). *Clinical ethics* refers to the day-to-day moral decision making of those caring for clients (Callahan, 1995).

People live in contexts. Although environs vary, everyone lives in some physical and social context. Thus, an *ethos* is always contextual and is itself surrounded by a wider range of meaning. It is a cluster of practices and activities, for those practicing them, which are in no need of any explanation or justification. In this sense, all *ethics* is culture-based and rooted in the practical beliefs of closed societies.

Moral Principles

What ethical standards should be used to determine what kinds of acts are right and which are wrong? When approaching moral decisions, is it important to hold moral principles that facilitate making wise or correct choices? Some philosophical traditions have placed an emphasis on *principlism*—the value of particular moral principles—in the actual making of decisions (Childress, 1989; Beauchamp & Childress, 1989). Moral principles are rules used by society for evaluating the behavior of individuals and groups. These principles are universally binding and fundamentally transcultural (Boss, 1998). Moral principles are universally binding on all people regardless of their personal desires, culture, or religion. Individual interests or cultural customs can influence how particular moral principles are carried out.

The advantage of moral principles is that in varying ways and to different degrees, they can be used to protect individuals against being harmed and to identify the good of people. Moral principles are grounded in broad theories of ethics. Historically, two theories of justification

of conduct have dominated. The utilitarian approach asks which consequences of a choice, action, or policy would promote the best possible
outcome (Boss, 1998). *Utilitarianism* maintains that moral conduct must
be evaluated in terms of the consequences of behaviors. Such an approach to health care rationing, for instance, would look for the collective social benefit rather than advantages to individuals (Buford, 1984;
Callahan, 1995).

The deontological theory holds that moral conduct must be evaluated in terms of standards alone, and that the consequences of conduct
are not germane to the evaluation of that conduct. *Deontology* focuses
on determining which choices most respect the worth and value of the individual, and particularly the fundamental rights of individuals (Boss,
1998; Buford, 1984). The question of our basic obligation to other individuals is central. Good consequences may occasionally have to be set
aside to respect inalienable human rights. For example, it would be
wrong to subject a human being to dangerous medical research without
his or her consent, even if the consequences of doing so might be to save
many other people's lives (Buford, 1984; Callahan, 1995).

So moral principles are self-imposed, universal, and formal. They
are abstract criteria for evaluating our behavior in its entirety (Table 6).
Moral principles are the duties or the *ought to:* "... a duty to perform a
certain action. A duty to perform certain actions—such as keeping prom-
ises and repaying favors—irrespective of our motive" (Boss, 1998, p. 325).

We can say that moral rules are plausible because they are supported by universal standards. Without moral principles or standards,
choices would be left to a whim, to an accident of circumstances, and to
the strongest desire of the individual (Buford, 1984). No one principle
stands by itself. Each is a necessary condition for the possibility of saying
that our conduct is morally correct. And collectively they are sufficient
for determining the correctness of any conduct. Yet, we are not compelled to engage them.

Moral Decision Making

Good intentions alone are insufficient to guide moral decision
making. Consequences matter when applying moral principles and making
a judgment. According to Callahan (1995) good individual moral decision
making encompasses three elements: self-knowledge, knowledge of moral
theories and tradition, and cultural perception. Self-knowledge is fundamental because beliefs, motives, inclinations, and interests both enlighten
and obscure moral understanding. Moral theories, traditions, and princi-

Table 6. Principles for Evaluating Moral Choices

Principle of Consistency	–the duty to choose consistently or logically
Principle of Self-Improvement	–the duty to improve your knowledge and virtue
Principle of Equality	–the duty to treat all humans equally
Principle of Justice	–the duty to give each person equal and fair consideration
Principle of Beneficence	–the duty to do good acts and to promote happiness
Principle of Autonomy	–the duty to respect the individual right for self-determination
Principle of Veracity	–the duty to tell the truth
Principle of Fidelity	–the duty to keep promises (confidentiality)
Principle of Nonmaleficence	–the duty to do no harm to an individual
Principle of Axiology	–the duty to make consistent, harmonious, and coherent choices
Principle of Consequences	–the duty to consider foreseeable consequences of actions
Principle of Altruism	–the duty to respect all persons and cooperate with others in the production and enjoyment of shared values

Note. The information in this table is synthesized from several useful references: Boss, J. A. (1988). Ethics for life: An interdisciplinary and multicultural introduction. Mountain View, CA: Mayfield Publishing; Buford, T. O. (1984). *Personal philosophy: The art of living.* New York: Holt, Rinehart, & Winston; Encyclopedias of Bioethics. (1995). New York: Macmillan; Veatch, R. M., & Flack, H. E. (1997). *Case studies in allied health ethics.* Englewood Cliffs, NJ: Prentice-Hall. Table by Shirley A. Wells

ples by themselves are not necessarily absolute or always the right ones to follow in every situation. As individuals we are social beings, reflecting the time in which we live, embodied in a particular society at a particular time. Our social embeddedness shapes the way we understand ourselves, the moral problems we encounter, and what we take to be plausible and feasible responses to them (Boss, 1998; Callahan, 1991; Callahan, 1995).

What are our duties and obligations to other individuals whose life and well-being may be affected by our actions? What do we owe to the common good, or the public interest, in our lives as members of society? These questions are general to all people and can be asked in any moral situation or context. When these general questions of ethics are posed in terms of health care decisions, two views arise. One holds that a moral decision in health care ought to be understood as the application of good moral thinking in general to the specific domain of health care. This argument stresses that it has a medical component does not make it a different kind of moral problem, but an application of more general moral values or principles (Clouser, 1978).

A more traditional view is that an ethical decision in health care is different from general ethical decisions because the domain of medicine is different from other areas of human life, and because medicine has its own moral approaches and traditions. It is argued that making a decision within medicine requires detailed and sensitive appreciation of the characteristics of health care practice and of the unique features of sick and dying persons (Pellegrino & Thomasma, 1981). It is not that the ethical principles and virtues of medicine are different from the more general principles of ethics; it is the combination and context of health care that give them a special bite.

Moral Conflicts

Moral choices are about what is objectively good in itself and for all people, what makes life worth living, or what is considered a good life (Fower & Richardson, 1996). There are moral rights and duties, which are dependent on race, culture, tradition, or form of government. These rights and duties can define, in terms of practice and action, human beings as human beings, citizens of this or that society (Becker, 1995). All choices involve values. A choice occurs whenever value options conflict. All values are culturally sensitive because they are contextually defined and dependent on a network of sociocultural relationships that provide meaning and significance (Buford, 1984).

When two values present themselves and we choose one rather than another, we are saying, on the basis of our cultural context and beliefs, that one is more valuable than the other. For example:

> A respect for patient autonomy stressing the right of competent patients to make their own choices based on their cultural context can conflict with the principle of beneficence if the choice to be made by a patient may actually be harmful.

There is no set formula for determining which action to take in a moral dilemma or conflict. You must carefully weigh the moral principles, decide which are the most compelling in that particular situation, and try to honor as many of the principles as possible. You must use creativity and reason to make a judgment. But, more importantly, moral decision making requires that you personally enter into the process. In the end, individuals, alone with their thoughts and private lives, must wrestle with moral problems. And once a decision is made, it must be acted on. A decision of conscience blends moral judgment and the will to act upon that judgment (Callahan, 1991). Good moral decision making requires moving back and forth among the necessary elements: the reflective self, the interpreted culture, and the contributions of moral theory.

Codes and Other Ethical Directives

When confronted with a moral conflict, choice, or decision, a health care professional may turn to the professional code of ethics of his or her profession or other ethical directives, such as oaths, prayers, and bills of rights. These are documents that articulate the idea and minimal standards of character and conduct for the profession. These codes of ethics generally reflect basic ethical principles relevant to professional practice. They often relate general moral values, duties, and virtues to the unique situations encountered in health care practice. Prayers, oaths, and codes are collective summaries of the moral ideals and conduct that are expected of the professional (Spicer, 1995; Veatch & Flack, 1997).

Professional codes of ethics serve a dual purpose—to maintain the profession and to serve society's well-being. They function as a promise to society that the profession will maintain specific standards of practice. They serve to protect the client from incompetent practice and at the same time safeguard the reputation of the profession. Professional ethic documents provide a moral framework for professional practice and define the ideal standard of practice. At the center of professional ethic codes and other ethical directives lies the value or values that the profession or public perceives to be the primary good, or the objective of something good. Some organizations focus on general values, such as benefits, well-being, or the greater good of the consumers and clients, as the fundamental value to be pursued (Spicer, 1995).

The moral duties articulated in ethic documents may be broad, such as respecting the dignity and self-determination of individuals; or they may be specific, such as maintaining client confidentiality or not engaging in sexual relations with a client. The more general duties permit a certain amount of interpretation in their implementation by the individual practitioner, whereas the more specific ones establish particular minimum standards for professional behavior. Many groups also provide accompanying guides for professional conduct that attempt to elaborate on behaviors consistent with their selected principles and virtues.

Professional ethics documents cannot make a practitioner ethical; they can only inform and guide. Moral guidelines may focus on a person's character, with the assumption that moral behavior will flow naturally from a moral person. Professional codes of ethics and other ethical directives, ideally, serve as guides, as something to aspire to.

Bioethics

Bioethics is a specific term referring not only to the intersection of ethics and the life sciences, but also an academic discipline; a political force in medicine, biology, and environmental studies; and a cultural perspective of some consequence (Callahan, 1995). Bioethics is a field that ranges from the private and individual dilemmas faced by health care workers, to the public societal choices faced by citizens and legislators as they try to devise equitable health or environmental policies. What should I do here and now? What should we do together, as citizens and fellow human beings?

As the field of bioethics has developed, four general areas of inquiry can be distinguished, even though in practice they often overlap and cannot clearly be separated.

1. *Health care ethics* is that part of bioethics that focuses on "the delivery of health care, on patient obligations and rights, and on the ethics of the providing professions, including medicine, nursing, dentistry, and allied health" (Anderson & Glesnes-Anderson, 1987). It is the process of a questioning approach to decision making that was formally governed by silent tradition, value, or emotion. It is a questioning of our treatment of human beings in medicine, rehabilitation, and other related fields in light of certain moral principles and rights that have universal acceptance and are based on our own values. Because of its context, health care ethics focuses on the individual case, seeking to determine what has to be done here and now with the client.

2. *Theoretical bioethics* deals with the intellectual foundations of the field. What are its moral roots and what ethical warrant can be found for the moral judgments made in the name of bioethics?

3. *Regulatory and policy bioethics* aim to fashion legal or clinical rules and procedures designed to apply to types of cases or general practices. This area seeks legal and policy solution to pressing societal problems that are ethically defensible and clinically sensible and feasible.

4. *Cultural bioethics* refers to the efforts to relate bioethics to the historical, ideological, cultural, and social context in which it is expressed.

How do trends within bioethics reflect the larger culture of which they are a part? What ideological leanings do the moral theories underlying bioethics openly or implicitly manifest?

Bioethics requires recognition of moral principles that cause conflicts or ethical dilemmas or moral choices in health care. What is the most just way to distribute scarce resources, such as health care technology? What is our obligation toward providing health care to the disadvantaged people of our society? What is the obligation of health care providers to treat clients in ethically acceptable ways? Bioethics deals with the daily moral dilemmas and ethical puzzle that are a part of contemporary health care and environmental protection. It helps shape the social context in which those dilemmas and puzzles play themselves out. And it moves back and forth between the concreteness of individual and policy decisions and the broad notions and dynamic of the human situation.

Cultural Issues

Ethical dilemmas and conflicts can arise frequently in culturally plural settings. Most questions center on whether health care providers are obligated to act in accordance with what contemporary medical ethics dictates in the United States, or to respect the cultural difference of their clients and act according to the family's wishes (Macklin, 1998; Kaufert & Putsch, 1997). Problems arise when the participants in the health care setting have a different interpretation of illness and treatment, hold disparate values in relation to death and dying, and use language or decision-making frameworks differently.

The mainstream culture in the U.S. view of the good life generally includes a large measure of individual autonomy and mastery, rewarding associations with family and chosen friends, financial success, and personal happiness (Fowers & Richardson, 1996). Health care ethics in the United States operates mainly within a modern, Western philosophical framework that also emphasizes autonomy and individual rights (Becker, 1995; Longmore, 1995; Macklin, 1998; Yesley, 1995). Bioethics principles reflect Western notions of the sovereignty of the individual person and of the individual life (Kaufert & Putsch, 1997). Renee Fox (1990, p. 206), an American sociologist, said:

> From the outset, the conceptual framework of bioethics has accorded paramount status to the value-complex of individualism, underscoring the principles of individual rights,

autonomy, self-determination, and their legal expression in
the jurisprudential notion of privacy.

Autonomy and Individual Rights

The *ethos* of autonomy and individual rights can be at odds
with the values of different cultures and religions. The moral principle
of autonomy holds that an action or practice is morally wrong insofar
as it attempts to control the actions of *substantially autonomous* persons on the basis of a concern for their own welfare (Veatch & Flack,
1997). In other words, this principle says that people have a right to be
self-determined insofar as their actions affect only them. The importance attached to individual rights and respect for persons in consent
laws assumes the existence of autonomous decision makers (Gostin,
1995). Currently, the principle of autonomy is at the center of medical
decision making, especially those that deal with truth-telling, advance
directives, and informed consents (Macklin, 1998; Murphy, Palmer,
Azen, Frank, Michel, & Blackhall, 1996).

Yet much of the world, if not most, embraces a value system that
places the family, the community, or the society as a whole above that of
the individual. Alternative values, such as the good or primacy of the
community, take precedence over the autonomy of the individual in
many other cultures (Kaufert & Koolage, 1984; Kaufert & Putsch, 1997;
Macklin, 1998). Solidarity rather than autonomy would be their highest
value (Fox, 1990).

By focusing monistically on the individual, clients can be cut off
from their families, religious practices, or cultural values. For example:

> A 52-year-old Nigerian immigrant, with an abiding fear of
> cancer, visited his physician because of a small growth on his
> lip. The pair has a long-standing physician-patient relation-
> ship, and the physician is aware of the patient's fear of cancer.
> When the biopsy was completed, the patient's son and daugh-
> ter were informed of the patient's condition and terminal prog-
> nosis. The children asked that all information be withheld
> from the patient. They reported a strong cultural prohibition
> against the *telling of bad news*. They explained that disclosure
> would abate hope and might hasten the patient's death.

Does the physician have an obligation to inform the client of the
condition, thereby placing autonomy above all other values? Is the physician obligated to follow the family's wishes, thereby respecting their cul-

tural customs? The client and family are recent immigrants from a culture in which the health care providers normally inform the family rather than the client of a condition. The family's perspective clearly prohibited communication of terminal prognosis. This perspective appears to reflect their cultural values. Most clients want and need the support of their families. Recognition of the culturally important role that families play when a loved one is ill demonstrates respect for individual autonomy.

According to Gostin (1995), research in this area has raised questions about whether principles of autonomy and individual rights are *truly respectful of all people in all cultures*. A heavy emphasis on the moral principle of autonomy and self-determination can be viewed as a display of the political and ideological bias of culturally individualistic societies. Other societies—in Central and Eastern Europe, Asia, and Africa—give societal rather than individual concerns a more pronounced priority (Fox, 1990). "Countries with strong paternalistic traditions may not consider it necessary to consult with clients about some kinds of decisions; they will not see the issue at all—yet they may have a far livelier dedication to equality of access to health care" (Callahan, 1995, p. 251).

It is important to realize that the boundaries of beliefs and reactions to illness are not simply described by lines of language, education, class, and ethnicity. Issues of autonomy and individual rights, ethical and cultural value systems, and family processes influence the position and assumptions that clients and health care providers carry into, and through, the process of delivering health care.

Truth-Telling and Advanced Care Directives

The predominant norm of the United States of disclosing a diagnosis of serious illness to the client is not universally accepted among citizens comprising some ethnic or religious subcultures. A study by Blackhall, Murphy, Frank, and Azen (1995) found that Korean Americans and Mexican Americans tend to have a negative sentiment toward telling a client that they have a terminal illness. They believe the family, not the client, should make important health care decisions. They believe the family, not the client, should be told the truth about the his or her condition. They tend to place great emphasis on family-centered, as opposed to client-centered, decision-making styles. Blackhall et al. also cite data from other countries that bear out a similar gap between the predominant *autonomy* model in the United States and the *family-centered* model prevalent in European countries as well as in Asia and Africa. They concluded that health care providers should ask clients whether they want to receive information and make decisions regarding treatment, or whether they prefer that their families to handle such matters.

A study by Murphy et al. (1996) found that, when compared to European Americans, Mexican Americans and Korean Americans as a group have a negative attitude and reaction toward the concept of advanced care planning and decision making. These groups are more likely to endorse the notion that "physicians should not discuss death and dying with their clients because doing so could be harmful to the patient," and "it is not necessary for people to write down their wishes about medical care because their family will know what to do when the time comes" (p. 114). They suggest that the concept of advanced care documents may appeal only to certain groups of the population. This limits the clinical usefulness of living wills and durable powers of attorney for health care. These documents, at least as they are currently formulated, may not be appropriate for many culturally diverse clients.

Informed Consent

Disclosure of risks during an informed consent discussion and offering clients the opportunity to make advanced directives can pose a problem for adherents of traditional cultural beliefs. In a study by Carrese and Rhodes (1995), Western biomedical and bioethical concepts and principles came into conflict with traditional Navajo Native American values and ways of thinking. The traditional Navajo belief is that health is maintained and restored through positive ritual language. When health care providers disclose risks of a treatment in an informed consent discussion, they speak *in a negative way*, thereby violating the Navajo prohibition *to think and speak in a positive way*. The Navajo believed that thought and language had the power to shape and control events. Therefore, advanced care planning and discussions on end-of-life treatment are a dangerous violation of traditional Navajo values. Should providers adhere to the ethical and legal standards pertaining to informed consent as accepted in the United States and risk harming their Navajo client by talking in a negative way? Or should they adhere to the Navajo belief system to avoid harm to their client and at the same time violate the ethical requirement of disclosing potential risk?

Disparaging Views

Travel and migration of both health care providers and recipients have increased the number and variety of cross-cultural contacts and ethical situations. This has resulted in many challenges in providing care to recent immigrants, culturally distinct ethnic groups, and other diverse populations. Clients and health care providers often come from different educational, cultural, or class backgrounds. The providers and clients may not agree on a common set of cultural values. What may be regarded as morally wrong in one culture may be morally praiseworthy in another culture. For example, the sick role in occupational therapy is viewed as an active role, one in which the client achieves his or her optimal level of functioning through active participation. In Chinese society, the sick role is a passive role. It is sometimes believed that a person is chronically ill because of the sins committed by his or her family members. Thus, family members may try to do everything for the sick person, which means that maximum dependence is encouraged (Jang, 1995). Is it unethical to deny practices or treatments that are clearly unacceptable by the standards of Western culture, but acceptable by the standards of another culture?

Power and Dominance

Ethical dilemmas and conflicts can be further complicated by the unequal distribution of power in the relationship between the involved client and health care provider. The health care provider–client relationship is one in which the provider has the ultimate responsibility for developing conclusions and proposing alternative treatments. Health care providers often reframe human realities according to learned practices, rules, and guidelines as well as their own biases (Kaufert & Putsch, 1997). Clients faced with medical decisions are often subject to being over- or under-influenced by the health care system and its code of ethics. The decision can range from how to maximize independent function in keeping with the individual potential to advice on beginning invasive or aggressive treatment therapies (Wilson, 1998).

In summary, conflicts around issues, such as autonomy, individual rights, truth-telling, informed consent, and advanced directives, have raised questions about whether principles of autonomy and veracity are *truly respectful of all people in all cultures*. These issues can lead to dilemmas in which the institution or health care provider must either accede to the family's wishes or withdraw care. It is not the cultural tradition that should determine whether disclosure to a patient is ethically appropriate, but rather the client's wish to communicate directly with the provider, to leave communications to the family, or something in between. To ask clients how much they want to be involved in the decision-making process shows respect for their autonomy (Macklin, 1998;

Veatch & Flack, 1997). "Negotiation does not, and should not, always lead to acquiescence to Western views of informed consent, truth-telling or patient's autonomy" (Kaufert & Putsch, 1997, p. 84).

What would show disrespect for persons at a fundamental level? It is for health care providers to make decisions without consulting the client at all, or failure to respect a person's wishes because of traditional religious or cultural beliefs. When beliefs can cause harm to others, attempts to prevent those harmful consequences are justifiable. Respect for autonomy grants clients, who have been properly informed in a manner appropriate to the client's beliefs and understanding, the right to refuse a proposed medical treatment. Western medicine does not have all the answers. Some traditional healing practices are not only not harmful but may be as beneficial as those of Western medicine.

Multiculturalism says that all cultural groups should be treated with respect and as equals; however, it does not say that all of the beliefs and practices of all cultural groups must be equally respected. "We ought to able to respect cultural diversity without having to accept every single feature embedded in traditional beliefs and rituals" (Macklin, 1998, p. 19). This in itself creates another cultural ethical dilemma.

Ethical Responsibility

As health care providers do we have a moral obligation or social responsibility to ensure the just distribution of and access to health care to all people? The state of health care in the United States is insufficient for many poor, women, and ethnic groups. For many it is a continuous struggle to access adequate health care; to make copayments for the health care; and to receive the same dignity and respect that more affluent, educated, or politically informed persons demand and receive (Dula & Goering, 1994). Access to health care is related to the status of a full-time job in a large corporation or to the social merit of having served in the armed forces. It can be diminished by divorce. Children have access to health care in direct proportion to the status of their parents, rather than in proportion to their needs. Medicare for the elderly is the only exception to statues-based access to health care (Miles, 1994; Dowling, 1994). Health status differences between poor and nonpoor, White Americans and people of color, and adults and children can be linked to differences in available services, the nature and quality of those services, and the ways people are helped to make use of them.

The United States has long recognized the specialness of health care and articulated the idea of a right to health care. Dowling (1994) says this has been supported by the generous public support for medical education, special programs for the medically needy, and in the past the insulation of health professionals from market pressure. According to Dowling this specialness is the foundation for creating public moral obligation on health care providers to locate in poor areas. According to Jennings, Callahan, and Wolf (1987), professional health care ethics involves more than obligations to individual clients and other appropriate constituencies; it includes obligation to the public as a whole. Health professions have an obligation and responsibility to control the cost of their services, to maintain (or allow for) an adequate supply of professionals, and to cultivate a professional culture that promotes service to others over self-interest.

Edmund Pellegrino (1987) believes that health professionals have an ethical responsibility to ensure that all segments of the population have access to health care. He states that each provider must establish some hierarchy of values and priorities that will define his or her individual and social ethical responsibility. The provider's first-priority is moral integrity in dealing with the clients he or she treats. The second-order responsibility is in helping shape policies that bear directly on the health of the larger community.

Ferguson (1994, p. 123) asks how physicians can provide medical care to *people whose language, culture, sexual orientation, and socioeconomic status are different from their own.* He states that this question places physicians in an ethical quagmire: How to serve the poor and get paid at the same time? He infers that not only the lack of an economic incentive for working with the poor but also cultural differences were to blame. Some physicians felt inadequate in dealing with clients who speak another language or have different views about compliance. Others cited the bureaucratic tangle of dealing with Medicaid and Medicare for reimbursement. Still, others complained about the client's lack of incentive to keep up with their appointments.

Health care providers must take responsibility for understanding attitudes and values that shape their delivery of health care. Personal views about racial and ethnic and diverse groups can either maintain or reduce the distance between provider and client. To resolve the question of ethical responsibility, we must weigh the rights of the individual provider against those of society. On one hand, providers have a right to serve and work where they please and should not be subjected to national and societal needs. On the other hand, the poor, people of color, and children have a right to basic health care necessary for equality of opportunity.

Dowling (1994, p. 138) asks: *Do [health care providers] have a micro responsibility to provide care to some individuals, or do they, in fact, have a macro or societal obligation as gatekeepers for the social good that is a prerequisite for equal opportunity?* In other words, does the health care provider's obligation to *do no harm* to clients on an individual level translate to a societal obligation to ensure access and just distribution of care to all because the absence of such does harm? The moral challenge to health providers according to McTernan (1989) is to remember that they exist to serve the health care needs of the community and that those needs do not simply exist to provide them with opportunities for achieving wealth and status.

Why should health care professionals acquiesce to the needs of various ethnic, diverse, and poor groups? Simply because we are all members of the human community, regardless of our different identities. Racism, social injustice, insensitivity, and irresponsibility on the part of society and the medical profession have given ethnic minorities and diverse groups a different perspective or outlook on life. To understand the morality and the real-life effects of unfair access and services, providers need to look at the health experiences of real people and different populations. We must be concerned with more than what can be seen in hospitals or clinics; we must also address the wider social issues that affect not only health physiologically, but also influence decisions about health care.

Summary

If the health care providers' views on the ethical principles that govern decision making are in conflict with the values that are held by clients, their families, or their communities, disagreement over cultural values may lead to confrontation. Conflicts that are based on cultural differences can be mediated with strategies that allow both the client and the provider the opportunity to clarify their values (Jecker, Carrese, & Pearlman, 1995). Negotiation does not, and should not, always lead to acquiescence to Western views of informed consent, truth-telling, or a client's autonomy.

When working with a client from a different background, practitioners must initiate systemic ways to communicate the *cultural context* as well as *cultural impact* of their advice and intervention. Providers should openly discuss their personal views and sources of those views. These types of discussions help clients better understand their options and help provide answers to frequent ethical dilemmas. Further, it can help the practitioners develop health approaches, systems, and policies that fully recognize and include the effects of the practitioner's and society's culture on the ethics of medical decisions (Dula & Goering, 1994; Stanfield, 1993; Wilson, 1998).

Medical ethicists need to discuss the obligation of health care providers to treat clients in ethically acceptable ways; they must also assume obligations to reassure the communities that, even though there are good reasons for the paranoia, suspicion must not stand in the way of beneficial treatments (Miles, 1994). "Health care providers must embody an ethic of caring and respect for all groups, a responsibility to condemn unjust medical practices, and a humility and an empathy regarding human suffering, which in the end transcends all cultural and racial prejudices and differences" (Dula & Goering, 1994, p. 8). We need to move toward a health system in which all people receive preventive and curative care—one in which widening disparities between ethnic minorities, women, and the poor are reduced and ultimately eliminated.

References

Anderson, G. R., & Glesnes-Anderson, V. A. (1987). *Health care ethics: A guide for decision makers.* Rockville, MD: Aspen.

Beauchamp, T. L., & Childress, J. F. (1989). *Principles of biomedical ethics* (3rd ed.). New York: Oxford University Press.

Becker, G. K. (1995). Asian and western ethics: Some remarks on a productive tension. *Eubios Journal of Asian and International Bioethics, 5,* 31–33.

Blackhall, L., Murphy, S., Frank, G., Michel, V., & Azen, S. (1995). Ethnicity and attitudes toward patient autonomy. *Journal of the American Medical Association, 274,* 820–25.

Boss, J. A. (1998). *Ethics for life: An interdisciplinary and multicultural introduction.* Mountain View, CA: Mayfield Publishing.

Buford, T. O. (1984). *Personal philosophy: The art of living.* New York: Holt, Rinehart, & Winston.

Callahan, D. (1995). History of bioethics. *Encyclopedia of Bioethics, I* (Rev. ed., pp. 248–256). New York: Macmillan.

Callahan, S. C. (1991). *In good conscience: Reason and emotion in moral decision making.* San Francisco: Harper San Francisco.

Carrese, J. A., & Rhodes, L. A. (1995). Western bioethics on the Navajo reservation, benefit to harm. *Journal of the American Medical Association, 274*(10), 826–829.

Childress, J. (1989). The normative principles of medical ethics. In Robert Veatch (Ed.), *Medical Ethics* (pp. 27–48). Boston: Jones & Barlett.

Clouser, K. D. (1978). Bioethics. In Warren T. Reich (Ed.), *Encyclopedia of Bioethics, Volume I* (pp. 115–127). New York: Free Press.

Davis, A. J., & Koening, B. A. (1996). A question of policy: Bioethics in a multicultural society. *Nursing Policy Forum, 2*(1), 6–11.

Dowling, P. (1994). Access to medical care: Do physicians and academic medical centers have a societal responsibility? In A. Dula & S. Goering (Eds.), *"It just ain't fair:" The ethics of health care for African Americans* (pp. 134–142). New York: Praeger.

Dula, A., & Goering, S. (1994). *"It just ain't fair:" The ethics of health care for African Americans.* New York: Praeger.

Ferguson, W. J. (1994). The physician's responsibility to medically underserved poor people. In A. Dula & S. Goering (Eds.), *"It just ain't fair:" The ethics of health care for African Americans* (pp. 123–133). New York: Praeger.

Fower, B. J., & Richardson, F. C. (1996). Why is multiculturalism good? *American Psychologist, 51*(6), 609–621.

Fox, R. C. (1990). The evolution of American bioethics: A sociological perspective. In George Weisz (Ed.), *Social science perspectives on medical ethics* (pp. 201–220). Philadelphia: University of Pennsylvania Press.

Gostin, L. O. (1995). Informed consent, cultural sensitivity and respect for persons. *Journal of the American Medical Association, 274*(10), 844–845.

Howell, W. S. (1981, November). *Ethics of intercultural communication.* Paper presented to the Speech Communication Association, Anaheim, CA.

Jang, Y. (1995, March). Chinese culture and occupational therapy. *British Journal of Occupational Therapy,* 103–106.

Jecker, N. S., Carrese, J. A., & Pearlman, R. A. (1995). Caring for patients in cross-cultural settings. *Hastings Center Report, 25*(1), 6–14.

Jennings, B., Callahan, D., & Wolf, S. M. (1987, February). The professions: Public interest and common good [Special supplement]. *Hastings Center Report, 17,* 3–10.

Kaufert, J. M., & Koolage, W. W. (1984). Role conflict among culture brokers: The experiences of Native Canadian medical Interpreters. *Social Science and Medicine, 18*(3), 283–286.

Kaufert, J. M., & Putsch, R. W. (1997). Communication through interpreters in health care: Ethical dilemmas arising from differences in class, cultures, language, and power. *The Journal of Clinical Ethics, 8*(1), 71–87.

Longmore, P. K. (1995). Medical decision making and people with disabilities: A clash of cultures. *Journal of Law, Medicine, & Ethics, 23,* 82–87.

Macklin, R. (1998). Ethical relativism in a multicultural society. *Kennedy Institute of Ethics Journals, 8*(1), 1–22.

McTernan, E. J. (1989). *Action in affirmation: Toward an unambiguous profession of nursing.* New York: McGraw-Hill.

Miles, S. (1994). Commentary. In A. Dula & S. Goering (Eds.), *"It just ain't fair:" The ethics of health care for African Americans* (p. 143). New York: Praeger.

Murphy, S. T., Palmer, J. M., Azen, S., Frank, G., Michel, V., & Blackhall, L. J. (1996). Ethnicity and advance care directives. *Journal of Law, Medicine, & Ethics, 24,* 108–117 (Michigan State University).

Paige, R. M., & Martin, J. N. (1996). Ethics in intercultural training. In D. Landis & R. S. Bhagat (Eds.), *Handbook of intercultural training* (2nd ed., pp. 35–60). Newbury Park, CA: Sage.

Pellegrino, E. D. (1987). Toward an expanded medical ethics: The Hippocratic ethic revisited. In J. B. Rogers (Ed.), *Search of the modern hippocratic* (pp. 45–64). Iowa City: University of Iowa Press.

Pellegrino, E. D., & Thomasma, D. C. (1981). *A philosophical basis of medical practice: Toward a philosophy and ethic of the healing professions.* New York: Oxford University Press.

Random House. (1988). *Random house college dictionary: Revised edition.* New York: Random House.

Reich, W. T. (1995). *Encyclopedia of Bioethics, I* (Rev. ed.). New York: Macmillan.

Spicer, C. M. (1995). Nature and role of codes and other ethics directives. *Encyclopedia of Bioethics, I* (Rev. ed., pp. 260–2612). New York: Macmillan.

Stanfield, J. H. (1993). Epistemological considerations. In J. Stanfield & R. Dennis (Eds.), *Race and ethnicity in research methods* (pp. 16–36). Newbury Park, CA: Sage.

Veatch, R. M., & Flack, H. E. (1997). *Case studies in allied health ethics.* Englewood Cliffs, NJ: Prentice Hall.

Wilson, G. (1998). Medical ethics and culture: Whose ethics should we follow? *Contemporary issues.* The Cleveland Clinic Foundation, Department of Bioethics. Retrieved from: www.ccf.org/ed/bioethic/biocon11.htm

Yesley, M. S. (1995). Diversity in bioethics. *Eubios Journal of Asian and International Bioethics, 5,* 87.

CHAPTER FOUR

Culture and Research

Key Points

• Research is a way of gaining and discovering knowledge about others. It is essential to providing the foundation for changing and improving health practices and health care policies.

• Research in the area of race, ethnicity, gender, and culture has been shaped by issues of researcher bias, inadequate data collection instruments and research designs, comparison with White, middle class European American standards or norms, and an insensitivity to cultural differences.

• Culturally linked research must be examined in terms of race and ethnic classification, methodological errors associated with population sampling, misinterpretation of findings, and measurement instruments—and just blindly accepted as fact.

• Research models for studying culture require the use of both an etic (cultural-specific) and emic (cultural-general) approach.

• Research on race, ethnicity, gender, and culture must be designed and conducted within the construct and context of the persons being studied.

• Culture must be considered a variable in all forms and types of research.

The examination of culture is not a new venture. There has been a fascination with other cultures over the decades. Generally, when the terms *culture* and *research* are invoked, many think of work concentrated in faraway places. Research is a way of gaining and discovering knowledge about others. It is essential to providing the scientific foundation for changes. It is needed for improvement in health practices and health care policies in the United States. Yet, research in the area of race, ethnicity, and nondominant cultures has been shaped by political expediency and cultural ideologies (Bhawuk & Triandis, 1996; Stanfield, 1993; Zane, Takeuchi & Young, 1994).

Until recently, our knowledge of the health status, characteristics, and behaviors of ethnic groups and women in the United States have been based on a few epidemiological activities and data that were not designed to focus exclusively on one or more minority groups but on the general population (USPHS, 1994; Zane, Takeuchi & Young, 1994; Williams, 1998). Minority populations and women were often inadequately or inaccurately represented in health research. Study samples either excluded or included them in numbers too small to provide an understanding of the context of health and illness to these groups. Because of this, questions have recently been raised about the validity and reliability of data on the health status and health-related behaviors of minorities and women (Brooks, 1998a; Frayne, Burns, Hardt, Rosen, & Moskowitz, 1996; McGraw, McKinlay, Crawford, Costa, & Cohen, 1992; Pinn, 1998; Williams, 1998). Advocacy groups working today to improve the health of racial and ethnic minorities, as well as women, have recognized that without data to document health problems, it is difficult to draw policymakers' attention and acquire the resources needed to tackle the problem (Carter-Pokras, 1998).

Historically, research about other cultures referred to comparison with middle-class European American as the standard or norm (Brookins, 1993). Along with researcher bias and other issues, data collection instruments, research designs, theories, and methodologies have been cited as reasons for the lack of empirical, realistic, and useful information on racial, ethnic, gender, and cultural differences (Carter-Pokras, 1998; McGraw et al., 1992; Meadow, 1998). Although a number of improvements have been and continue to be made, a number of data gaps and issues remains in the research on nondominate cultures and groups in the United States. This chapter will give a critical review to issues concerning research models and methodologies used in culture, gender, and health research, and to the effects of those issues on the formation of explanations about human life, health, and policies.

Emic and Etic

Culture is a very complex entity. There is no one way or clear road to studying cultures. In the study of culture, there are always two perspectives: (1) the *emic*, which is the native's (insider) point of view; and (2) the *etic*, which is the researcher's (outsider) view (Bhawuk & Triandis, 1996; Hughes, 1990; Stiens, 1990). For example:

> A Vietnamese woman has just delivered a beautiful healthy baby boy, but the new mother's reaction puzzles the delivery nurse attendant. The new mother ignores the baby when the nurse presents him to her. On the hospital records, the nurse describes the mother's response: *Bonding-0*.

The nurse and mother have different views about the event. The nurse (etic) observed the event as a lack of caring and appreciation for the child, though the mother (emic) beheld it as a form of protection rather than indifference. Many Asian persons believe a baby is in grave danger when first born. To recognize the child's presence by fussing over it would bring too much attention that might place the baby in jeopardy, a concept related to the evil eye (Dresser, 1996). Both perspectives involve trade-offs; the emic view provides the subjective experience but limits objectivity. Whereas the etic view is farther from the actual experience of the phenomenon. The culturally sensitive health care provider becomes skilled at gaining both etic and emic perspectives.

These two words also represent two distinct approaches to studying cultures. The *emic approach* (cultural-specific) believes that each culture has unique ideas, behaviors, and concepts and that its uniqueness must be the focus of the study. This approach is followed predominantly by anthropologists. Emics are essential for understanding a culture, but their uniqueness makes them inappropriate for cultural comparisons. The *etic approach* (cultural-general) believes that cultures have both specific and universal dimensions and that both dimensions should be studied. This approach is mainly followed by cross-cultural scientists—both anthropologists and psychologists. Etics are theoretical concepts that allow generalizations about relationships among variables across cultures (Bhawuk & Triandis, 1996).

When studying cultural similarities and differences, one can start with a construct generated in his or her own culture and use it in another culture *(etic approach)*. This is imposing the construct developed in one's culture on to another and is referred to as *psuedoetic* or *imposed etic*. This approach allows researchers to find out how the original construct changes in the second culture—for example, studying the growth and development of children of Asian refugees based on American standards of height, weight, and development. Thus, a derived emic of that culture can be identified (Berry, 1969).

The *emic approach* requires that one start with a theoretical construct. The etic and emic aspects of the construct should be identified. Measurement items for both should be developed by using focus groups and local standards. This provides equivalent measures of the theoretical construct (Triandis, 1994). Employing an *emic approach* and perspective protects against ethnocentrism. "Using a set of behavioral standards developed according to the norms of one culture to assess a client from another culture is a culture imposition based on ethnocentricity" (Kavanagh & Kennedy, 1992, p. 32).

The methods used for studying cultures depend on the research question, the knowledge of the investigators, the cultural acceptability of various techniques, the sophistication of the respondents, and many other variables (Bhawuk & Triandis, 1996; McGraw et al., 1992; Stanfield, 1993). In general, emic approaches, such as ethnographic techniques, systematic observations, and content analyses, should be used when the researcher knows relatively little about the culture and when a holistic picture is of interest. Data collection using these strategies tends to be maximally appropriate (Bhawuk & Triandis, 1996; Facio, 1993). "Although the data have depth and are usually collected ethically, one cannot really depend upon the findings" (Bhawuk & Triandis, 1996, p. 32).

Testing, experimentation, and questionnaires are useful when the researcher has limited goals, knows a great deal about the culture, and has some well-developed theory to test. These methods are often culturally inappropriate and obtrusive (Malpass, 1977). Surveys can accomplish what they try to do but often do not greatly increase the researcher's understanding of cultures (Bhawuk & Triandis, 1996; Patton, 1993). Survey analyses tend to oversimplify many of the differences among population groups and subgroups. This results in false homogeneity within the group: they are all presumed to think alike (Smith, 1993). Bhawuk and Triandis (1996, p. 32) suggest that combined approaches of etic and emic are the most useful:

> Unstructured interviewing, questionnaires based on the interviews, and validation with some method are the essential elements of studies of subjective culture. The amount of work required is great, but so is the payoff in terms of understanding cultural similarities and differences.

Research Models

Research models that portray persons from other cultures or diverse backgrounds as inferior serve as barriers and prevent the development of appropriate, culturally sensitive, and useful intervention strategies. White, middle class value systems have often been reflected in research regarding racial and ethnic groups.

> The act of imposing the experiences of the dominant on the subordinate as a logic for explaining their attributes and ignoring the relevance of subordinate experiences for explaining those of the dominant extend the parameters of folk racial ideologies (Stanfield, 1993, p. 34).

Historically, research regarding racial and ethnic groups has been guided by three harmful models (Ponterotto, 1988; Sue, Arredondo, & McDavis, 1992; Sue & Sue, 1990):

1. *Inferiority or Pathological Model*—The basic premise is that minorities are lower on the evolutionary scale (more primitive) and are more inherently pathological.

2. *Deficient Model*—Assumes that Blacks and other racial and ethnic minorities are deficient in desirable genes. And the differences between Whites and minorities are the reflection of biological and genetic inferiority.

3. *Deficient or Disadvantaged Model*—Blames the culture for the *minority problems*.

The underlying data and research regarding racial and ethnic minorities using these models have: (a) perpetuated a view that minorities were inherently pathological, (b) perpetuated racist research practices, and (c) provided an excuse not to take social action to rectify inequities in the system (Katz, 1985; Stanfield & Dennis, 1993; Sue, Arredondo, & McDavis, 1992).

All too often society's view of minorities depicts deprivation and emphasizes weakness. "One of the great difficulties with formulations like culturally deprived, disadvantaged, culturally handicapped, impoverished, and so forth, is that they connote inadequacy, rather than present a rounded picture of the culture that would have to include strengths as well as deficiencies" (Ayers, 1967, p. i). This deficit orientation and context denies that other cultures have their own unique integrity. Secondly, it affixes the problem within the *disadvantaged* person.

Relationship to Health Care

The U.S. health care delivery and policy targeting minorities have historically employed these models in terms of outcomes for care and services. The importance of race and gender have often been downplayed or negated in health analysis. The claim is made that minorities experience poor health and premature death because of pathological behaviors. The *blaming the victim* approach is reminiscent of earlier justifications used to defend health care policies that denied health care to African Americans during a time when racism was sanctioned by law throughout a majority of states in the Union. People thought that minorities were dying, so commitment to care for them would be wasted (Smith, 1998). Unfortunately, variations of these models and arguments continue to undergrid race, ethnic, gender, and cultural research as well as health policies.

New Research Models

New and conceptually different models of research are emerging to discover knowledge about nondominate cultures. These include the *Culturally Different Model* (Katz, 1985), *Multicultural Model* (Johnson, 1990), and *Culturally Pluralistic Model* (Ponterotto & Cass, 1991). These models have several premises and assumptions in common:

- There is the belief that to be culturally different does not equate with *deviancy, pathology, or inferiority.*

- There is a strong acknowledgment that racial and ethnic minorities are bicultural and function in at least two different cultural contexts.

- Biculturality is seen as a positive and desirable quality that enriches the full range of human potential.

- Individuals are viewed in relationship to their environment and the larger social forces (e.g., racism, oppression, discrimination) rather than the individual or minority group being the obstacles.

Ethnographic research design uses principles of and methods of cultural anthropology to study aspects of daily life within a social group. The orientation of an ethnographic study is descriptive. Its analytic procedures are open-ended. Its focus tends to be activity-based, and it occurs in social settings. It requires both emic and etic descriptions, and a cyclical collection and comparison of data.

Culturally linked research outcomes enable service providers to build on the strengths of the individual's culture and use the unique resources of that culture to effect solutions. The radical changes in this country and in world society require that we become proactive in establishing new models of research for studying racial, ethnic, gender, and diverse groups and adopt new ones that encourage refreshing and more adequate logic of inquiry.

Epistemological Issues

Moving forward in racial, ethnic, gender, and culture research requires more than reconsidering concepts and models. It must begin with reviewing, questioning, and finally creating new epistemologies to ground theories and test them. In terms of research, epistemology includes not only the methods used to obtain human knowledge but also ethics, human values, and politics, involving how researchers structure relationships with collaborators and with subjects (Stanfield, 1993).

Researchers are often unaware of the racial, gender, and cultural misperceptions they bring to research. Those inaccurate perceptions and associated ethnocentric biases influence what research questions are asked; how studies are designed; which research projects are funded; and how results are interpreted, disseminated, and applied. In addition to ethnocentric biases, there are other problems associated with conducting effective race, ethnic, gender, and cultural research, such as: (a) validity of racial and ethnic classification, (b) methodological errors associated with population sampling, and (c) misinterpretation of findings. Whether researchers take a quantitative or a qualitative approach, there are certain epistemological universals in race, ethnic, gender, and cultural relations research that must be considered in the design and execution of research processes.

Race and Ethnicity in Health Statistics

For decades data have been collected comparing health care in racial and ethnic groups. The use of such groups in health services research assumes that standard, reliable, and valid definitions of race and ethnicity exist; and these definitions are used consistently. The use of race and ethnic information in public health research and intervention is often taken for granted. They are routinely used with little attention given to the underlying problems of measurement that exist for current racial categories or how the data will be used. In health research, race, ethnicity, and gender are rarely studied, but rather used as a cause factor (Carter-Pokras, 1998; Centers for Disease Control and Prevention, 1993).

Race is a term often used but ill defined. It can incorporate biological, social, and cultural characteristics of clients. It can refer to both genetic and behavioral traits (Schulman, Rubenstien, Chesley, & Eisenberg, 1995). When race is used as a variable in research, there is a tendency to assume that the results obtained are a manifestation of the biology of racial differences. Race as a variable implies that a genetic reason may explain differences in incidence, severity, or outcome of medical conditions. Researchers, without saying so, lead readers to assume that certain racial groups have a special predisposition, risk, or susceptibility to the illness studied. Because this presupposition is seldom warranted, this kind of comparison may be taken to represent a subtle form of racism (Osborne & Feit, 1992). Many studies use race as a proxy for other socioeconomic factors not collected in the research effort. The question to ask is, *Is race being used as a biogenetic variable or as a proxy variable for environmental variables?*

Race is an unscientific, societally constructed taxonomy that is fluid and without boundaries (Centers for Disease Control and Prevention, 1993; Feinleib, 1993). It is based on an ideology that views some human population groups as inherently superior to others on the basis of external physical characteristics or geographic origin (Williams, Lavizzo-Mourey, & Warren, 1994). The concept of race is socially meaningful, but of limited biological significance. Racial or ethnic variations in health status stem primarily from variation among races in exposure or vulnerability to behavioral, psychosocial, material, and environmental risk factors and resources (Scribner, 1996; Williams et al., 1994; Wray, 1992). The scientific pitfalls that stand in the way of ethnic research are formidable because racial status is highly correlated with social, economic, and political factors (Osborne & Feit, 1992).

There are ethical problems with the search for genetic reasons to explain certain types of diseases. Kumanyika and Golden (1991) suggest genetic explanations of differences can play into stereotypes and can even be interpreted as reasons for not addressing environmental risk factors; environmental explanations may be viewed as evidence of negative lifestyle practices that are the responsibility of the individual, not service institutions. Others may view environmental explanations of racial and cultural differences as indications of institutional racism.

If we assume that *race* suggests *biologic differences* and *ethnicity* suggests *nonbiologic differences,* then the value of race information in health research is limited. Ethnicity becomes more important, but only as a marker of social, environmental, and cultural risks. A *risk factor* is an aspect of personal behavior or lifestyle, an environmental exposure, or an inborn or inherited characteristic that is associated with an increased occurrence of diseases or other health-related event or condition. In contrast, a *risk marker* simply indicates the increased likelihood of the presence of a particular risk factor, but is itself not related to the disease or condition. The risk factor is the true cause, though the risk marker is an indicator of the cause that is itself not the cause (Centers for Disease Control and Prevention, 1993). For example, the risk factor for sickle cell anemia is the presence of the hemoglobin S gene. The Black race is a risk marker. For a relatively small number of diseases and conditions, genetic factors related to race are important (e.g., sickle cell anemia, gallbladder cancer, and hepatitis B and its sequelae.) For other diseases and conditions, race becomes a proxy measure for factors related to class, lifestyle, and socioeconomic status (Feinleib, 1993; Hahn, 1992; Osborne & Feit, 1992; Scribner, 1996; Williams et al., 1994; Wray, 1992). Information on race and ethnicity is used in public health research for describing health status, for designing and targeting intervention programs, and for assuring equality in health status for all Americans (USPHS, 1994). Schulman et al. (1995) suggest that health services researchers focus on nonracial, socioeconomic characteristics that might be more informative and more useful in guiding policy formation.

Measuring Race and Ethnicity

Because the measurement of race and ethnicity are not scientific, rules are necessary to guide assignment of race so that there can be some understanding of resulting statistics. Using race as a means of classifying the population has a long statistical tradition in the United States. For more than 20 years, the Office of Management and Budget's (OMB) Statistical Policy Directive No. 15, *Race and Ethnic Standards for Federal Statistics and Administrative Reporting,* have provided a common language for uniformity and comparability in the collection and use of data on race and ethnicity by federal agencies. These categories are required for use in all federally sponsored data collection and reporting activities involving questions on race and ethnicity. Although most Public Health data and epidemiological research activities include the OMB standard race and ethnicity categories, they are not universal.

After an extensive and lengthy review process, in October of 1997, OMB revised the standards for classification of race and ethnicity in federal data. The standards have five categories for data on race— (1) American Indian or Alaska Native, (2) Asian, (3) Black or African American, (4) Native Hawaiian or Other Pacific Islander, and (5) White—and two categories on ethnicity—*Hispanic or Latino* and *Not Hispanic or Latino* (Table 7). The categories in this classification represent a sociopolitical construct designed for collecting data on the race and ethnicity of broad population groups in this country, and they are not anthropologically or scientifically based (OMB, 1998).

Although the OMB standard categories are extremely valuable in promoting uniform and comparable health data, the categories are broad and some encompass many different subpopulations (Evinger, 1995). Use of the OMB standards may mask major differences within racial and ethnic populations (USPHS, 1994; Yu & Liu, 1994). For example, the National Center for Health Statistics (NCHS) collects and publishes data on births and deaths in the United States; however, ethnic identifiers for Asians and Pacific Islanders only recognize Japanese, Chinese, and Filipinos. There are no codes for the fastest growing and more recent Asian immigrants and refugees—Koreans, Vietnamese, Cambodians, Hmongs, Laotians, East Indians, Thais, Burmese, Malaysians, and Indonesians. General grouping of ethnic populations does not always get at those subgroups that may be at risk. Thus, a population that may be at risk remains unidentified and underserved.

In addition, persons of mixed racial and ethnic backgrounds have difficulty responding to the standard OMB classification. Given the current rates of interracial marriages, the question of how to classify individuals whose parents are of different races continues to be a debated topic. Persons and parents of multiracial children are asked to choose a single racial category. Proponents of a multiracial category

Table 7. Office of Management and Budget—Standards for the Classification of Federal Data on Race and Ethnicity

---
Race

American Indian or Alaska Native—A person having origins in any of the original peoples of North and South America, including Central America, who maintains tribal affiliation or community attachment

Asian—A person having origins in any of the original peoples of the Far East, Southeast Asia, or the Indian subcontinent, including, for example, Cambodia, China, India, Japan, Korea, Malaysia, Pakistan, the Philippine Islands, Thailand, and Vietnam

Black or African American—A person having origins in any of the Black racial groups of Africa. Terms, such as *Haitian* or *Negro*, can be used in addition to *Black* or *African American*.

Native Hawaiian or Other Pacific Islander—A person having origins in any of the original peoples of Hawaii, Guam, Samoa, or other Pacific Islands

White—A person having origins in any of the original peoples of Europe, the Middle East, or North Africa

---
Ethnicity

Two Categories—(1) *Hispanic or Latino* and (2) *Not Hispanic or Latino*

Hispanic or Latino—A person of Cuban, Mexican, Puerto Rican, South or Central American, or Spanish culture or origin, regardless of race. The term *Spanish origin* can be used in addition to *Hispanic* or *Latino*.

Source: *Federal Register Notice,* 62 FR 36874–36946, July 9, 1997.

argue that the current categories force people to deny the racial heritage of one parent when they must choose one race, thereby adversely affecting their self-esteem, sense of family and pride, and psychological well-being. Users of health data argue that a multiracial category would result in data that are not useful in analyzing the health status of population groups that historically have been at risk for certain diseases—for example, hypertension within the African American population. Health uses of racial and ethnic data from multiracial categories with no races indicated would become increasingly problematic with marriages between multiracial persons. Racial and ethnicity classification questions will apply to an ever-increasing proportion of the population (Evinger, 1995; Williams, 1998).

The new OMB standards recommend that self-identification be used where possible, that they allow persons to report more than one race, and that Hispanic ethnicity be asked as a separate question from race. Guidelines for the implementation of the new standards for racial and ethnic data—including comparisons of data collected using the old and new standards—are being developed by OMB.

Quality of Racial and Ethnic Data

Another problem with measuring race and ethnicity that has an important effect on the quality of cultural data is the process of ascertaining the race and ethnicity of a person. Race and ethnicity are assigned through two methods: (1) self-identification or (2) another's perceptions of the person's race and ethnicity. The reliability of data on race and ethnicity becomes of particular concern when this information is obtained from records that may be completed by someone other than the individual of interest. Methodological research reveals inaccuracies in the classification and coding of race and ethnicity on vital records (USPHS, 1994).

Birth certificates in the United States have never listed the race of the child. They include the race of both parents. Before 1989, NCHS used an algorithm to determine the race of a newborn. The person completing the birth certificate was to elicit information from the parents and to provide the race of both parents. If both parents were White, the child was considered to be White. If the father was White and the mother belonged to a different race, the child would be given the race of the mother. But if the father was non-White, the child would be assigned the race of the father. If one parent was Hawaiian, then the child was Hawaiian. Thus, unlike the assignment of race for all other racial groups, the child would be White only if both parents were White. If the race of one parent was unknown, the race of the other parent was assigned. If racial information on both parents was lacking, the child was assigned the race of the child in the preceding record of the NCHS computer file. NCHS no longer reports vital statistics by the race of the child, but it reports all birth data by the mother's race. The race of the father is only used if the mother's race is unknown. The ethnicity of the child, both before and after 1989, is determined by the ethnicity of the mother (Hahn, 1992).

Respondent self-report is not an option on the death certificate. Officials (e.g., funeral director, medical examiner, coroner) who complete these forms make a decision based on their own judgment instead of obtaining the race of the deceased from the next of kin. Even though it is recommended that the next of kin be consulted, many funeral directors consider requesting racial information as an imposition on the family

(Williams, 1998). The last name of the individual is commonly used to determine ethnicity of the person.

According to Williams (1998), discrepancy between race as observed and self-reported was seen in a 1978 Health Interview Survey. Racial information was collected both by an interviewer and self-report. Analysis revealed that 6% of persons who reported themselves as Black, 29% as Asian, 62% as American Indians, and 80% as *other*, were classified by the interviewer as White.

The reliability of self-identification of race and ethnicity is also questionable. Studies have shown that an individual's perception on race and ethnicity changes over time (Centers for Disease Control and Prevention, 1993; LaVeist; 1997). The most dramatic evidence of change in self-identification has been among American Indians. Between 1960 and 1990 there was a six-fold increase in the Indian population. This growth cannot be explained by biological growth or international migration. According to Williams (1998, p. 4), it appears to reflect a change in self-definition, with more adults of mixed ancestry identifying themselves as American Indian. There may well be periods when an individual identifies more closely with different races and ethnicities.

Regardless of the options for response to race and ethnicity questions, the method of response is different for each data set. Self-perceptions, next of kin identification, and the use of algorithms to determine race may well lead to conflicting results. It is important that comparison data sets be identified early in a research project so that data might be collected appropriately. Our current approach to race identification for statistical purposes expects identification of one race per person. This forces individuals who perceive themselves to be of mixed race ancestry to choose. It may well increase the number of respondents who identify as *other race*. And it may lead persons to change their reported race over time as they identify more closely with one particular race as there are political, social, or economic reasons to do so.

Methodological Errors

Too many studies are published claiming to be *American Studies* that are rooted in White American populations and sampling, with short notes explaining the reasons for excluding persons of color, whose presence in the study would just complicate the analysis (Stanfield, 1993). It has been viewed both appropriate and normative for social researchers to select male Euro American populations or samples for studies with no or little regard for populations or samples made up of persons of color or women.

In selecting a sample, researchers are concerned about the representativeness of the persons they choose to interview or study. It is difficult in epidemiological studies of racial and ethnic groups to defend the selection of respondents for health surveys using less than scientifically rigorous sampling methods and still obtain the critical approval of statisticians who are accustomed to using conventional sampling schema. Thus, insufficient attention has been directed to improving the ability of our basic health surveys and epidemiological activities to develop strategies to ensure the inclusion of sufficient numbers of minorities and women in study samples to support estimates (USPHS, 1994).

The issue of sampling from small populations has been one of the reasons little or no large-scale health epidemiological study has been conducted for racial and ethnic minorities. Most large-scale studies include only small samples of ethnic individuals. Large-scale studies usually weigh the data to the population figures of the community, geographic region, or the nation as a whole. These factors may disguise the fact that ethnic samples are actually quite small. A small sample does not have sufficient statistical power to detect important health needs. Complex multivariate analyses are not possible to identify high-risk subgroups. When a large sample of Asian Americans, Hispanics, or American Indians are collected, they are often collapsed into one category. Because these groups are quite heterogeneous, the use of a general category makes it difficult to assess their needs accurately (Andersen, 1993; Stanfield, 1993; Zane, Takeuchi & Young, 1994).

According to McGraw et al. (1992), a valid, reliable, and efficient research study can only be mounted when researchers pay attention to the procedures used to identify and locate study subjects. Because members of minority groups can be small and highly dispersed in any given geographic area, existing sampling frames can misidentify or misrepresent members of some minority groups. Census data often undercount minority populations. Commercial directories and government lists omit many dwelling units and multiple-dwelling unit structures in low-income, urban minority communities. Some researchers have resorted to the use of telephone or ethnic directories or marketing firms to obtain a universe of ethnic populations (Zane, Takeuchi & Young, 1994). But the accuracy as well as differential biases of these lists must be addressed if the surveys are to be credible.

Generally in health research, the population sample tends to include only those individuals who are receiving health services. Data based on clinic populations offer insight into the health problems of those ethnic individuals who use the services, but no information as to how representative that clinic population is of the ethnic community in any single region of the country (Yu & Liu, 1992). It is also well documented that ethnic groups delay seeking professional care for their health problems (Brooks, 1998a; Ponce, 1992; Zane, Takeuchi & Young, 1994). Because of this pattern of behavior, researchers often conclude that ethnic populations underuse health services rather than ask, *Is the sample size sufficient enough to generalize about a whole ethnic population? Why do certain groups use or not use health services? Are there differences in need among ethnic and diverse groups? Why are services underused? Is there a cultural mismatch between those in need and service strategies used?*

Frayne et al. (1996), reviewed studies from 1989 to 1991 to determine how often non-English-speaking (NES) persons were excluded from medical research. They surveyed all original investigators whose methodologies involved direct interaction between researchers and subjects (number of subjects = 216). Of the respondents, 22% had included NES persons, 16% had not considered the issue during the study design process, and 32% thought including the NES had affected their study results. Among the 40% who excluded the NES, the most common reason was not having thought of the issue (51%) followed by translation issues and recruitment of bilingual staff. The remaining 35% indicated that there were no NES persons in their study areas. The authors concluded that NES persons are often excluded through oversight. The exclusion of NES persons from provider–client communication studies greatly limits the generalizability of the findings.

Guidelines on the inclusion of women and minorities in clinical studies have been recommended and in place since 1989 at the National Institutes of Health (NIH). In 1987 a policy encouraging the inclusion of women and minorities was first published. According to Pinn (1998), in 1990 the General Accounting Office (GAO) conducted an investigation into the implementation of the guidelines at NIH. The results indicated that the implementation of the policy was lacking, slow, not well communicated, that gender analysis was not implemented, and that the effect of this policy could not be determined. The GAO study also indicated that there were differences in the implementation of the policy and that not all institutes factored adherence to these policies into the scientific merit review.

After the GAO report and the establishment of the Office of Research on Women's Health (ORWH)—which has a legislative mandate to ensure that women and minorities are included in NIH-supported clinical research—the NIH strengthened and revitalized its inclusion guidelines. The ORWH is responsible for overseeing as well as monitoring the implementation of the guidelines in NIH-supported clinical trails to ensure adequate representation.

The USPHS (1994, p. 40) said that oversampling strategies may work for some populations; but this approach is not a panacea, and a multifaceted strategy is needed. Other approaches may involve the addition of minority group follow-back surveys to existing survey mechanisms, or the conduct of special targeted surveys like the Hispanic HANES or the survey of American Indians and Alaska Natives. In large-scale registries or community-based epidemiological research studies, it may be necessary to add study sites that include adequate numbers of minority groups of interest. For some small subpopulations, smaller scale targeted epidemiological studies may offer the best data development strategy (USPHS, 1994).

Individual Researchers

Another important issue of concern is the cultural similarity or disparity between the researcher and the study population. Researchers are often unaware of the racial and cultural misperception they bring to research.

The studies on the health of Asian Americans and Pacific Islanders face major obstacles, including a lack of communication among qualified mainstream and Asian American and Pacific Islander health investigators, and intense competition among trained Asian American and Pacific Islander researchers for limited resources, as well as the *town-and-gown* conflict between *community advocates* and *academics* on the objectives (Yu & Liu, 1992, p. 46).

Researchers in mainstream disciplines rarely reflect on the effects their racial, ethnic, gender, and cultural identities and consciousness might have on what they see and interpret in their studies. By constructing supposedly value-neutral methods of data collection and interpretation, they are able to rationalize and justify their claims rather than acknowledge the intrusions of their life histories and cognitive styles in research processes (Andersen, 1993; Stanfield, 1993).

Study across race, class, and gender lines poses unique methodological problems for both researchers and subjects. The problems of doing research within ethnic communities are compounded by the social distance imposed by class and race-relations when interviewers are White and middle-class and those being interviewed are not (Andersen, 1993; Facio, 1993). Community leaders often see researchers as exploiters whose studies are divorced from real issues and real life problems (Zane, Takeuchi & Young, 1994).

Research data are also limited by interviewer reliability. Often evaluations are made by a number of interviewers or investigators. Different interviewers create biases, especially when they must rate subjects on a number of dimensions. Some investigators may be more thorough in their evaluations than others, and some subjects may describe their problems more openly with some researchers than others (McGraw et al., 1992; Zane, Takeuchi & Young, 1994; Williams, 1998). Some studies have noted that investigators are more effective when they reside in the study neighborhoods or at least share the culture under investigation (Aneshensel et al., 1989; Salber & Beza, 1980). "Those who study minorities can encounter problems in establishing rapport with the community, especially when the survey work is conducted over an extended period of time in a specific geographic site" (McGraw et al., 1992, p. 284). Some have found that the investigators' ethnicity had notable effects on responses to racially sensitive questions (Campbell, 1981; Cotter, Cohen, & Coulter, 1982; Schaeffer, 1980). The beliefs and values of researchers will shape the answers to the questions more than any *objective data* that might be collected and analyzed (Cultural Diversity in Rehabilitation, 1994).

Memories of the Tuskegee Syphilis Study and the health consequences associated with the use of DES and Thalidomide by pregnant women have created biases and cultural barriers against medical research for many Americans, especially minority populations and women (Brooks, 1998a; Pinn, 1998). Mistrust of the health system and White researchers accounts for some of the under-representation of minorities in clinical trials (Meadows, 1998). According to Brooks (1998a), several studies have shown differences in attitude toward medical research between African Americans and White Americans. In *Barriers to Black Women's Participation in Cancer Clinical Trails* (Mouton et al., 1997), African American women were more likely to believe that clinical research was unethical. They also believed that the researcher did not care about them, and that by participating in the research they would not have access to better care. They indicated they would be more likely to participate in a clinical trial if the researcher was also African American. African American men were found to hold similar attitudes toward

Tuskegee Syphilis Study

In 1932, the Public Health Service, working with the Tuskegee Institute, began a study in Macon County, Alabama, to record the natural history of syphilis in the hopes of justifying treatment programs for Blacks. It was called the "Tuskegee Study of Untreated Syphilis in the Negro Male." The study involved 600 Black men—399 with syphilis and 201 who did not have the disease. Researchers told the men they were being treated for "bad blood," a local term used to describe several ailments including syphilis, anemia, and fatigue. In truth, they did not receive the proper treatment needed to cure their illness. In exchange for participation in the study, the men received medical exams, free meals, and burial insurance. The study was originally projected to last 6 months; it actually went on for 40 years.

Although the men had agreed freely to be examined and treated, there was no evidence that researchers had informed them of the study or its real purpose. The men had been misled and had not been given all the facts required to provide informed consent. They were never given adequate treatment for their disease. Even when penicillin became the drug of choice for syphilis in 1947, researchers did not offer it to the subjects. It was also found that the men were not even given the choice to quit the study when this new and effective treatment became widely used. An Ad Hoc Advisory Panel, appointed by the Assistant Secretary for Health and Scientific Affairs, in October 1972, concluded that the Tuskegee Study was "ethically unjustified"—the knowledge gained was sparse when compared with the risks posed to its subjects. The study was ended in November of that year. (For more information see: Centers for Disease Control and Prevention, *Historical time line of the Tuskegee Study,* URL: http://www.cdc.gov.)

DES (diethylstilbestrol)

DES is a synthetic estrogen drug that was given to millions of pregnant women from 1938–1971 to prevent miscarriage, bleeding, or premature birth. It was thought to ensure a healthy pregnancy, but it did not work. Women who took DES and the children they carried are at risk for certain health problems. Women who took DES have a high risk for breast cancer; DES daughters have an increased risk of cervix and vaginal cancer, infertility, pregnancy problems, and structural changes in their reproductive organs; and DES sons face an increased risk of problems with their genital organs, such as testicular problems, epididymal cysts, microphallus, hypospadias, and testicular varicoceles. (For more information see: DES Action, http://www.desaction.org.)

Thalidomide

Thalidomide, a teratogen drug, was used in the 1950s and 1960s by pregnant women to treat morning sickness. It was sold as a sedative for pregnant women in 48 countries—but not in the United States. Regardless, some Americans got the drug overseas or in clinical trials. Before scientists discovered the danger, as many as 12,000 children worldwide were born with horrific birth defects. Just one pill in early pregnancy could result in a baby with no limbs or with flipper-like arms and legs, serious facial deformities, and defective organs.

prostate cancer clinical trials. A study on *Attitudes of African Americans Regarding Prostate Cancer Clinical Trails* (Robinson et al., 1996), showed that African American men lacked confidence in physicians with non-American accents.

Misinterpretation of Findings

Interpretation of racial and ethnic population differences can be particularly problematic. Misinterpretation becomes a barrier to the development of new knowledge and more effective services. Often race and ethnic research results overemphasize between-group differences and underemphasize within-group differences (Smith, 1993). Racial and ethnic data analysis and the interpretation of results must take into consideration the social context of the subjects studied (McGraw, et al., 1992; Stanfield, 1993; Dennis, 1993).

Cultural standards of data generalization are the basis of researcher presumptions regarding the racial, ethnic, or female population source of constructing universal statements. It has been the norm to assume that male Eurocentric empirical realities can be generalized to explain the realities of persons of color and women. For decades researchers, using Eurocentric norms, have applied Eurocentric concepts of families, deviance, social movements, psychological development, behavior, stratification, health, and even spirituality to the experiences of persons of color (Stanfield, 1993). The realities of persons of color are not considered legitimate standards of generalizations to Eurocentric realities.

> It is rare for mainstream scholars to select empirical observations about persons of color, such as religious behaviors or a female-headed family structure, to explain Eurocentric realities. Yet, researchers have relived deviant and pathological patterns of the poor and of people of color and normalize such trends when they become dominant middle class Euro-American patterns (Stanfield, 1993, p. 28).

Measurement Instruments

It is well established that culture affects all perceptions of life, including physical and emotional conditions. The measurement of similarities and differences across cultures relies on the development and use of standardized instruments. Medical technology can reliably detect physical disease, but cultural factors can constrain the ways individuals define and evaluate their health problems, present their problems to the physician, and seek help for their problems. Researchers, assuming that concepts and measurements of health and illness are universal from one cultural group to another, have used standardized instruments without assessing the reliability and validity of these instruments for specific ethnic, racial, or gender populations. Because cultural groups vary in their definitions of normality and abnormality, and these variations affect models of health and illness, this assumption is unwarranted (Zane, Takeuchi & Young, 1994). Some of the cultural factors affected by culture include types and parameters of stressors, coping mechanisms, personality patterns, language systems, and expressions of illness. Without proper consideration of these issues, errors are often made in diagnosis, evaluation, and treatment, as well as the understanding of the group being studied.

If the study population does not speak the primary language of the researcher and interviewer, which is usually English, the problems of translating the instrument into another language must be considered. Because of the existence of diverse languages and dialects, researchers must pay attention to regional and ethnic group differences when translating data collection instruments. According to Yu & Liu (1994), in a major health study, an instrument was translated from English to Spanish. Upon field use of the Spanish instrument, the researchers noted that Latinos were scoring very low on one particular question: *How often do you kiss your child?* After checking and double-checking the original questionnaire, someone checked the translation and found that the translated question read: *How often do you kiss your puppy?* Attention must be given to establish the equivalence difference between the dialect and language versions of an instrument.

Beside the translation considerations, researchers must also be concerned with conceptual, scale, and norm equivalence (McGraw et al, 1992; Zane, Takeuchi & Young, 1994). For example, do ethnic minorities and White Americans think of well-being, depression, or self-esteem in the same way? Are recent immigrants or individuals not educated in United States familiar with answering survey questions using responses along a scale that includes *strongly agree, agree,* and so on, or with a true-false dichotomy? Are the standards of weight and height developed among White Americans suitable for Asian Americans?

If a large proportion of the study population is bilingual or uses multiple languages, then researchers must also be careful to employ bilingual or multilingual interviewing staff. This strategy is preferred over conducting interviews through interpreters, a procedure that severely compromises the quality of the data (Fray, et al., 1996; McGraw et al., 1992).

Health Data Systems

In promoting the health of the U.S. population, having reliable and timely data is crucial. The Public Health Service (PHS) relies on a wide variety of data sources (see chapter 2, "Health Disparities and Inequalities"). Yet, limitation exists in collecting and providing accurate data on ethnic minority populations and subgroups (Feinleib, 1993; USPHS, 1994; McGraw et al., 1992; Yu & Liu, 1992). Carter-Pokras (1998) identified several possible reasons for this lack of data: (1) data may have never been collected from a national data system; (2) national data systems may have insufficient numbers of a particular group to make reliable estimates; (3) Puerto Rico, the U.S. Virgin Islands, and the U.S. Public Insular areas are generally not included in national data systems; and (4) only racial and ethnic minority groups with a documented disparity versus the total population are included in national data surveys. "The lack of data is likely to have a negative impact on availability of [research] resources" (p. 8).

In general, national health survey data have oversampled for Black and White populations but not for others (Feinleib, 1993). Delgado & Estrada (1993) examined 21 major health data systems of the U.S. Department of Health and Human Services (HHS) and concluded that data on Hispanics are not included in several of their national health data collection systems. Of the 21 data systems, 6 did not collect Hispanic population data, including the Medicare statistical system. Even when collected, data on Hispanic subpopulations were found in few of the systems. Only the National Vital Health Statistics System was found to collect data for all major Hispanic subpopulation groups.

Routine health collection data systems tend to focus exclusively on specific types of diseases that are well defined in terms of pathological manifestations and clinical diagnoses. They cannot address a broader array of concepts, such as (1) *health status*, (2) *health behaviors*, or (3) *health utilization*. These data are almost always collected in selective locations and are therefore of limited use in providing a national picture of the health status of ethnic populations. Missing data are a common problem in public records, especially data on income, occupational status, and educational level. These three variables are important in determining whether differences in health status among groups can be attributed to ethnicity or socioeconomic status. Some variables that are critical to understanding the health status of ethnic populations may not be recorded or collected on health clinic forms, such as primary language, place of birth, and generation (USPHS, 1994; Yu & Liu, 1992).

Estimates based on data systems, which do not routinely use self-identification to collect racial and ethnic data, such as mortality data, may significantly underestimate the burden of disease, disability, and death for certain racial and ethnic groups. Racial and ethnic data are descriptive and do not get at the underlying reasons behind the health disparities (Carter-Pokeras, 1998). Additional information on socioeconomic status, program participation, behavioral risk factors, cultural differences, birthplace and generation, and the effects of racism and discrimination are needed.

The importance of obtaining and seeking health information and data for the understudied population, such as women and minorities, has been seen through the passage of the Disadvantaged Minority Health Improvement Act of 1990 (P.L. 101-527); the 1991 Cooperative Agreement issued by the Center for Disease Control to the Asian and Pacific Islander American Health forum; and the National Coalition of Hispanic Health and Human Services Organizations to advance the understanding of the health of racial and ethnic populations or subpopulations, authorized under Section 306 (42G U.S. 242K) of the Public Health Service Act. This agreement provides unprecedented opportunities for researchers to analyze previously collected health data and improve existing research methodologies or test innovative methodological techniques used in gathering information on special populations.

In October of 1997, the Secretary of HHS issued an inclusion policy that requires all data systems funded and maintained by the federal government to collect racial and ethnic data. Public hearings have been held to address the needs of Puerto Rico, the Virgin Islands, and the U.S. Insular areas. OMB and USPHS have already begun concerted efforts to standardize data collection, improve funding for data systems, and strengthen the quality of data to meet the objectives of Healthy People 2010.

Other Considerations

The moral dilemmas in race, ethnicity, and gender research are numerous. According to Stanfield (1993), considering the history of race and ethnicity as a field of study, the research processes of social sciences involve powerful relationships between dominant (researcher) and subordinate (subject) parties that can be studied empirically, like any other form of social inequality. Research on persons of color has been based on researchers asking subjects embarrassing and inappropriate questions that even the researchers themselves would never answer and would certainly never ask their own relatives, friends, or colleagues. Research on the poor, in which subjects receive services in return for consenting to be part of a research study or clinical practice, involves taking advantage of the marginal resources and communities of the poor by developing exploitative exchange relationship—for instance, exposure of their bodies in exchange for free access to teaching hospital clinics. Such abuse of subjects is what Stanfield calls *legal unethical behaviors*.

  New immigrants and refugees from politically controlled areas in Asia understandably associate surveys and research with police interrogations or punitive political actions. They may refuse to give written consent because they are unable to write their own name; others simply cannot understand why they must sign their names to answer a series of harmless questions (Yu & Lui, 1994). Does the signature violate the promise of anonymity and confidentiality?

Summary

  One problem that contributes to the state of services and health disparities in the United States is a lack of research and data. Just as important as the lack of adequate research is the unfortunate manner in which research has been conducted in the past when it came to racial and ethnic populations and women. Too often, research was conducted without the consent, consultation, or participation of the subject population; and the resulting information never found its way back into those communities. The legacy of past studies is not positive, and suspension of researcher's hidden agendas presents unique challenges to our ability to gain and discover knowledge about others.

  Horror stories have left a distrust of research in many communities. Numerous authors have cited the use of overgeneralization from research findings as a source of stereotyping. Classification of groups as *other* in research findings is another example of insensitivity to cultural differences. Current research too often fails to consider culture as a variable. Funding sources historically have not been sensitive to the needs of the different cultural groups in this country, and thus, they do not follow their directions or input for research.

New methods of research that involve the community—from planning to dissemination—need to be developed and implemented. New epistemological assumptions and methods that encourage refreshing and more adequate logic of inquiry are needed. The future of research on race, ethnicity, gender, and culture must be designed and conducted on the construct of the persons being studied. We need new ways of thinking and explaining to the world of the new century. Our ability to understand the health as well as the people of the nation is dependent on the strength and breadth of our research and data collection systems.

References

Andersen, M. (1993). Studying across difference: Race, class, and gender in qualitative research. In J. Stanfield & R. Dennis (Eds.), *Race and ethnicity in research methods* (pp. 39–52). Newbury Park, CA: Sage.

Aneshensel, C. S., Becerra, R. M., Fielder, E. P., & Schuler, R. H. (1989). Participation of Mexican-American female adolescents in a longitudinal panel survey. *Public Opinion Quarterly, 47,* 567–575.

Ayers, G. E. (1967). *Rehabilitating the culturally disadvantaged.* Mankato, MN: Mankato State College.

Berry, J. W. (1969). On cross-cultural comparability. *International Journal of Psychology, 4,* 119–128.

Bhawuk, D., & Triandis, H. C. (1996). The role of culture theory in the study of culture and intercultural training. In D. Landis & R. S. Bhagat (Eds.), *Intercultural Training* (2nd ed., pp. 17–34). Newbury Park, CA: Sage.

Brookins, G. K. (1993). Culture, ethnicity, and bicultural competence: Implications for children with chronic illness and disability. *Pediatrics, 91*(5), 1056–1062.

Brooks, J. (1998a, December/January). Cancer clinical trials: Barriers to African American participation. *Closing the Gap: Office of Minority Health Newsletter,* p. 7.

Brooks, J. (1998b, December/January). Minority participation in clinical trials: The impact of the Tuskegee syphilis study. *Closing the Gap: Office of Minority Health Newsletter,* p. 3.

Campbell, B. A. (1981). Race of interviewer effects among southern adolescents. *Public Opinion Quarterly, 45,* 231–244.

Carter-Pokras, O. (1998, August/September). How do we fill the data gaps? *Closing the Gap: Office of Minority Health Newsletter,* p. 8.

Centers for Disease Control and Prevention. (1993). *Race/ethnicity and public health statistics: An interactive case study.* Hyattsville, MD: Author.

Cotter P. R., Cohen, J., & Coulter P. B. (1982). Race of interviewer effects in telephone interviews. *Public Opinion Quarterly, 46,* 278–284.

Delgado, J. L., & Estrada, L. (1993). Improving data collection strategies. *Public Health Reports, 108*(5), 540–545.

Dennis, R. M. (1993). Participant observations. In J. H. Stanfield & R. M. Dennis (Eds.), *Race and ethnicity in research methods* (pp. 53–74). Newbury Park, CA: Sage.

Disadvantaged Minority Health Improvement Act of 1990, P.L. 101-527, 42 U.S.C.A. §254c-1 *et seq.* (West 1993).

Dresser, N. (1996). *Multicultural manners: New rules of etiquette for a changing society.* New York: Wiley.

Evinger, S. (1995). How shall we measure our nation's diversity? *Chance, 8*(1), 7–14.

Facio, E. (1993). Ethnography as personal experience. In J. H. Stanfield & R. M. Dennis (Eds.), *Race and ethnicity in research methods* (pp. 75–91). Newbury Park, CA: Sage.

Feinleib, M. (1993). Data needed for improving the health of minorities. *Annals of Epidemiology, 3*(2), 199–202.

Frayne, S. M., Burns, R. B., Hardt, E. J., Rosen, A. K., & Moskowitz, M. A. (1996). The exclusion of non-English-speaking persons from research. *Journal of General Internal Medicine, 11*(1), 39–43.

Hahn, R. H. (1992). The state of federal health statistics on racial and ethnic groups. *Journal of the American Medical Association, 267*(2), 268–271.

Hughes, C. C. (1990). Ethnopsychiatry. In T. M. Johnson & C. F. Sargent (Eds.), *Medical anthropology: A handbook of theory and methods* (pp. 132–148). New York: Greenwood Press.

Institute on Rehabilitation Issues. (1992). *Cultural diversity in rehabilitation: Nineteenth institute on rehabilitation issues.* Hot Springs, AR: University of Arkansas.

Johnson, S. D. (1990). Toward clarifying culture, race, and ethnicity in the context of multicultural counseling. *Journal of Multicultural Counseling and Development, 18,* 41–50.

Katz, J. (1985). The sociopolitical nature of counseling. *The Counseling Psychologist, 13,* 615–624.

Kavanagh, K. H., & Kennedy, P. H. (1992). *Promoting cultural diversity: Strategies for health care professionals.* Newbury Park, CA: Sage.

Kumanyika, S. K., & Golden, P. M. (1991). Cross-sectional differences in health status in U.S. racial/ethnic minority groups: Potential influence of temporal changes, disease, and life-style transitions. *Ethnicity & Disease, 1,* 50–59.

La Veist, T. A., Sellers, R. M., Brown, K. A., & Nickerson, K. J. (1997). Extreme social isolation, use of community based senior support services and mortality among African American elderly women. *American Journal of Community Psychology, 25*(5), 721–732.

Malpass, R. S. (1977). Theory and methods in cross-cultural psychology. *American Psychologist, 32,* 1069–1079.

McGraw, S. A., McKinlay, J. B., Crawford, S. A., Costa, L. A., & Cohen, D. L. (1992). Health survey methods with minority populations: Some lessons from recent experience. *Ethnicity & Disease, 2,* 273–287.

Meadow, M. (1998, December/January). Searching for an AIDS vaccine, searching for volunteers. *Closing the Gap: Office of Minority Health Newsletter,* p. 4–5.

Mouton, C. P., Harris, S., Rovi, S., Solorzano, P., & Johnson, M. S. (1997). Barriers to women's participation in cancer clinical trials. *Journal of the National Medical Association, 89*(11), 721–727.

National Medical Association. (1997). Barriers to women's participation in cancer clinical trials. *Journal of the National Medical Association.*

Office of Management & Budget. (1997). *Race & ethnic statistical policy directive standards for federal statistics and administrative reporting, No. 15.* Washington, DC: Author.

Osborne, N. G., & Feit, M. D. (1992). The use of race in medical research. *Journal of the American Medical Association, 267,* 275–280.

Patton, J. (1993). Psychoeducational assessment of gifted and talented African Americans. In J. H. Stanfield & R. M. Dennis (Eds.), *Race and ethnicity in research methods* (pp. 198–216). Newbury Park, CA: Sage.

Pinn, V. W. (1998, June/July). Improving the health of minority women: The role of research. *Closing the Gap: Office of Minority Health Newsletter,* p. 3.

Ponce, N. (1992, September 21–22). The cultural dimensions of getting health care. *Partners in Human Service: Shaping Health Care and Civil Rights Policy for Asian and Pacific Islander Americans* [Conference proceeding]. Washington, DC.

Ponterotto, J., & Casas, M. (1991). *Handbook of racial/ethnic minority counseling research.* Springfield, IL: Charles C Thomas.

Robinson, S. B., Ashley, M., & Haynes, M. A. (1996). Attitudes of African Americans regarding prostate cancer clinical trials. *Journal of Community Health, 21*(2), 77–87.

Salber, E. J., & Beza, A. G. (1980). The health interview survey and minority health. *Medical Care, 18*(3), 319–326.

Schaeffer, N. L. (1980). Evaluating race of interviewer effect in a national survey. *Social Methods Research, 8,* 400–419.

Schulman, K. A., Rubenstien, L. E., Chesley, F. D., & Eisenberg, J. M. (1995). The roles of race and socioeconomic factors in health services research. *Health Services Research, 30*(1), Part 2, 179–195.

Scribner, R. (1996). Paradox as paradigm—the health outcomes of Mexican Americans. *American Journal of Public Health, 86*(3), 303–305.

Smith, A. W. (1993). Survey research on African Americans: Methodological innovations. In J. H. Stanfield & R. M. Dennis (Eds.), *Race and ethnicity in research methods* (pp. 217–229). Newbury Park, CA: Sage.

Smith, M. B. (1998, March). Race, ethnicity, class, and culture. *Closing the Gap: Office of Minority Health Newsletter,* p. 2.

Stanfield, J. H. (1993). Epistemological considerations. In J. H. Stanfield & R. M. Dennis (Eds.), *Race and ethnicity in research methods* (pp. 16–36). Newbury Park, CA: Sage.

Stanfield, J. H., & Dennis, R. M. (Eds). (1993). *Race and ethnicity in research methods.* Newbury Park, CA: Sage.

Stiens, H. F. (1990). Psychoanalytic perspectives. In T. M. Johnson & C. F. Sargent (Eds.), *Medical anthropology: A handbook of theory and methods* (pp. 73–92). New York: Greenwood Press.

Sue, D. W., Arredondo, P., & McDavis, R. J. (1992). Multicultural counseling competencies and standards: A call to the profession. *Journal of Counseling & Development, 70,* 477–485.

Sue, D. W., & Sue, D. (1990). *Counseling the culturally different: Theory and practice.* New York: Wiley.

Triandis, H. C. (1994). *Culture and social behavior.* New York: McGraw-Hill.

University of Arkansas. (1994). *Cultural diversity in rehabilitation.* Hot Springs, AR: Author, Department of Rehabilitation Education and Research, Arkansas Research & Training Center in Vocational Rehabilitation.

U.S. Public Health Services. (1994). *Improving minority health statistics: Report of the public health task force on minority health data.* Washington, DC: U.S. Department of Health and Human Services, Office of Minority Health.

Williams, D. (1998). The quality of racial data. *Closing the Gap: Office of Minority Health Newsletter,* Vol. 4.

Williams, D. R., Lavizzo-Mourey, R., & Warren, R. C. (1994). The concepts of race and health status in America. *Public Health Reports, 109*(1), 26–41.

Wray, L. A. (1992). Health policy and ethnic diversity in older Americans. Dissonance or harmony? *Western Journal of Medicine, 157*(3), 357–361.

Yu, E. S., & Liu, W. T. (1992). U.S. national health data on Asian Pacific Islanders: A research agenda for the 1990s. *American Journal of Public Health, 82*(12) 1645–1652.

Yu, E. S., & Liu, W. T. (1994). Methodological issues. In N. Zane, D. Takeuchi, & K. Young (Eds.), *Confronting critical health issues of Asian and Pacific Islander Americans* (pp. 22–50). Newbury Park, CA: Sage.

Zane, N., Takeuchi, D., & Young, K. (1994). *Confronting critical health issues of Asian and Pacific Islander Americans.* Newbury Park, CA: Sage.

CHAPTER FIVE

Global Perspective

Key Points

- Many countries have and are becoming more racially diverse through immigration. We are becoming nations of immigrants.

- Issues of global economic changes have had a detrimental effect on the state of world health (i.e., a decrease of access to health services).

- Global changes and cooperation call for increased tolerance and appreciation of other cultures and inability to understand persons who are different from us at individual, group, organizational, national, and international levels.

- It is necessary to look at the world from a perspective that does not equate difference with inferiority.

- We must commit ourselves to building a global village and global society where human dignity and equality of all will be respected.

- We must commit ourselves to changing attitudes and values to those that uphold the dignity of the human person in all cultural contexts.

s the new century develops, the world is becoming smaller and smaller. Every day the rapid developments in transportation and the effects of technology link us with almost any part of the globe. Like the United States, many countries around the world have and are becoming more racially diverse through immigration. Recent political and economic events both within and among countries are shifting the players in international affairs. Other languages, such as Chinese, German, Spanish, French, Swahili, Arabic, and Japanese, are making their way into international business meetings and college campuses. These changes have made the different regions of the world highly interdependent and interactive with one another.

Wealthy countries that once were overwhelmingly White have become much more racially diverse, mostly because of a flood of immigrants from poorer countries—former colonial subjects, refugees from war zones, economic migrants looking for better opportunities, and *guest workers* who will do the jobs that natives find unsavory (Robinson, 1998). Immigrants and persons with at least one immigrant parent comprise one eighth of Sweden's population. During the last few decades, immigrants have been primarily political and economic refugees from a variety of nations, including Chile, Peru, Argentina, Iraq, Vietnam, Somalia, Ethiopia, Bosnia, and Croatia (Rothermel, 1998). Among the more than 150 million people in Russia, 82% claim to be Russian, with Tatars making up the second largest group and Ukrainians the third largest group (Singatulin, 1998). There are an estimated three million people of ethnic minority origin living in England and Wales. They make up 6% of the population. Indians are the largest ethnic group, followed by Black Caribbean, Pakistani, Black African, Bangladeshi, and Chinese (U.S. Department of Health and Human Services, 1998).

American businesses must understand the values and cultures of other countries if they are to be successful in their global undertakings. Not only is the potential workforce of this country becoming increasingly diverse, but as Europe moves closer to the implementation of its common market, and Japan and Germany continue to become increasingly competitive with the United States, American businesses must evaluate their productivity and ability to compete inside as well as outside of the United States. It is anticipated that American companies will begin to establish more and more facilities outside the country or cater to a world population rather than just an American one. Because 90% of the world's population is non-White, ethnicity and differing cultures will become particularly important if productivity and profits are to be realized.

American businesses will have to adapt their approaches and routines to account for different cultural and ethnic practices and values (Isaacs & Benjamin, 1991; Kabagarama, 1993).

Issues of global economic changes have affected health and development at the international, national, and local levels. According to Long (1997), economic policies influenced by international institutions, such as the World Bank and International Monetary Fund, have had a detrimental effect on the state of the world's health. They have led to

- a decline in living standards for large numbers of people;

- the widening of the gap between the rich and the poor;

- the resurgence of known infectious diseases, such as cholera, yellow fever, and tuberculosis; and aggravation of new diseases, such as Ebola and AIDS;

- the deterioration and even collapse of public health services in *underserved* countries; and

- environmental destruction and degradation on a massive scale.

Overall cuts in public sector spending, reprioritization of government budgets away from health and education, increased privatization of public services, and reductions in the number of health personnel, along with the introduction of user fees, have all contributed to the decrease of access to health services and health status in developing countries.

With the emergence of a global society, local or regional problems and conflicts around the world take on global implications. Basic cultural knowledge is important, but equally important is the ability to use such knowledge to understand the effects of the cultural heritage of different groups on the deeper fabric of society. "Governments, educators, and parents have begun to realize that younger generations must be prepared to face this global concern with the knowledge, values, and skills that will enable them to interact effectively in an international and interdependent world with people different from themselves" (Singatulin, 1998, p. 25). These rapid changes in the world call for educational institutions to seize the opportunity to equip students with skills that will enable them to deal effectively with persons from diverse backgrounds. As we move into the era of globalization, educators need to teach students survival techniques for the internationalization of society (Freeman, 1986; Kabagarama, 1993; McCrann, 1998; Rothermel, 1998).

Global changes penetrate all areas of human activity, including population, business, health, technology, lifestyle, role of women, and work relations. In order for global cooperation to be effective, people's beliefs, behavior, and modes of interaction must change greatly. These international changes call for greater tolerance and appreciation of other cultures and an ability to understand persons who are different from us at the individual, group, organizational, national, and international levels.

Developing an appreciation of other cultures is a difficult process. We need to look at the world from a perspective that does not equate difference with inferiority (Seely & Wasilewski, 1996). Such an approach sees human beings the world over as striving to make meaning out of life and adapting to their environments. It takes a conscious effort to understand and respect fellow human beings regardless of whether they are like us or different from us. It also calls for empathy toward those whose conditions are less desirable than our own. By being objective and nonjudgmental, we gain a better understanding of world conditions (Kabagarama, 1993; Seely & Wasilewski, 1996).

The world is shrinking in terms of geographical, psychological, and sociological distances. No longer can we sit comfortably in our small corners of the globe and watch the world go by. Catastrophes, such as AIDS, world hunger, environmental degradation, conflicts of all sorts, and the possibility of a nuclear disaster pose a threat to all of our existence. The connection between health, race, ethnicity, gender, and socioeconomic status is not unique to the United States. This is a global condition that is well documented by international health literature. As health care providers, we must establish collaborative initiatives with other countries to develop a cooperative process for improving the health of all persons. We have to share information, guidelines for data collection, and ways to improve the exchange of health information.

With many international countries becoming more demographically diverse and nations of immigrants, it is clear that at the individual and social levels overcoming linguistic and cultural barriers is fundamental. Viewing ourselves within only national boundaries of race, gender, class, and other classifications will limit our ability to contribute to the expansiveness of thought and our role in influencing the world order. We must strive for global citizenship—in which all citizens have a thorough knowledge of the world in which they live, a knowledge of its human dimensions, and its sociocultural characterization (Matriano, 1998). Cultural competence will provide a framework for knowledge, skills, self awareness, confidence, objectivity, interpersonal relations, and acceptance of all persons and cultures. It will also enrich and enhance one's capability for intercultural studies and transnational communication.

Organizations and community structures, nationally and internationally, need to sensitize persons about not only their human rights, but also health rights and responsibilities. We need to commit ourselves to building a *global village* and *global society* where human dignity and equality of all will be respected. The new multiculturalism must be committed to changing the attitudes and values that currently exist to ones that uphold the dignity of the human person in all cultural contexts.

References

Freeman, R. E. (1986). *Promising practices in global education.* New York: National Council on Foreign Language and International Studies.

Isaacs, M. R., & Benjamin, M. P. (1991). *Towards a culturally competent system of care: Programs which utilize culturally competent principles.* Washington, DC: CASSP Technical Assistance Center, Georgetown University Child Development Center.

Kabagarama, D. (1993). *Breaking the ice: A guide to understanding people of other cultures.* Newton, MA: Allyn and Bacon.

Long, P. (1997). The impact of global economic changes on health and development. *Women's Health Project, 22,* 6.

Matriano, E. C. (1998). NAME: Where art thou in globalization? *Multicultural Education, 4*(5), 4.

McCrann, T. O. (1998). Japanese enough? A Korean's journey to Japanese identity. *Multicultural Education, 4*(5), 17–19.

Robinson, E. (1998, July 5). Blending in, or wiping out? *The Washington Post,* p. A01.

Rothermel, B. A. (1998). Salad bars & smorgasbords: The management of culture in Sweden & the United States. *Multicultural Education, 4*(5), 6–11.

Seely, H. N., & Wasilewski, J. H. (1996). *Between cultures: Developing a self-identity in a world of diversity.* Lincolnwood, IL: NTC Publishing Group.

Singatulin, I. (1998). Diversity and multicultural education: A glance at the Russian front. *Multicultural Education, 4*(5), 24–25.

U.S. Department of Health and Human Services. (1998, March). British government efforts on ethnic minority health. *Closing the Gap: Office of Minority Health Newsletter,* p. 3.

Effects of Inequality   *II*

*"Knowledge should be examined not
only for the ways in which it might
misrepresent or mediate social reality,
but also for the ways in which it
actually reflects the daily struggle
of people's lives."*

—Peter McLaren

Objectives

The information in this section is intended to help the reader

- understand the concept of sociopolitical power and how it maintains
  a hierarchy of privilege and oppression in American society;

- differentiate among the concepts of prejudice, stereotyping, and
  discrimination;

- recognize that the use of language is a powerful act, reflecting one's
  status within the power structure of society, while at the same time
  helping to maintain one's power position, or lack thereof;

- realize the power and challenges of White privilege in the current
  sociopolitical climate; and

- appreciate the importance of the awareness of power issues when
  dealing with clients within the health care arena.

CHAPTER SIX

Power, Privilege, and Prejudice

Key Points

- The issue of sociocultural power must be explored in the education of health professionals.

- Sociocultural power gives status and control to the dominant social group, which continues to be White, middle and upper class, heterosexual males. Today's White men did not cause the current power structure, but nevertheless they benefit the most from it.

- Power and privilege are also awarded (at varying levels) to any person who claims any of the characteristics listed above.

- All Whites experience unearned privilege simply as a result of the color of their skin.

- People who are not part of the dominant group suffer varying levels of prejudice, stereotyping, and discrimination because of their differences.

- Prejudice is a general feeling of dislike or hatred for people on the basis of some characteristic they have or are believed to possess.

- Discrimination is the overt action one takes to exclude, avoid, or distance oneself from others.

- Discrimination may be unintentional and may not be motivated by conscious prejudice.

- Discrimination can occur at multiple levels—personally, institutionally, and structurally.

- Health care professionals must be aware of their own sociocultural power and how it may affect consumers and colleagues.

- Each practitioner and educator must evaluate her own values, beliefs, biases, and prejudices so that they never engage in discriminatory practices.

ower, or the lack of it, is an issue we deal with daily whether we are aware of it or not. Although in the health professions we tend to talk more about empowerment, especially when discussing the client–therapist relationship or client treatment (Joiner & Hansel, 1995; Stewart, 1993; Crepeau, 1994; MacKinnon & Froehlich, 1994), the reality is that as long as we are in a position of authority there is a power differential between us and our clients. There are also issues of power among various cultural groups that influence the way we deal with one another. Power issues are also apparent in our classrooms among students and between students and teachers, and power is maintained almost invisibly by the language that we use. It seems obvious that the issue of power must be explored in health professions' practice and education, and especially when discussing issues of diversity and multicultural content within a curriculum.

Sociocultural Power and Privilege

The history of this country is a story about power and control—success and growth for some, loss and despair for others. It is a story that has been revisited in the past thirty years to include the perspectives of all of the participants, rather than of just a privileged few. The following short summary is woefully inadequate, but it provides a point of view that is becoming more prevalent. This is not a story about blame, but one that presents the facts of this country.

Before being colonized by the Spanish, British, and other Europeans, native people originally inhabited the United States. The White immigrants brought with them a sense of entitlement and ownership that devalued the lives lived by the native inhabitants. White men of power arrived in this country not only with their families and material goods, but also laden with their own ideas, beliefs, and values that quickly became the dominant manner of thinking and acting. They believed in independence, self-control, and mastery. This ultimately resulted in control of the land, control of the goods and products of the land, control of education and commerce, control of religion, and control of others. This need for ownership, control, and power soon resulted in the possession of other human beings as slaves and the development of a hierarchy that placed prominent White men at the top and others in inferior positions, depending on one's sociocultural and economic status.

Although slavery has been legally eradicated in this country, racism, sexism, classism, heterosexism, ageism, and ableism are the legacies that remain as a result of the effects from the first colonizers. These societal issues are held in place by sociocultural power and politics and supported by the economics of capitalism. Sociocultural power gives status and control to the dominant social group, which continues to be White, middle and upper class, heterosexual, Protestant men. Although today's White men did not cause the sociopolitical power structure in which we all participate, they do benefit the most from it. Power and privilege are also meted out at varying levels to those who hold any of the characteristics of the dominant group (i.e., White Americans in this country, whether they are men or women, are awarded unearned privileges because of the color of their skin). Maleness, being a privileged characteristic, gives Hispanic men more power than Hispanic women. Heterosexual women and men of any race or ethnicity have more freedom and opportunities than do homosexual women and men. However, as these characteristics become blended and multilayered, the complexity of the issue of power and access becomes dependent upon the context of the social situation.

Privilege and Insider Status *as a Member of the Dominant Group*

Being a member of the dominant group affords one sociopolitical power and privilege. Power in this context is "the capacity to produce desired effects on others; it can be perceived in terms of mastery over self as well as over nature and other people" (Pinderhughes, 1989, p. 109). Sociopolitical power gives dominant group members not only mastery over self and others, but also access to better jobs, better education, better housing, better health care, and better material goods. It allows people to more easily become decision makers, participants in the dominant discourse of a society, and policymakers.

Being part of the dominant group affords people certain privileges, which many authors identify as *unearned* (McIntosh, 1988; Haney, 1994; Frankenberg, 1993). Unearned privilege, says Haney, includes "freedoms or other benefits given to us simply because we are White, heterosexual, or born into middle strata economic and social location. Such unearned privilege allows us to generalize from our own experience, to assume that everyone else's is like ours" (Haney, 1994, p. 5). McIntosh (1988, pp. 1–2) compellingly writes about the privilege of being White when she states:

> I have come to see White privilege as an invisible package of
> unearned assets which I can count on cashing in each day,

but about which I was *meant* to remain oblivious. White privilege is like an invisible weightless knapsack of special provisions, assurances, tools, maps, guides, codebooks, passports, visas, clothes, compass, emergency gear, and blank checks.

One of the amazing things about being White, or being a man, or possessing other characteristics of power or privilege, is that they are often invisible to those who have them. People who are White are taught not to see the mantle of privilege within which they are wrapped, reminiscent of the emperor and his new clothes. By not looking at these unearned privileges, White individuals can evade recognizing the power they represent and the responsibility that comes from that awareness (Frankenberg, 1993).

On the other hand, those who do not share the privileges enjoyed by the dominant group are very aware of the differences in power and access. Sometimes these oppressive differences are readily apparent as in the blatant racism that denies persons of color access to education or to adequate health care. More often oppression is subtle, affecting each of us in ways that are apparent only to those who are slighted or misused. One of the authors was walking with an African American friend in a well-known department store, when they passed a cosmetic counter where foundation cremes were displayed in various shades of beige and cream. When the author commented on the lack of dark skin tones, the friend stated that it was frustrating and typical, and that she retaliated by never shopping in that store. This interaction clearly exemplified one of the many subtle ways that our society treats Whites and persons of color differently.

McIntosh (1988, pp. 5–8) identifies 46 ways that she as a White woman benefits from skin color privilege that most persons of color cannot count on. Some of these are noted below:

- If I should need to move, I can be pretty sure of renting or purchasing housing in an area that I can afford and in which I would want to live.

- I can go shopping alone most of the time, fairly well assured that I will not be followed or harassed.

- I can turn on the television or open to the front page of the paper and see persons of my race widely represented.

- I can be sure that my children will be given curricular materials that testify to the existence of their race.

- I can do well in a challenging situation without being called a credit to my race.

- I am never asked to speak for all the persons of my racial group.

- I can choose blemish cover or bandages in *flesh* color and have them more or less match my skin.

- I can be pretty sure that if I ask to talk to *the person in charge*, I will be facing a person of my race.

Those who are White may recognize that these few items are not aspects of their lives that they have to think about. Because they have privileged status, they expect to be responded to in a particular way without even being aware of these expectations or the status associated with them. Most White people unconsciously expect that all persons are treated as they are, but the previous list is a reminder that that is not the case.

People assume that they know things about others in groups different from their own on the basis of what they have learned from family and friends, from the media, and from books and formal education. But what they know, or what they think they know, may be only partial truths. Those in privileged groups are often seen as the *insiders* whereas others are seen as *outsiders*. Merton (1972) used these terms while discussing his concept of the validity of group knowledge. He stated that insiders claim that their knowledge of the group is more valid because they understand the group's values, perspectives, and culture. Those who function outside of the group, however, claim that they have a more valid and objective understanding of the group. "The perspectives of both outsiders and insiders provide important insights into social reality. Our understanding of a group remains incomplete when the perspective of either the insider or the outsider is overlooked" (Banks, 1996, p. 8). Just as McIntosh (1988) had to consult with many of her friends of color to develop the list of privileges enjoyed by Whites, each of us must listen to both insider and outsider voices to understand the truth about any group of persons.

The multilayered nature of our lives belies the simplicity of the theory discussed previously. Many of us maintain both insider and outsider status concurrently because of our social location and the groups of which we are part. A Franco American man from rural Maine who was raised in near poverty may theoretically understand the concept of White privilege and may actually enjoy many of its effects; but because he has had to work so hard to be where he is today, he does not believe he is especially privileged. A study by Blank & Slipp (1994) found that many White men say they often believe they are powerless and vulnerable. The young female engineer may be considered a social insider because she is White, but she may certainly sense the results of being an outsider in her field because of her gender. The Black health care provider might be considered an insider because of the authority of her position; but when a White client refuses her treatment, she is once again reminded of her outsider status. It is the constant fluctuation and negotiation between and within levels of sociocultural power that complicates the concepts of privilege and insider and outsider status. Social location and standpoint theory provide another avenue to examine these ideas.

Social Location and Standpoint Theory

Each person born in this country comes into this world at a particular *social location*. The term *social location* does not just refer to one's geography, but rather how people are shaped by our participation in class, gender, racial, age, geographical and national groups. Within these groupings, "we are fundamentally shaped by the power and authority (or lack thereof) of roles given to us and expectations on us in those groups and by the access to social rewards and resources available to us as members of those groups" (Haney, 1994). Because one of the authors is a White, single, middle-class, heterosexual, fifty-something, educated woman from the rural Northeastern section of the country, she is viewed in a particular way by others and her own worldview differs from that of anyone else. As a White woman she will be awarded certain (unearned) privileges solely because of the color of her skin (McIntosh, 1988), and will have freer access to the things she covets and needs in this world than will her sisters of color.

Social location produces subjectivity and influences one's construction of knowledge (Banks, 1996). The way we understand the world is influenced by our intersection with race, class, gender, age, and sexual orientation; and the sociocultural value placed on those characteristics. Feminist standpoint theory developed from the understanding that women, because of social location within U.S. culture, understand and interpret their world in a particular way (Harding, 1991; Hekman, 1997). However, Harding points out that there is no one "woman's way" of thinking and responding, but that there are contradictory social locations for feminists in particular. Where women stand socioculturally determine the expectations for certain behaviors. Women traditionally have been relegated to an inferior place where excellence in thinking not only is not expected, but also is often negated and punished in subtle ways. Harding (1991, p. 275) notes that a *woman thinker is a contradiction in terms;* and *bearing an identity or speaking from a social location that is perceived as a contradiction in terms can be a serious disadvantage within political, economic, and social structures.* Collins (1991) further explains how differently African American, feminist women think and experience their world, not only from a woman's viewpoint, but also from the experience of being African American in a racist society.

Each specific cultural characteristic of every person elicits varying responses *from* and *of* the society of which we all are part. Although we can change some aspects of our social location, such as geography, education, language, dialect, marital status, and sometimes class, other aspects, such as race, gender, sexual orientation, age, and ability, are not so easily altered. It is often these aspects that may result in discrimination.

Prejudice, Stereotyping, and Discrimination

One element that helps determine and maintain positions of power is prejudice. Prejudice is an erroneous judgement, usually negative, which is based on incomplete or faulty information (Bennett, 1995). When used to label most or all members of a particular group, prejudice becomes a stereotype. Ageism prejudice, for example, leads one to stereotype all elders as frail and senile, with nothing left to contribute to society.

None of us is born with prejudicial thoughts, and most of us would choose not to be prejudiced. But prejudice is learned, and each of us has been taught well. Many people are unaware of their prejudices; they may not realize that they hold members of a particular group in low esteem. They may not even be aware that it is prejudice that disallows them to accept someone into their own insider status. Rothenberg (1998, p. 132) more completely defines prejudice as a *general feeling of dislike for people, perhaps even hatred of them, on the basis of some characteristic they have or are believed to possess. Prejudice may be based on race, gender, or ethnicity; or on hair color, religion, or style of dress; or just about any imaginable characteristic.* Using Rothenberg's definition, someone may be prejudiced about young men with long hair, or about men or women with tattoos, or about persons in wheelchairs. She differentiates between this kind of prejudicial thought and that which is encompassed in racism or sexism: *Racism and sexism require not* prejudice alone *but* prejudice plus power. "When we use these terms rather than prejudice or discrimination, we highlight the unequal distribution of power in U.S. society and draw attention to the elaborate, interlocking system of rituals, stereotypes, institutions, punishments, and rewards that have functioned historically to reinforce male privilege and White skin privilege" (Rothenberg, 1998, p. 132). The authors suggest that prejudice plus power is seen not only with racism and sexism, but also with heterosexism, classism, ageism, and ableism. The unequal distribution of power in the United States is apparent when we examine laws that do not support the safety of homosexuals or those in poverty, and lack of access to health care and productive work for older Americans and persons with disabilities.

Young-Bruehl (1996) recognizes that not all prejudices are the same. She argues that "racism, anti-Semitism, sexism, and homophobia differ in their internal (il)logic; that is, although all expressions of prejudice are oppressive, they may differ in intensity and scope" (Marsiglia & Hecht, 1998, p. 290). This becomes clear when we hear and read daily reports from the media of hate crimes perpetuated by White American supremacist groups against African Americans, Jews, and homosexuals.

Within multicultural literature we often see the terms *discrimination, stereotype,* and *prejudice* used somewhat interchangeably when discussing sociocultural power. The simplest way to differentiate these terms is to recognize prejudice as a belief or attitude about a particular group; a stereotype as a particular belief we hold about a disempowered group; and discrimination as the overt action we take to exclude, avoid, or distance ourselves from others (Hecht, 1998).

Stereotyping occurs when one uses a characteristic seen in one or a few members of a particular group and generalizes it to the entire group. Some common stereotypical statements include

- all African Americans can dance,

- all Native Americans are alcoholics,

- all Jewish Americans are good with money,

- all White Americans are racists,

- all single mothers are on welfare, especially if they are African American,

- the poor population does not want to improve its lot in life,

- women are emotional,

- obese people are morally weak, and

- people in wheelchairs are powerless.

Although these statements may be true for a few members of the groups mentioned, by assuming that all members of the group carry these characteristics, we negate the individuality of each member of the group. Stereotyping may provide a means of categorizing and classifying a group of persons that are different from ourselves, but it also renders the individuals within that group invisible. Allport (Hecht, 1998) believes that categorization is necessary to daily functioning because it enables people to react quickly to new, incoming stimuli. For instance, knowing that most White Americans are taught to shake hands when greeting one another enables a stranger to respond appropriately when first introduced. However, Allport suggests that the categorization done with stereotyping is overgeneralization. The difficulty with overgeneralization is that it actually impedes the process of encoding, storing, and retrieving information (Hecht, 1998). For example, if we expect an Asian woman to be shy and self-effacing, that is what we will see, even if there is evidence to the contrary. We then treat the person on the basis of what we expect to be true, rather than on what the reality actually is, often resulting in what Neuberg (1991) and others refer to as a self-fulfilling prophecy. If an Asian woman is in our clinic, we may overlook a vital factor of her condition during evaluation, if we unwittingly stereotype her and do not probe for important information.

Prejudice (one's attitude) and stereotyping (one's beliefs about a group) lead to discrimination (overt action). Lott (Hecht, 1998, p. 9) argues that whereas prejudice and stereotyping are *deplorable*, discrimination is the *social problem*. Although people may hold prejudicial thoughts and attitudes and stereotypical beliefs, it is only when they act on these that we see the evidence of sociopolitical power. Discrimination occurs in many forms and at multiple levels. Although it is maintained through individual actions, discrimination is evident in national patterns of inequality and under-representation as well. Rothenberg (1998) identifies three levels of discrimination, which she labels (1) individual discrimination, (2) organizational discrimination, and (3) structural discrimination.

At an individual or interindividual (i.e., face-to-face) level, discrimination may be either intentional or unintentional and may not be motivated by conscious prejudice (Lott, 1995). Although some people are clearly aware of their prejudicial thoughts, others are not. Nevertheless, these discriminatory acts "build on and support prejudicial stereotypes, deny their victims opportunities provided to others, and perpetuate discrimination, regardless of intent" (Rothenberg, 1998, p. 137). A few examples of individual discrimination include

- personnel officers whose stereotyped beliefs about women, minorities, and persons with handicaps justify hiring them for low-level and low-paying jobs exclusively, regardless of their potential experience or qualifications for high-level jobs;

- teachers who interpret linguistic and cultural differences as indications of low potential or lack of academic interest on the part of minority students; and

- medical office receptionists who make lower-income clients wait longer than paying clients, even when they have made appointments (Rothenberg, 1998, p. 136).

Banks & Banks (1997, p. 392) point out that individual prejudice and discrimination does not occur in only one direction, for example, from Whites to African Americans. It occurs in all directions and even within groups. But they believe that, as hurtful as individual discrimination can be, it does not have *the long-range and life-limiting effects of institutional [discrimination] and bias.*

Institutional discrimination, referred to as organizational discrimination by Rothenberg (1998), reinforces individual discrimination by instituting rules, policies, and practices of the organization that have an adverse effect on nondominant groups, such as minorities, women, homosexuals, elders, and persons with disabilities. These may include

- height and weight requirements that are unnecessarily geared to the physical proportions of White men, and therefore exclude women and some minorities from certain jobs;

- the use of standardized academic tests or criteria, geared to the cultural and educational norms of the middle-class Whites, that are not relevant indicators of successful job performance;

- preferences shown by many law and medical schools in the admission of children of wealthy and influential alumni, nearly all of whom are White; and

• questioning of mental illness on a job application, which then affects the applicant's chance of being hired (Rothenberg, 1998, p. 137).

Many times organizational discrimination is not an act of conscious prejudice but is considered just the *normal* way in which things are done. It becomes part of the organizational climate. Therefore, people are unaware that the practices must be changed, despite the discriminatory results, making organizational discrimination harder to change than is individual discrimination.

Rothenberg's (1998) last level of discrimination is what she names *structural discrimination*. This occurs when discrimination is found between the fields of employment, education, housing, and government. She describes a classical style of structural discrimination that reproduces itself in the following way: "Discrimination in education denies the credentials to get good jobs. Discrimination in employment denies the economic resources to buy good housing. Discrimination in housing confines minorities to school districts providing inferior education, closing the cycle in the classic form" (Rothenberg, 1998, p. 140). Structural discrimination is systemic, and the integration of all aspects of the system (e.g., employment, education, housing, and government) results in lack of access to all places within the system for those who are discriminated against. The complexity of structural discrimination makes it very difficult to change.

Having an awareness of the varying levels of prejudice that leads to discrimination is important, but this awareness must be coupled with the means to reduce or eradicate the prejudice altogether.

Prejudice Reduction Strategies

The literature identifies many approaches to help reduce prejudicial attitudes as they relate to sociocultural issues. Hecht (1998) identifies four locations at which intervention can occur. These are (1) at the personal and interpersonal level, (2) within organizational structures, (3) through educational interventions, and (4) through changes in public policy. This chapter discusses intervention at the personal level and through educational methods.

At the personal level some believe that if we have an opportunity to meet and work with persons from other groups, our attitude toward members of that group will shift. Supporting this idea, one of the earliest, most well-known theories was the *contact hypothesis* developed by Allport (1954). This theory, now further developed and recognized as social contact theory, provided students with useful guidelines for the development of more positive interracial attitudes and actions. Allport believed that contact between groups will improve intergroup relations, but the contact must be characterized by these conditions: (1) Members of various groups must share equal status; (2) the contact situation should lead people to work cooperatively rather than in competition with one another; (3) there should be institutional sanction and support by authorities, such as teachers and administrators, or there must be a social climate that encourages intergroup contact; and (4) contact must be characterized by interpersonal interactions in which students become acquainted as individuals in such a way to produce reciprocal knowledge and understanding between groups (Banks & Banks 1997, p. 22; Bennett, 1995, p. 31).

One of the most difficult of Allport's four conditions to establish is an equal status environment for different racial groups. Within schools, where most of this theory applies, there are often major socioeconomic differences as well as differences in the initial achievement levels between Whites and other students of color (Bennett, 1995). These discrepancies are often seen in higher education as well, although socioeconomic differences are less pronounced. Unrecognized institutionalized racism may also contribute to unequal treatment between Whites and students of color. Admission policies, school tradition, and dorm rules may privilege Whites more than others. Less visible, more hidden problems of inequality may also occur, such as "a mutual lack of knowledge about communication modes, values, and perceptions, among culturally different students and teachers, which often leads to misunderstanding and conflict" (Bennett, 1995, p. 32). The lack of understanding about Black English Vernacular (see chapter 7, "The Power of Language") may cause Whites to view Blacks as *low class* or *uneducated,* constructing barriers to the development of reciprocal knowledge necessary to prejudice reduction.

Social contact theory can and does work to reduce prejudicial attitudes, but not without serious planning and commitment by those who are attempting to make a difference. Without a climate of respect and openness that supports equal status, having contact with someone from a different cultural group may not reduce prejudice at all.

Another way to shift prejudicial attitudes is through education where positive aspects about groups that differ from oneself are taught. Banks (1996) identifies prejudice reduction as one of five dimensions of multicultural education. In his viewpoint, prejudice reduction may occur when teachers develop lessons and activities that *help students to devel-op positive attitudes toward different racial, ethnic, and cultural groups* (Banks, 1996, p. 338). His research indicates, however, that certain con-ditions must occur for this to be successful. These include "positive im-ages of the ethnic groups in the materials and the use of multiethnic materials in a consistent and sequential way" (p. 338). These lessons are more successful if the objective is on cognitive learning for the students rather than *one-shot treatments* focused on prejudice reduction. Nieto (1996, p. 330) cites research that supports this idea, concluding "that the least effective approach was a direct antiprejudice teaching unit, proba-bly because students sensed that they were being manipulated and re-sented it . . . one of the most effective ways of reducing prejudice is not through the study of prejudice or ethnicity, but rather through coopera-tive learning."

Summary

Power and privilege are awarded to members of the dominant so-ciocultural group in this country, simply because they are part of the group by virtue of their race, ethnicity, class status, gender, heterosexual-ity, and religion. Those people who do not possess the valued character-istics of the dominant group are often not treated with equal respect, are stereotyped, and often endure prejudice and discrimination. It is vital that the health care practitioner be aware of the differences in sociocul-tural power and treat each person in a fair and equal manner.

Equal status environments are also difficult to achieve in the clin-ic. When the health practitioner and the client come from different racial and ethnic groups and one is a White American, not only is there an un-equal racial relationship, there is inequality in the level of authority. It is doubly challenging for the practitioner to establish a more equitable cli-mate when there are multiple levels of hierarchy to deal with.

It is imperative that health care professionals who strive to be culturally competent be aware of issues of power within American so-ciety, and how those issues become reflected within each health care setting. White American practitioners must be sensitive to their own White privilege and how that may influence client–practitioner interac-tion and rapport, especially if the client is non-White. Each of us must evaluate our own values, beliefs, biases, and prejudices, so that we never engage in discriminatory practices (whether conscious or uncon-scious) in the workplace. It is the responsibility of each of us to work towards sociopolitical equality and justice within our professional and personal lives.

References

Allport, G. W. (1954). *The nature of prejudice.* Reading, MA.: Addison-Wesley.

Banks, J. A. (1996). *Multicultural education, transformative knowledge, & action.* New York: Teacher's College Press.

Banks, J. A., & Banks, C. A. M. (1997). *Multicultural education: Issues and perspectives* (3rd ed.). Newton, MA: Allyn and Bacon.

Bennett, C. I. (1995). *Comprehensive multicultural education: Theory and practice* (3rd ed.). Newton, MA: Allyn and Bacon.

Blank, R., & Slipp, S. (1994). *Voices of diversity: Real people talk about problems and solutions in a workplace where everyone is not alike.* New York: American Management Association.

Collins, P. H. (1991). *Black feminist thought: Knowledge, consciousness, and the politics of empowerment.* Boston: Routledge & Kegan Paul.

Crepeau, E. B. (1994). Uneasy alliances: Belief and action on a geropsychiatric team. Doctoral Dissertation, University of New Hampshire.

Frankenberg, R. (1993). *White women, race matters: The social construction of Whiteness.* Minneapolis, MN: University of Minnesota Press.

Haney, E. (1994). *Social location and alliance building.* Unpublished paper.

Harding, S. (1991). *Whose science? Whose knowledge? Thinking from women's lives.* Ithaca, NY: Cornell University Press.

Hecht, M. L. (1998). *Communicating prejudice.* Newbury Park, CA: Sage.

Hekman, S. (1997). Truth and method: Feminist standpoint theory revisited. *Signs: Journal of Women in Culture and Society, 22*(2), 341–365.

Joiner, C., & Hansel, M. (1995). Empowering the geriatric client. Paper presented at the American Occupational Therapy Association's Annual Conference & Exposition, Denver, CO.

Lott, B. (1995). Distance from women: Interpersonal sexist discrimination. In B. Lott & D. Maluso (Eds.), *The social psychology of interpersonal discrimination* (pp. 12–49). New York: Guilford.

MacKinnon, S., & Froehlich, J. (1994, January 6). Cultural diversity: Empowerment: Empowering others by empowering yourself. *OT Week, 8*(1), 18–19.

Marsiglia, F. F., & Hecht, M. (1998). Personal and interpersonal interventions. In M. L. Hecht (Ed.), *Communicating prejudice.* Newbury Park, CA: Sage.

McIntosh, P. (1988). *White privilege and male privilege: A personal account of coming to see correspondences through work in women's studies* (Working Paper No. 189). Wellesley, MA: Wellesley College Center for Research on Women.

Merton, R. K. (1972). Insiders and outsiders: A chapter in the sociology of knowledge. *The American Journal of Sociology, 78*(1), 9–47.

Mish, F. H. (Ed.). (1995). *Merriam Webster's Collegiate Dictionary* (10th ed.). Springfield, MA: Merriam-Webster, Inc.

Neuberg, S. L. (1991). Expectancy-confirmation processes in stereotype-tinged social encounters: The moderating role of social goals. In M. P. Zanna & J. Olson (Eds.), *Ontario Symposium on Personality and Social Psychology, Volume 7: The psychology of prejudice* (pp. 103–130). Hillsdale, NJ: Lawrence Erlbaum.

Nieto, S. (1996). *Affirming diversity: The sociopolitical context of multicultural education* (2nd ed.). White Plains, NY: Longman.

Pinderhughes, E. (1989). *Understanding race, ethnicity, & power: The key to efficacy in clinical practice.* New York: The Free Press.

Rothenberg, P. S. (1998). *Race, class, and gender in the United States: An integrated study* (4th ed.). New York: St. Martin's.

Shor, I. (1992) *Empowering education: Critical teaching for social change.* Chicago: University of Chicago Press.

Stewart, A. M. (1993). Empowerment and enablement. *The British Journal of Occupational Therapy, 56*(12), 433.

Young-Bruehl, E. (1996). *The anatomy of prejudices.* Cambridge, MA: Harvard University Press.

The Power of Language

Key Points

- Discourse is a socially accepted interaction among language usage, thinking, and acting that can be used to identify oneself as a member of a social network.

- Those who engage in the dominant discourse are empowered in our society, and those in power have access to the dominant discourse.

- Social status and differentiation among persons correlate with differences in speech patterns, and differences in language are used as an indicator of social segmentation.

- One's words, linguistic style, and use of voice contribute to differences in language and power.

- Health professionals must find ways to break down linguistic barriers, so that all consumers have a voice and are heard.

- All health professions have their own specialized language, sometimes referred to as "jargon."

- Jargon provides a shortcut way of communicating among professionals.

- Jargon is not an effective way of communicating with clients, and it serves to emphasize the difference between the authorities (the professionals) and the disempowered client.

- When speaking with clients
  - communicate in a language that is clear and at their level of understanding,
  - define any medical terms,
  - listen well to the client's questions and stories,
  - carefully observe the client's body language,
  - do not assume understanding—ask for clarification, and
  - always communicate in a respectful manner.

Sticks and stones may break my bones,
but words will never hurt me. . . .

Many of us grew up reciting this phrase, usually after a time when our feelings had been hurt by someone calling us names or teasing or berating us. Despite our use of this angry or prideful retort, the truth was then, and continues to be, that words can and do indeed hurt us. We are aware of that hurt when we are spoken to in anger or derision or when we are slandered or reviled; but language can also *hurt* us when we may not even be aware of its power to do so. For in fact, language has power.

As health professionals we must be aware of the words we choose to use when dealing with one another and with our clients. We cannot establish rapport nor effectively communicate with people who are different from ourselves if the words we use unwittingly hurt or oppress. Being aware of and sensitive to not only our own words and language, but also to those of our clients is essential for the culturally competent therapist.

The information in this chapter is the distillation of a large body of work that cannot possibly be fully explored in this context. The authors have chosen to identify only specific areas related to power and language that affect health professionals with the caveat that the choice of topics is itself a political act. What one speaks about, what one chooses to eliminate as topics, and the words and language spoken indicates one's perception of power and control and one's actual power within a sociocultural context.

Sociocultural Correlation With Language

Someone once said that whoever does the naming has the power. Historically in this country, the *naming* has been done by those who have been dominant, and thus those who have been in powerful positions. The English language that has developed in the United States, with its European roots, has been developed by persons in powerful positions; and it has helped maintain the social hierarchy that was discussed in the last chapter. Learning and control of language can be defined as literacy, and according to Bennett (1991, p. 14) "literacy is intricately tied up in the maintenance of vested interests in an already existing structure of power." When discussing the concept of literacy, Gee (1989, p. 18) identifies the importance of *discourse* as a socially accepted association among ways of using language, of thinking, and of acting that can be used to identify oneself as a member of a socially meaningful group or *social network.*

Several important points can be made about discourses: (a) discourses involve a set of values and viewpoints from which one must speak and act; (b) any discourse puts forth certain concepts, viewpoints, and values at the expense of others, resulting in the diminishing or marginalization of other discourses; and (c) "discourses are intimately related to the distribution of social power and hierarchical structure in society. Control over certain discourses can lead to the acquisition of social goods (money, power, status) in a society" (Gee, 1989 p. 19). Therefore, those who engage in the dominant discourses are empowered within a particular society and, concurrently, those who hold sociocultural power have access to the dominant discourses.

Not everyone born in the United States, however, has immediate access to the dominant discourses identified by Gee. Although certain discourses can be learned, such as those of the health professions of which we are all a part, we acquire our first and primary discourse from our families. This discourse is socioculturally defined and determines the way we use our native language during face-to-face communication. Sociolinguistics is a method of studying communication behavior that holds the assumption that there is a dynamic relationship between language and social factors. Two complementary processes that are recognized within the discipline of sociolinguistics are that social status and differentiation among persons correlate with differences in speech patterns, and that differences in language are used as an indicator of social segmentation. "Speakers of socially ordered groups exhibit differences in frequency of use of certain sounds, words, and grammatical features" (Bonvillain, 1997, p. 131). Each person has a unique way of speaking that reflects his or her gender, class, geography, race, and ethnicity. Additionally, most persons in a given social group are aware of these speech differences and where it places them within the social structure. For example, women's speech patterns tend to differ from those of many men, and in a patriarchal society those differences in language have been given a value that places women (and men) with feminine speech patterns within a lower social status than most men. Therefore, many women, in an effort to appear more authoritative or powerful, learn to modulate their voices so as not to sound *too feminine.*

There are several characteristics that contribute to differences in language and power, a few of which include the words we choose to use, our linguistic style, and our use of *voice*.

Words, Linguistic Style, and *Voice*

The *words* one chooses to use hold cultural, societal, and personal meaning for the user and the person(s) addressed. Tanno (1997, p. 80) states that *words—labels—convey volumes about assumptions and perceptions*. Many words indicate bias and prejudice, serving to demean and maintain persons within oppressed positions. Herbst (1997) has written a reference book that identifies and defines more than 850 ethnic and racial terms and expressions that indicate bias in today's multicultural society. He states that "all of the words here will—in one of their senses, in some ways or context—restrict, misrepresent, or distort how people are known" (p. ix). Every American has grown up knowing, hearing and sometimes using some of these words. People may not mean to be prejudiced or show bias towards someone from another group, but because we live in a society that harbors institutionalized racism, sexism, homophobia, and all the other *ism's*, it is difficult not to make verbal mistakes. Sometimes the slurs are intentional; but often people will use biased language without being aware of the hurt that it causes, mainly because it has become part of the accepted vernacular. How many of us have referred to elder women as *cute little old ladies* without considering the fact that that language diminishes them and negates the wisdom and experience that are the result of many years of life? Biased language is so much a part of American English that most of us do not even realize we are using it.

Linguistic style is another unique feature of one's use of language. It is the manner in which one uses words and language and incorporates features such as pronunciation, intonation, grammatical variants, and choices of vocabulary (Bonvillain, 1997). All people in this society are socialized to express themselves in different ways according to the cultural norms that teach and reinforce differentiated roles related to age, gender, race, ethnicity, class, and other characteristics. Although a person may speak English, the style in which he or she speaks immediately identifies his or her place in society. Although there are many ways this could be represented, for the purposes of this chapter, the authors will use only examples related to gender and to the use of *Black English*.

Linguistic Differences Related to Gender

Differences between the way White American men and women speak have been studied for years. Although the increased numbers of women in the workplace have altered some of those differences, there are still specific speech patterns and styles that are identified as more masculine or feminine. No patterns are exclusive of either gender, but particular styles are culturally associated and often stereotyped for each. Bonvillain (1997, p. 172) reports on the differences in pronunciation between men and women, summarizing that pronunciation relates to class differentiation and that

> women are socialized to behave with propriety and politeness (reflected by *middle-class speech*), and given a system of gender stratification in which men are privileged and in which men who act like women are strongly criticized, men consciously or unconsciously strive toward speech norms that reject styles associated with women. Because women model their behavior on *middle-class* styles, men covertly prefer *working-class* speech.

The *polite style* of feminine speech puts women at a disadvantage in the workplace where more masculine modes of conversation and interaction are valued.

Women generally use more dynamic intonation than do men. Intonation is "a complex combination of rhythm, volume, and pitch overlaying entire utterances." Women tend to employ "a wider range of pitches within their repertory and a more rapid and marked shift in volume and velocity" (Bonvillain, 1997, p. 173). Research on gender differences in intonation indicate that dynamic patterns are interpreted as indicating emotionality and natural impulses, which are ascribed to women; whereas use of narrow intonational ranges is taken to indicate control and restraint, seen as more masculine qualities (McConnell-Ginet, 1983). The more controlled (masculine) speech patterns are given more cultural value in American society whereas the more expressive, dynamic patterns used more often by women have identified women as more unstable and unpredictable, substantiating and maintaining the cultural stereotypes of women in the United States.

The research on grammatical variants has been inconclusive regarding gender differences, although Bonvillain (1997) cites class differences in grammatical patterns. However, choice of vocabulary has generally been found to differ in men and women. Studies have found that women use more specific terms than do men when denoting colors (e.g., using terms like *magenta* and *turquoise*), and that women tend to use less profanity than men or use milder expletives. Women also tend to use more modifiers (i.e., adjectives and adverbs) in their speech. Although this last characteristic has also been given the negative connotation of superficiality, Bonvillain comments that many of the modifiers are affective in nature (e.g., words such as *wonderful* or *lovely*). This increased expressiveness signifies that women in our culture have been allowed to display emotions and emotional thought more than men have, and this is reflected in their language.

One additional and interesting area of vocabulary differences noted with women is the tendency to use hedge words in discourse. Bonvillain (1997, p. 178) defines hedge words as *words or expressions that covertly comment on assertions in one's statements*. The following are some examples:

• *Maybe* I *could try* to call at a later time.

• I've been *sort of wondering whether* I should go.

• *Well,* I *assume* it's *approximately* seventy degrees out.

This style of speaking signals a speaker's uncertainty about the validity of her statements; in so doing, it makes her appear indecisive, ineffective, and weak. Many women do this, even those who are in positions of power or leadership as reported by McIntosh in her fascinating article entitled "Feeling Like a Fraud" (1985). Although she focuses on women's sense of fraudulence when placed within the center of the public's attention, the phrases McIntosh highlights are essentially hedge words as identified by Bonvillain.

In summary, the linguistic styles of White men and women not only indicate their sociocultural status within the society, but also serve to maintain the difference in status by supporting stereotypical cultural roles. The message to women is to be aware of one's mode of discourse and how it affects those around you. Then a choice can be made to either continue to verbally present oneself pridefully in the usual manner, to alter one's style of speaking to adopt a more culturally valued (and more masculine) style, or to vary one's style depending upon context and people. Any choice can be seen as positive as long as the speaker is aware of the effect she is having.

Many female health professionals assume a *professional* voice and style that tends to diminish gender differences in speaking. With a linguistic style and discourse that is accepted by all other health professionals, a woman might be perceived as more of an equal with the men on the health care team.

The Linguistic Style Associated with Black English

Many African Americans in this country speak a variety of English known *as Black English, Black English Vernacular* (BEV) (Bonvillain 1997), or as it has recently been named, *Ebonics*. Some use their own dialect in all their communications, whereas others use it only in certain familiar contexts such as with family or friends. However it is used, *Black English* is never regarded as part of the dominant discourse. Some of the differences from Standard English are in the structure and linguistic style of the language.

Grammatical differences include the following: BEV reduces the final consonants in words using *las' night* rather then *last night,* sometimes omits the past tense ending of *-ed,* and often omits the final *-s* when it indicates a possessive form. The language form also uses the contraction and deletion of the verb *to be* in a particular stylistic form (Bonvillain 1997). The following are some examples:

• Why you *be* running in the street so much?

• He *be* hiding when she *be* mad.

• He fast in everything he do.

• We on tape.

Although this usage does not reflect Standard English format, linguists have determined that it does maintain its own grammatical rules. Nevertheless, because this style of speaking is not part of the dominant discourse, persons who speak it are often devalued and stereotyped, much as women are for their linguistic style. Consider the word *standard* in the phrase *Standard English*. If something is the standard it becomes the yardstick by which everything else in that category is measured. If something competes with that standard and does not *measure up* to it, it is then seen as diminished, devalued, or less than that with which it is compared. *Black English* fits into that category. Additionally, African Americans' historical status as an oppressed minority has resulted in the tendency of Whites to "perceive Black English as a mass of random errors committed by Blacks trying to speak English" (Labov, Cohen, Robins, & Lewis, 1968, p. 366). However, the student of diversity must always question who sets the standard for any category. In many cases the *standards* were set early on by the dominant power group, which historically has been White, middle-class, or elite men of European descent.

African American children who are more comfortable with *Black English* are often stigmatized and may become quiet or even silent in a formal situation such as school where standard English is the expected norm. Some of these children become hostile in an environment that does not seem to meet their needs. They run the risk of being misjudged and labeled by teachers (the majority of whom are White), who then may place them in special education settings or lower their expectations for success for these students. Orvando (1997) reports that historically, speakers of *Black English* have been misperceived as language deficient and cognitively impaired. Perhaps this is one of the many factors that limit the numbers of African American students that are found in health professions' academic programs.

Whether or not an African American child who speaks *Black English* should be taught standard English or *Black English* in school is controversial. However, many authors support the idea that even though their native discourse should be honored and encouraged in a variety of tasks and settings, African American children should be taught standard English to empower them to be successful in the dominant culture (Delpit, 1995). "Both linguistic forms have been demanded for Black survival—Black language for use in the Black community where *talkin proper* is negatively equated with *talkin White,* White language for use in attempts to get admitted to the White American mainstream" (Smitherman, 1984, p. 108).

Smitherman's comment is important. Within a sociocultural context one must speak in a particular way to have access to the dominant discourse. In summary, one's linguistic style has an effect on the perception and reality of one's social status. In a health profession context, practitioners will be judged and evaluated by their superiors, colleagues, and clients by the manner of their speech. White American women need to be aware of their linguistic style and how it affects others' perceptions of them as professionals. White American men and women also must be sensitive to their response to the linguistic style of their clients, particularly if the clients are persons of color. Is one making assumptions about clients' abilities based solely on their manner of speech? Are they inadvertently being treated differently because they speak English in a nonstandard manner or with an accent? Black male practitioners must consider whether their linguistic style differs from the dominant discourse; and if so, does it cause others to view them as less able or less intelligent? And if one is living with the *double jeopardy* of being a woman of color and a health care professional, she must be aware of all of the above in her communication with others to evaluate the affect she has within her interpersonal communications. Although one probably cannot, nor should one try to change his or her manner of speaking and linguistic style for each person with whom one communicates, establishing rapport with clients, colleagues, and supervisors will be easier if each has an awareness of how he or she may be perceived by others because of the way one speaks.

Voice

The term *voice* is defined in *Webster's* dictionary (Merriam-Webster, 1995, p. 586) not only as "sound produced through the mouth by vertebrates and esp. by human beings in speaking and shouting," but also as "the power of speaking or the right of expression." It is these latter definitions that we speak of in this section. Considering the power of speaking, having a voice means speaking and being heard. In the 1993 edition of her seminal work, *In a Different Voice* (1982/1983, p. xvi), Gilligan defines *voice* as follows.

> ...I mean something like what people mean when they speak of the core of the self. Voice is natural and also cultural. It is composed of breath and sound, words, rhythm, and language. And voice is a powerful psychological instrument and channel, connecting inner and outer worlds. Speaking and listening are a form of psychic breathing. This ongoing relational exchange among people is mediated through language and culture, diversity and plurality. For these reasons, voice is a new key for understanding the psychological, social, and cultural order—a litmus test of relationships and a measure of psychological health.

In the previous paragraph, Gilligan emphasizes the necessity of having a voice for one's psychological health, yet many disempowered people in this society do not believe that they have a voice in the matters of their lives. They do not think that they are heard when they speak, nor do they have access to the dominant discourse where their voices might make a difference. Many believe they are silenced and subsequently powerless and hopeless. Others do not have a voice because there are cultural restrictions regarding speaking and silence (Goldberger, 1996). Without a sensitive recognition of cultural differences, many people's needs will go unspoken and unheard.

Often within the health care arena, clients think they are disempowered and silenced, especially within an institutionalized setting. They no longer believe they have a voice in what happens to them. If they are persons of color within a predominantly White American setting, or from a different cultural or ethnic group, more barriers are raised that prevent adequate communication and the development of rapport between them and their caregivers. As culturally competent health care providers we must find ways to break down or bypass these barriers so that all our clients will believe they are supported and are thus safe enough to tell us what they need. They must be encouraged to speak and to have a voice in their own health care.

Political Correctness

One cannot discuss language, power, and multiculturalism without addressing the political correctness—or *PC* as it is known in the vernacular-movement. PC became popularized on American university campuses around 1990 and is defined as "a set of ideas, concerns, principles, and directives that stresses social nonoppressiveness, inclusiveness, and sensitivity to diverse groups of people" (Herbst, 1997, p. 183). A somewhat simplistic and superficial understanding of the beginnings of this political movement is that the purposes were to limit language that was sexist, racist, and homophobic, and to find a common way to engage in multicultural discourse across various groups without resorting to oppressive language. As a result, words such as *Native American, African American,* and *nondominant group* began to be used in place of other labels that may have been considered pejorative. Although using PC language appears to be a worthwhile endeavor—after all, it encouraged people to think about the words they were using and forced them through societal pressure to *clean up their act,* so to speak—a deeper analysis reveals that there has been, and continues to be much controversy regarding this movement.

In fact, the PC controversy is a political *hot potato* that is far too complex and convoluted in its arguments to be addressed fully in the context of this chapter and book. We will try, however, to outline some of the prevalent ideas with the conflicting *voices* of the theorists.

First of all, one must recognize that the PC movement is indeed political. It addresses power and power relationships and attempts to shift power from one *side* to another through its rhetoric. Although there are many voices, the *sides* of this debate line up with either the *neoconservatives* (a term used by Epstein, 1995; Bernal, 1997) or with the *liberatory theorists*. The neoconservatives are described as right-wing conservatives (Bernal, 1997, p. 19), who are White, male, and elitist. The liberatory theorists are feminists, multiculturalists, and critical theorists. The neoconservatives are perceived to hold much of the dominant power, whereas the liberatory theorists are viewed to be more marginal.

The neoconservative *voice* cries out with the following anti-PC rhetoric and themes:

- Before the 1960s there was pure and objective (i.e., without political context or bias) scholarship relating to the *Great Books* and academic literary canon, which has been polluted by left-wing radicals who bring in feminist and multicultural scholarship and *voices* that do not meet the previous standards (Bernal, 1997; Allsup, 1995).

- The Western canon defines intellectual excellence; the one version of *truth* is liberal thought that is derived from this canon; and multiculturalism, which is equated with anti-Intellectualism, opposes *truth* (Epstein, 1995).

- Being *forced* to use PC language takes away the right of free speech. Those pushing for PC are *feminazis* or *radical militants* who are *thought police* that reside in the universities (Allsup, 1995).

- Feminists and multiculturalists are degrading the concept of the one, common, binding culture and value system, which has provided the "unique source of those liberating ideas of individual liberty, political democracy, the rule of law, human rights, and cultural freedom that constitute our most precious legacy and to which most of the world today aspires" (Schlesinger, 1991, p. 32).

The responsive *voice* of those who argue against the above criticisms replies that fear is the emotion that drives the rhetoric. Howard (1996) believes that there is a history of fear of diversity in this country, and the anti-PC neoconservatives fear "the loss of European and Western cultural supremacy in the school curriculum" (p. 328). In reality, the PC movement was an effort to increase equality, equity, and inclusiveness to the language of the academy and to society. It was an attempt to "introduce the voices and experiences of those who have been excluded from academic curricula and intellectual discourse" (Epstein 1995, pp. 5–6). The rash of articles and books by neoconservatives who vehemently argued against the PC movement sound to Epstein like "a group of men who are terrified that their world is falling apart, that their worldview is being rejected" (p. 6).

One way that opponents of the PC movement have attacked the movement is to mock, trivialize, and discredit the language and the ideas. What this does is deflect the focus from the real issues, which are efforts to reduce racism, sexism, homophobia, and other kinds of oppression. Lindsley (1998, p. 196) reports that the media attacks PC by *trivializing* and *exaggerating* PC language in an effort to pervert the meaning of the words and language; and as a result,

> an interesting role reversal emerges: Those who are members of traditionally privileged groups are construed as victims of academic liberals who are mandating impositions on individuals' freedom of speech. Thus, tolerance is artfully construed as an attack on basic human rights and, in particular, on the rights of the most powerful members of our society. The actual effects of intolerance on targeted groups are lost in the margins of this media discourse. . . . Thus, mass-mediated constructs juxtapose intolerance as more desirable than tolerance.

Howard (1996, p. 328) sees the attack against PC as an attack against diversity. In response he states, *It is not multiculturalism that threatens to destroy our unity—as some neoconservative academics would have us believe—but rather our inability to embrace our differences and our unwillingness to honor the very ideals we espouse [equality, freedom, and justice for all people].*

Perhaps the lesson in all of this is that words and language can be and are used to influence others in a sometimes subtle and often covert manner. It is important that, as culturally competent professionals, we each become aware of the power we wield (and sometimes yield) each time we open our mouths to speak.

Professional Language, Jargon, Authority, and Power

Although the specialized languages we use as health professionals are not meant to diminish or oppress or to be biased, they do in fact separate us from our clients in a hierarchical fashion. A recent article in a leading health magazine charted the public's understanding of many common terms used in today's health arena and found that more than half of those persons responding to a recent poll do not know or only have a *rough idea* of the meaning of the words (*Business & Health*, 1997). For example, 51% of the general public does not understand universal health care; 63% does not know what "PPO" means; 75% does not understand COBRA health insurance, and 84% cannot tell you the meaning of "POS" (p. 56). If the results of this poll are representative, how then are we communicating with our clients and with each other?

Because one of the characteristics of a profession is specialized knowledge (Curry, Wergin, & Associates, 1993), each profession has its own specialized language. This common language defines the technical aspects and uniqueness of each separate profession and allows the members to communicate and understand one another. For those of us who are health care professionals, the specialized language is rooted in the medical model, allowing us to use medical terminology to speak to one another across disciplines. Yet each separate health care profession also employs its unique specialized language. This specialized language helps the members of a profession form a kind of elite community whose language is only known to one another. The interesting thing about communities or the sense of community, however, is that they are both inclusive and exclusive. To its members, a community provides a sense of belonging, a sense of *us*. A specialized language helps maintain that awareness and sense of inclusion. However, it is important to remember that inclusiveness, that sense of *us*, alternately means that others are excluded and become the *them*.

As health care professionals, one way that we separate ourselves from *them* is through the use of jargon. Jargon is defined as "nonsensical, incoherent or meaningless talk" and as "the specialized or technical language of a trade" (Houghton Mifflin, 1993). Therefore, jargon is simply another word for the specialized language we use as health care professionals. As such, the use of it is not valued as either bad or good. Within a particular group jargon becomes a *shorthand* way of communicating more efficiently.

When speaking with others outside of the professional community group, however, the use of jargon has mixed results. Some believe that jargon is acceptable to use as long as it is defined (McGlade, Milot, & Scales, 1996). When medical terms are used and then defined in lay terms to clients, it serves to educate them about the health care arena, empowering them to have clearer understanding and to make more informed decisions.

Others believe that jargon and abbreviations are used not only to separate health care professionals from their clients, but also used "as an artificial means of defining staff status levels with the [nursing] profession—from consultant to auxiliary" (Leitch, 1992, p. 50). Hammond (1993, p. 26) states that the jargon used by doctors "transforms common-sense medicine into a cosy (sic), elite world that is impenetrable to all but the ever-so-clever."

Jargon is often used as a way to remind ourselves that we are part of a professional group and may be viewed as part of the developmental process of learning to talk as a professional. In an article about occupational therapy language, Gilfoyle (1979) identifies four developmental stages that one's communication patterns go through during the transition between an entering and a seasoned therapist: (1) representational language, (2) private language, (3) socialized language, and (4) communicative language. Gilfoyle believes that to reach the fourth stage (i.e., communicative language) where the speaker communicates well with another person whose language style may differ, though not compromising a sense of professionalism, the inexperienced professional learns to speak jargon (i.e., representational and private language). One reason for this may be "to provide ourselves with some element of control, as if to know and use impressive terms adds to the credibility we seek" (p. 8). The following use of jargon was selected from Gilfoyle's article.

> J. Diagnosed as MR, with a birth history of Hyelines and RDS was referred for an OT eval.... OT eval included SCSIT, SCPRN, DDST, reflex testing and ADL. J. Has CP, spastic diplegia with hypertonicity. He has severe SID. His PPL is 2 yr. below age. He has a positive footing, TLR, ATNR. STNR: primitive righting, poor protective and equilibrium reaction. Recommend OT 3x weekly using SI and NDT techniques.

Although the paragraph above may communicate fully with other rehabilitation professionals, it should not be presented to the client or family in that manner. Whatever the reasons for speaking jargon, it rarely allows health care professionals to communicate well and fully with our clients. Rather, it is a subtle reminder to them that the professionals are part of the dominant group—the authorities, the ones with the knowledge—whereas clients and families are the *other*—the recipients of services and knowledge, the disempowered ones.

Using this "private language" with clients and families may silence and intimidate them. Instead of communicating in a way that stimulates dialogue, this kind of language only emphasizes the differences between the health professional and the client. It does not contribute to a conversation, but it strengthens the sense of hierarchy.

We can change this by *communicating* with our clients *in a language that is clear and at their level of understanding*. If it is necessary to use jargon or professional or specialized language, *define the terms* until the meaning is clear to the recipient. *Listen well* to the client's questions and stories, and *carefully observe* the body language that accompanies his or her discussion. If the client is from a cultural or subcultural group that is different from our own, *we cannot assume to understand* the meaning behind the words. *Ask for clarification.*

Summary

The language we use as health professionals has the power to separate us from or connect us to our colleagues, administrators, and clients. We must be aware that language has power; the words we use, the linguistic style of our speech, and the way we use our voice all influence others around us. All of these language characteristics reflect who we are and how we are viewed by others just as they influence how we perceive our clients and colleagues. It is imperative that health care professionals be aware of the importance of their language and speech and how it may affect others.

Professional language and jargon must also be used judiciously in conversation with clients. When considering the effects of the authority of professional language combined with the sociopolitical privilege and power afforded those of us who are White, it is imperative that as health professionals we acquire and maintain a sensitivity to those who are different from us. Not only must we be culturally aware and sensitive to the language we use and the authority it commands, but also we must develop the skills necessary to become culturally competent practitioners. Those skills will be outlined in the following chapters.

References

Allsup, C. (1995). Postmodernism, the politically correct, and liberatory pedagogy. In C. E. Sleeter & P. L. McLaren (Eds.), *Multicultural education, critical pedagogy, and the politics of difference*. Albany, NY: State University
of New York Press.

Bennett, A. T. (1991). Discourses of power, the dialectics of understanding, the
power of literacy. In C. Mitchell & K. Weiler (Eds.), *Rewriting literacy:
Culture and the discourse of the other*. New York: Bergin & Garvey.

Bernal, M. (1997, Winter/Spring). Politically correct: Mythologies of neocon-
servatism in the American academy. *New Political Science, 38–39,* 17–28.

Bonvillain, N. (1997). *Language, culture, and communication: The meaning of
messages* (2nd ed.). Englewood Cliffs, NJ: Prentice Hall.

Curry, L., Wergin, J. F., & Associates. (1993). *Educating professionals*. San
Francisco: Jossey-Bass.

Delpit, L. (1995). *Other people's children*. New York: The New Press.

Darnovsky, M., Epstein, B., & Flacks, R. (1995). *Cultural politics and social
movements*. Philadelphia, PA: Temple University Press.

Editors of the American Heritage Dictionaries (Eds.). (1993). *American Heritage College Dictionary* (3rd ed.). Boston: Houghton Mifflin.

Epstein, B. (1995). Political correctness and collective powerlessness. In
M. Darnovsky, B. Epstein, & R. Flacks (Eds.), *Cultural politics and social
movements*. Philadelphia, PA: Temple University Press.

Gee, J. (1989). What is literacy? *Journal of Education, 171*(1), 18–25.

Gilfoyle, E. (1979). Occupational therapy language. *Training: Occupational
therapy educational management in schools, a competency-based educational program: Volume 4. Modules Six, Seven, Eight*. Bethesda, MD:
American Occupational Therapy Association.

Gilligan, C. (1982/1993). *In a different voice: Psychological theory and
women's development*. Cambridge, MA: Harvard University Press.

Goldberger, N. R. (1996). Cultural imperatives and diversity in ways of knowing. In N. Goldberger, J. Tarule, B. Clinchy, & M. Belenky (Eds.), *Knowledge, Difference, and Power*. New York: BasicBooks.

Hammond, P. (1993). Communication breakdown. *Nursing Times, 89*(20), 26.

Hecht, M. L. (Ed.). (1998). *Communicating prejudice*. Newbury Park, CA:
Sage.

Herbst, P. H. (1997) *The color of words: An encyclopedic dictionary of ethnic
bias in the United States*. Yarmouth, ME: Intercultural Press.

Howard, G. (1996). Whites in multicultural education: Rethinking our role. In J. A. Banks (Ed.), *Multicultural education, transformative knowledge and action.* New York: Teachers College Press.

Labov, W., Cohen, P., Robins, C., & Lewis, J. (1968). *A study of the non-standard English of Negro and Puerto Rican speakers in New York City, report on Cooperative Research Project 3288.* New York: Columbia University.

Leitch, C. (1992). Understanding sweet nothing. *Nursing Standard, 6*(48), 50–51.

Lindsley, S. (1998). Communicating prejudice in organizations. In M. L. Hecht (Ed.). *Communicating prejudice.* Newbury Park, CA.: Sage.

Makau, J. M., & Arnett, R. C. (1997). *Communication ethics in an age of diversity.* Urbana and Chicago, IL: University of Illinois Press.

McConnell-Ginet, S. (1983). Intonation in a man's world. In Thorne et al., *Language, Gender and Society* (69–88). Rowley, MA: Newbury.

McGlade, L. M., Milot, B. A., & Scales, J. (1996). Eliminating jargon, or medicalese, from scientific writing. *American Journal of Clinical Nutrition, 64,* 256–257.

McIntosh, P. (1985). Feeling like a fraud. *Work in Progress #18.* Wellesley, MA: Stone Center for Developmental Services and Studies at Wellesley College.

Mish, F. H. (Ed.). (1995). *Merriam Webster's Collegiate Dictionary* (10th ed.). Springfield, MA: Merriam-Webster, Inc.

Orvando, C. (1997). Language diversity and education. In J. A. Banks & C. A. Banks (Eds.), *Multicultural education: Issues and perspectives* (3rd ed.). Newton, MA: Allyn and Bacon.

———. (1997, March). Parlez-vous health speak? In Data Watch (Ed.), *Business & Health, 15*(3), 56.

Schlesinger, A. (1991, Winter). The disuniting of America, what we stand to lose if multicultural education takes the wrong approach. *American Educator* (pp. 14–33).

Smitherman, G. (1984). Black language as power. In Kramarae, Schultz, & O'Barr (Eds.), *Language and power* (pp. 101–115). Newbury Park, CA: Sage.

Tanno, D. V. (1997). Ethical implications in the ethnic 'text' in multicultural communication studies. In J. M. Makau & R. C. Arnett (Eds.), *Communication ethics in an age of diversity* (pp. 73–78). Urbana and Chicago, IL: University of Illinois Press.

CHAPTER EIGHT

The Challenge of Being White

Key Points

- Whiteness is a racial category.

- Whiteness as a cultural construct often is the standard by which other ethnic and racial groups are measured.

- For cultural competence, White health care workers must examine what it means to be White.

- Some people get "stuck" at the emotional stage of White guilt. Whites must move beyond this in order to become agents of change.

- Examining one's Whiteness often results in cognitive dissonance. Some respond to this state by choosing to remain unaware of sociocultural injustice or by denial, hostility, and fear of diversity.

- None of the above emotions have a place within the client–practitioner interaction.

- Practitioners must engage in self-analysis, knowledge about people who differ from themselves, and culturally competent skills in order to interact effectively with all clients.

- White educators of diversity can be important allies for nondominant students and others.

- Culturally competent skills include

  - using inclusive language;

  - making no assumptions about people based on race, ethnicity, gender, class, sexual orientation, age, and ability;

  - learning about each client's culture, beliefs, and customs during the assessment process;

    – seeking a translator if there is a language barrier; and

    – approaching each client with openness to difference and a willingness to learn.

• Effective White educators of diversity possess the following characteristics:

    – Courage

    – Humility

    – Open-mindedness

    – Introspection

    – Hunger for knowledge

lthough a preceding chapter discusses the privileges and benefits that White Americans are given solely because of the color of their skin, there are challenges and problems inherent in these so-called benefits, especially as we consider the task of becoming culturally competent. Much of the work being done in race relations or multicultural theory has been focused on understanding the lives and cultural experiences of nondominant groups: African Americans, Hispanics, Asians, and Native Americans (Howard, 1993). "Studies of racial and cultural identities have tended to view the range of potential subjects of research as limited to those who differ from the (unnamed) norm" (Frankenberg, 1993, p. 17). White Americans have been allies for decades with oppressed groups and have written about and spoken up for social justice. Yet little of the rhetoric has actually examined what it means to be White. Only recently have White American authors focused on Whiteness as a racial category. McLaren (1997), in an extensive, in-depth, sociopolitical analysis believes that *Whiteness* became racialized in the mid-seventeen and early-eighteen hundreds, after the establishment of racism in this country. By the early 1860s, "Whiteness had become a marker for measuring inferior and superior races" (p. 259). Today, the broadened concept of Whiteness as a cultural construct "constitutes and demarcates ideas, feelings, knowledge, social practices, cultural formations, and systems of intelligibility that are identified with or attributed to White people and that are invested in by White people as White" (p. 267). What is not defined here is that with all of the above, Whiteness within American culture comes with an "invisible knapsack of unearned privileges" (McIntosh, 1988, p. 11).

The earlier lack of self-analysis may have occurred because, as a privileged, dominant group, White Americans have not had to examine or think about what it means to be White. White just is! It is the standard by which others are measured. The privileges of being White are generally invisible to White Americans. There are numerous unexamined expectations that White Americans hold, some of which have been delineated by McIntosh (1988).

White is generally not an adjective used to describe a specific person or group. One rarely hears the *White teacher* or *White doctor* or *White lawyer* because in our society White is the expected standard, the dominant group. On the other hand, it is common to hear others described by their race or ethnicity, the *African American teacher*, the *Hispanic doctor*, or the *Asian lawyer,* indicating that a person is identified by their race or ethnicity as the *other,* as non-White.

To become culturally competent, White American health care practitioners, in an effort to have a better understanding of themselves and their values and beliefs, must also examine what it means to be White. It is imperative that those of us who are White are aware not only of the power and authority we are given by virtue of our positions as health professionals, but also the inherent power and privilege we have simply because of the color of our skin.

One thing that plays a part in the maintenance of unexamined Whiteness is the emotion that is elicited when people begin to evaluate what being White means in the sociopolitical reality of this society. When discussing racism or multiculturalism, an examination of the privilege and power of Whiteness often brings with it feelings of guilt, shame, embarrassment, and hopelessness, which often lead to fear, anger, defensiveness, or confusion (Kivel, 1996). *White guilt* is often a byproduct of this examination (Holzman, 1995), and some White Americans seem to get *stuck* there, never moving to another level from which they can become agents for change. In a culture that extols the virtues of strength, confidence, and rational thinking, the feelings mentioned above result in a sense of vulnerability and discomfiture. These are not the expected reactions of those who are seen as the dominant and powerful individuals of a society. Rather, these feelings are more representative of those expressed by nondominant and oppressed groups. It is important at this point to remember the words of Kivel (1996, p. 14).

> There's absolutely nothing wrong with being White or with noticing the difference that color makes. We were born without choice into our families. We did not choose our skin color, native language or culture. We are not responsible for being White or being raised in a White-dominated, racist society in which we have been trained to have particular responses to persons of color. We are responsible to how we respond to racism . . . and we can only do that consciously and effectively if we start by realizing that it makes a crucial difference that we are White.

However, White Americans do not always respond to racism or oppression in responsible ways. As a White American learning about the sociopolitical power of Whiteness, feelings of security, pride, and satisfaction are challenged by new information that shifts the reality of who we think we are. This results in what Howard describes as a *classic state of cognitive dissonance* (1993, p. 38). This cognitive dissonance, combined with the emotions listed above, is often hard to bear. One way that many White Americans deal with this is by choosing to remain unaware. Howard (1993) reports that this *luxury of ignorance* is only available to members of a dominant group. He states that "throughout most of history, there has been no reason why White Americans, for their own survival or success, have needed to be sensitive to the cultural perspectives of other groups" (p. 41). Yet this luxury is not available to non-Whites in this society. If you are African American, Hispanic, Native American, or Asian in America, your success and daily survival depends on knowing the expectations and behaviors of the White American community.

Another strategy that many White Americans adopt to deal with the realities of our oppressive history is denial. By denying the reality of White privilege, discrimination, or inequitable resources or access for minority groups, White Americans can abdicate any responsibility for changing the social injustices that occur. In their blindness they can avoid eye contact with the panhandler on the street; refuse to acknowledge the racial discrimination that occurs in public school classrooms (Kozol, 1991); and choose not to see the poverty and lack of access to health care for many Native Americans, Hispanics, and single, African American mothers.

Along with denial, Howard (1993) identifies two other *emotions that kill* as hostility and fear of diversity. The exacerbation of blatant hostility to violence is apparent daily in the media and on our streets as we recall the recent killing of a gay man in Wyoming, the dragging of an African American man to his death by White American supremacists, the murder of a Jewish talk show host by neo-Nazis in Denver, and increased racial incidents and other hate crimes on college campuses.

Howard (1993) believes that it is the fear of diversity that underlies the denial and hostility of many White Americans. Historically, humans have always feared those who were different from themselves. Fear turns to hatred—the kind of hatred that is apparent in White American supremacist groups today. Fear also comes from ignorance—an ignorance that is supported by a lack of information and education about diverse groups in today's society; and ignorance that is kept in place by neoconservative and other groups that fear a loss of sociopolitical power and control.

As White American health professionals working with diverse groups of people, denial, hostility, and fear of diversity have no place.

Rather, a knowledge of self, including an awareness and understanding of the power and reality of Whiteness, openness to and respect for difference that leads to knowledge about groups different from our own, and a commitment to providing equitable and just care to all people, is what we each must strive for.

Thoughts on Being a White Clinician

What must White American health practitioners be aware of in their practice? There are many things to consider. First of all, although the demographics of the United States are rapidly changing, the majority of the work force in the major health professions remains White American. Because White Americans will no doubt remain the dominant majority in medicine and allied health, policies and practices will continue to reflect the values and beliefs of that group. Attitudes, language, and expectations will be representative of White Americans, leaving the increasing numbers of non-White clients less well represented. This will automatically place nonmajority groups of persons in a vulnerable and unequal power position, simply because of their race or ethnicity.

Additionally, health care practitioners are in an authoritative position because of their role in the client–practitioner dyad. Clients are in a vulnerable state physically, emotionally, and socially; and they depend on the health care practitioner to treat them effectively and fairly. Most do. But the experience of being a non-White client places that person in a *double jeopardy* situation that often disempowers them even more than a White client.

It then becomes the responsibility of the practitioner to try to lessen this power inequity as much as possible within the context of the health care system. We can do this by achieving an attitude of acceptance and developing skills that demonstrate this.

An accepting attitude is based on honesty, humility, and respect. Howard (1993) believes that White Americans must face the fact that we have benefited from racism and that we are given sociocultural privileges as a result. Within a client–practitioner relationship, honesty is enhanced when the White American practitioner examines his or her own beliefs and values, and determines whether he or she harbors biases or prejudices that would affect the care offered the client.

> Awareness of one's attitudes and behavior becomes a critical component of preparation to remove barriers for effective

cross-cultural interaction. Such awareness means identifying distortions born of cultural indoctrination as well as psychological need, and it requires an in-depth understanding of one's own cultural background and its meaning (Pinderhughes, 1989, p. 20).

If there are cultural differences between the client and practitioner, an honest attempt to learn more about the client's culture and beliefs will assist the development of trust and rapport, and reduce the possibility of cultural misunderstandings and mistakes.

Humility, or giving up one's power, and humbly admitting the need for additional knowledge about a client's cultural background, is also necessary for the White American practitioner. In a client-centered approach to treatment, the health care professional must recognize the client's uniqueness, and work collaboratively with that person to develop treatment goals and a therapeutic plan. To do this effectively, there must be shared knowledge regarding the client's desires as well as his or her beliefs about wellness, illness, therapeutic care, and independence. These beliefs are grounded in one's culture.

Respect for the individual provides the foundation for honest and humble interactions. "One of the greatest contributions White Americans can make to cultural understanding is simply to learn the power of respect" (Howard, 1993, pp. 39–40). Respecting the dignity and uniqueness of each client is a necessary attitude for the culturally competent therapist. Without respect there can be no mutuality or social equality within the client–practitioner relationship.

Additionally, there are skills that are necessary for the White American practitioner to practice to be effective within a diverse environment. Although not exhaustive, the list in Table 8 is a place to begin.

In conclusion, being a White American is a privilege and a challenge. To be an effective and culturally competent White American health care practitioner, one must have an awareness of self, of one's beliefs and attitudes, and an understanding of the power inherent within the Whiteness of one's skin. Additionally, the White American practitioner has a responsibility to develop the attitudes and skills necessary to competently and effectively establish rapport and trust within a cross-cultural client–practitioner relationship. It is vital to "know how to manage the dynamics of race, ethnicity and power in ways that celebrate the differences among people while also promoting mutual understanding, empathy and respect" (Pinderhughes, 1989, p. 210).

Table 8. Skills for the White American Practitioner

Use inclusive language.

Make no assumptions about a person.

Ask culturally inquisitive questions.

Listen well.

If there is a language barrier, seek a translator.

Learn about the client's culture.

Explain what you are doing and why.

Engage the client's family if appropriate.

Approach each client with openness and a willingness to learn.

Table by Roxie M. Black

Can a White Teacher Teach About Diversity?

The answer to the question above is often an enthusiastic, *Of course! Good teachers can teach about anything!* But any White American teacher who is sensitive to issues of diversity and is aware of the power of Whiteness often questions his or her ability to present these concepts effectively and with an awareness and appropriate use of power that supports the empowerment of students (Kivel, 1996; McLaren, 1998; Paley, 1989; Sleeter, 1995). Many White American teachers of diversity question their ability to teach students how to critically analyze the power structure of White America when they are not only a part of that structure and benefit from it, but also do it from the authoritative and powerful position of teacher. It is a conundrum, and their concerns echo those of Kivel (1996, pp. xi–xii):

> People of color have addressed all the issues much more powerfully than I could. I would make mistakes. I would leave important pieces out. People of color would be angry with me. Other White people would call me racist.... People would expect me to have all the answers. The entire task felt formidable, scary, fraught with problems, and I felt ill-equipped to carry it out successfully.

So, what is a teacher to do?

First of all, White American teachers must continue to teach about diversity simply because there are more of them to do so. In health

Table 9. Characteristics of a Multicultural Teacher

Courage	Open-mindedness	Hunger for
Humility	Introspection	knowledge

Table by Roxie M. Black

professions' educational programs, White American teachers are present in a far greater majority than are teachers of color. Therefore, given the mandate that diversity issues be included in health professions' curricula, more White American teachers will be teaching about diversity than will non-Whites.

Additionally, many White Americans are sincerely interested in becoming culturally competent, and in facilitating students towards cultural competence as well. Sensitive and knowledgeable White American teachers make excellent allies for those who are non-White. If there is interest and knowledge, there is also a responsibility to make a difference. A quote by Rabbi Tarfon (as quoted in Kivel, 1996, p. xii) supports this: "It is not upon you to finish the work. Neither are you free to desist from it."

White American health care educators have a responsibility to present an inclusive and multicultural curriculum to all students. If they are concerned that they do not have enough knowledge, then it is important to get it. Many of the references and resources in this book provide a place to begin. Another way to meet the need for increased numbers of knowledgeable professors who will teach about diversity issues is to identify one person on the faculty who has an interest in this area, and provide that person with the support (e.g., funding and time) to increase his or her knowledge and the time to present it to colleagues and students.

There are multiple ways to present this kind of information in an academic setting, many of which are described in a later chapter within this book. However, the attitude of the White American teacher will determine the success of any of the approaches used. The following is a list of characteristics that are important for a teacher to maintain to effectively do this work (Table 9).

1. *Courage:* As was mentioned earlier, White American teachers of diversity are often concerned whether they can be most effective. It takes courage to put oneself in a situation where one feels vulnerable. Yet teachers must take a bold stance to be successful. They must be

willing to make mistakes, to offer unpopular theories and ideas, to sometimes say the wrong thing, and to become co-learners in the classroom. This means giving up some of their authority. For some faculty members, particularly those who are not confident in their role as teacher, this may be very difficult.

2. *Humility:* Giving up one's power results in humility (Howard, 1993). White American teachers must become aware of the unearned power of Whiteness and its effect on those who are non-White, and be willing to share authority with the students. Shor (1992) discusses a student-centered approach that he calls *democratic authority,* where students are collaborators with the teacher in the teaching and learning process. To listen well and be willing to learn from the students, a teacher must approach the classroom with humility.

3. *Open-mindedness:* Although it is difficult to give up the ethnocentric beliefs and ideas that come from being White American in this society, White American teachers of diversity must be willing not only to listen to comments and ideas from persons who are different from them, but also to honestly believe that there is much to learn from others, and that perspectives different from their own still have value. This characteristic may result in students and teachers questioning many of the assumptions, beliefs, attitudes, and behaviors of American society that have heretofore been accepted without critique. This, in turn, may result in cognitive dissonance described by Howard (1993).

4. *Introspection:* Developing a multicultural, empowering classroom, and dealing with the topics of diversity may be emotional for both the students and for the teacher. It is important for the teacher to be skilled in self-awareness and be honest (especially to oneself) about his or her responses to the emotional climate in the classroom. Hidalgo (1993) believes that teachers must explore how their own cultural perspectives shape their thinking and actions and begin this process by "specific introspective information gathering" (p. 101). Introspection, therefore, is a process that happens before developing a curriculum on diversity, and during the process of teaching as emotions become evident and *buttons get pushed.*

5. *Hunger for knowledge:* Information on diversity is a burgeoning, interdisciplinary body of knowledge that can be found in feminist, multicultural, and critical pedagogy literature, as well as in the literature of cultural studies, communication ethics, language, literacy, and oth-

ers. It is impossible to read it all, yet the more the White American teacher reads from a variety of sources, the more he or she begins to comprehend the issues. Information and knowledge can also be gathered by visiting, talking with, and interviewing non-White Americans; watching documentaries and other video and film presentations; attending conferences; doing research; and discussing the issues with colleagues, friends, and families. The teacher of diversity must always be a student of diversity.

There are many characteristics that could be included in this list, but for the purposes of this book, these five become the foundation for any others that might be considered important. Being an effective White American teacher of diversity is challenging; but it is also exciting and invigorating, bringing a fresh new perspective to the educator and education of health professionals.

Summary

White Americans in this country have sociocultural status based solely on the color of their skin. This status results in unearned privilege and easier access to the things they desire and need in life. But this elevated status also comes with challenges. Because the White American middle-class culture is dominant in the United States, Whites often do not recognize that nondominant people are not afforded the same privileges as they. In order to be culturally competent, it is important for White American health care providers to recognize the differences in sociocultural status among various people, and to be sensitive to the privileges they are given. They must examine what it means to be White American.

As health care practitioners or educators, White Americans must develop characteristics and skills that enable them to be effective in the workplace with all clients and students. Cultural competency requires that we each know ourselves, learn about others who are different from ourselves, and develop skills for effective intercultural communication. This is a lifelong process for most of us, and especially challenging for those who experience the privilege of being White American.

References

Frankenberg, R. (1993). *White women, race matters: The social construction of Whiteness.* Minneapolis, MN: University of Minnesota Press.

Hidalgo, N. M. (1993). Multicultural teacher introspection. In T. Perry & J. W. Fraser (Eds.), *Freedom's plow: Teaching in the multicultural classroom.* Boston: Routledge & Kegan Paul.

Holzman, C. (1995). Rethinking the role of guilt and shame on White women's anti-racism work. In G. M. Enguidanos & J. Adleman (Eds.), *Racism in the lives of women: Testimony, theory and guides to antiracist practices.* New York: Harrington Park Press.

Howard, G. (1993, September). Whites in multicultural education: Rethinking our role. *Phi Delta Kappan* (pp. 36–41).

Kivel, P. (1996). *Uprooting racism: How White people can work for racial justice.* Philadelphia, PA: New Society Publishers.

Kozol, J. (1991). *Savage inequalities: Children in America's schools.* New York: Harper Perennial.

McIntosh, P. (1998). *White privilege and male privilege: A personal account of coming to see correspondences through work in women's studies.* (Working Paper No. 189). Wellesley, MA: Wellesley College Center for Research on Women.

McLaren, P. (1997). *Revolutionary multiculturalism: Pedagogues of dissent for the new millennium.* Boulder, CO: WestView Press.

McLaren, P. (1998). *Life in schools: An introduction to critical pedagogy in the foundations of education* (3rd ed.). White Plains, NY: Longman.

Paley, V. G. (1989). *White teacher.* Cambridge, MA: Harvard University Press.

Pinderhughes, E. (1989). *Understanding race, ethnicity, & power: The key to efficacy in clinical practice.* New York: The Free Press.

Shor, I. (1992). *Empowering education: Critical teaching for social change.* Chicago, IL: The University of Chicago Press.

Sleeter, C. (1995). Reflections on my use of multicultural and critical pedagogy when students are white. In C. E. Sleeter & P. L. McLaren (Eds.), *Multicultural education, critical pedagogy, and the politics of difference.* Albany, NY: State University of New York Press.

Framework for Cultural Competency III

"If we wonder often,
the gift of knowledge will come."

—Arapaho

Objectives

The information in this section is intended to help the reader

- identify the various approaches to multicultural education and select one that matches the curricular goals of one's health professional educational program;

- identify the skills and characteristics needed to be a culturally competent health care provider;

- understand the variety of stages that one goes through to become culturally competent;

- understand and use the Cultural Competency Education Model to develop the awareness, knowledge, and skills necessary to be a culturally competent health care provider; and

- establish a plan of action for becoming culturally competent that focuses on activities for self-exploration and awareness, knowledge, and skills.

CHAPTER NINE

Defining Cultural Competency

Key Points

- Cultural competence is an evolving and developing process that depends on self-exploration, knowledge, and skills.

- One major source of cultural misunderstanding and conflicts lies in the clash of deeply rooted, conditioned perceptions of reality.

- Culture is the sum total of ways of living built up by a group of human beings and transmitted from one generation to another.

- Competence is the skills, knowledge, and experience to function in a particular way or within the realm of integrated patterns of human behaviors as defined by the group.

- Cultural competence is lifelong learning designed to foster understanding, acceptance, knowledge, and constructive relations between persons of various cultures and differences.

- The resistance to self-learning lies at an emotional, unconscious level.

- The steps taken toward cultural competence as an individual or system are varied, but they all require exploring perceptions, behaviors, and communication patterns.

- As an individual moves toward cultural competence, attitudes become less ethnocentric and biased; behaviors become more open, spontaneous, and flexible, and perceptions become more neutral and appreciative of all persons.

- As a system moves toward cultural competence, policies become more flexible and culturally impartial, and the practice becomes more congruent with the culture of their clients.

Many millions of people have roots in two or more distinct cultures. Your multicultural credentials for inclusion may be caused by being raised in a home where the language or culture differed from those of the *mainstream* society. Maybe each of your parents came from a distinct culture, or you married someone from another culture. You may have lived in different regions of the country or attended a variety of schools. You may have lived abroad for years, or worked or lived in an atmosphere of culture diversity. You may have been a health care provider or educator serving multicultural clients and families. Whatever the cause, you have been affected and molded by more than one culture. You are, therefore, a multicultural being.

The great challenge of our time is to view diversity as a resource and not a problem. Cultural diversity enriches our ability to survive. Because our species relies on cultural adaptations more than biological change for its survival, it is this cultural diversity that provides the best chance for the survival of humans. We all need to develop and enhance our ability to deal with diversity in positive ways. We must learn how to develop multiple perspectives, critical reasoning, and acceptance of differences. With differences rooted in age, culture, health status, ethnicity, race, experience, education, gender, sexual orientation, disability, religion, and appearance, the variability and combination are nearly limitless (Seely & Wasilewski, 1996).

We can take pride in the multicultural roots of our ancestors and in the heritage and accomplishments they achieved. Although we all can count multicultural ancestors on our family trees, pressures to conform exclusively to the norms of one society or another have pushed many persons to allow the gifts of multicultural skills and perspectives to atrophy. This chapter will examine the skills as well as goals of cultural competency. It will look at a variety of learning models and processes for becoming culturally competent.

What Is Cultural Competence?

The different languages spoken around every corner; the broad culinary fairs that are offered; and recommended health regimes, such as yoga, tai chi, herbal medicine, acupuncture, and meditation, all tempt us to think we are totally at home with diversity. The image of America as a *mosaic* of cultures misleads us into believing that we are culturally competent. The notion of *cultural-blindness* only leads to services and practices that do not value differences. To truly understand and interact with persons whose dominant culture is different from the majority or main-stream culture, one must become culturally competent. But what is *cultural competence?*

There are many definitions of *cultural competence.* Central to most are the ideas of culture and competence. *Culture,* as put forth by Linton (1945), is the configuration of learned behavior whose components and elements are shared and transmitted by the members of a particular society. It is the common patterns of interaction and perception shared by a group of persons (Hecht, Collier, & Ribeau, 1993). Culture implies the integrated pattern of human behaviors that includes thoughts, communications, actions, customs, beliefs, values, and institutions of a racial, ethnic, religious, or social group (Cross, Bazron, Dennis, & Isaacs, 1989). It is the sum total of ways of living built up by a group of human beings and transmitted from one generation to another.

Competence refers to having suitable and sufficient skills, knowledge, and experience for some purpose (Houghton Mifflin, 1996). It applies to having the capacity to function in a particular way, within the realm of culturally integrated patterns of human behaviors as defined by the group (Cross et al., 1989). Hence, *cultural competence* is the capacity to respond to the needs of populations whose cultures are different from what might be called *dominant* or *mainstream.* It is "a set of congruent behaviors, attitudes, and policies that come together in a system, agency, or among professionals and enable that system, agency, or those professionals to work effectively in cross-cultural situations" (Cross et al., 1989). Cultural competence is the process of actively developing and practicing appropriate, relevant, and sensitive strategies and skills in interacting with culturally different persons (AOTA, 1995).

According to Walker (1991), cultural competence is the ability of people to see beyond the boundaries of their own cultural interpretations; the ability to maintain objectivity when faced with persons from cultures different from their own; and the ability to interpret and understand the behaviors and intentions of persons from other cultures nonjudgmentally and without bias. Cultural competence refers to a program's ability to honor and respect the beliefs, interpersonal styles, attitudes, and behaviors of both the families who are clients and the multicultural staff members who are providing services (Roberts, 1990).

Cultural competence is an evolving and developmental process that depends on self-exploration, knowledge, and skills. It is an ongoing process that assumes that its goal of creating a multicultural environment will never be completed. Cultural competence is lifelong learning, designed to foster understanding, acceptance, knowledge, and constructive relations between persons of various cultures and differences. A culturally competent person has mastered the knowledge and developed the skills necessary to feel comfortable and communicate effectively with persons of any culture, as well as being able to bridge the differences (Cultural Diversity in Rehabilitation, 1992).

Goals of Cultural Competence

The expected outcomes of cultural competency are embedded in its definitions, justifications, and assumptions. There are numerous goals and related objectives, which vary only according to contextual factors, such as audiences, timing, purposes, and perspectives. They tend to cover the domains of learning (e.g., cognitive, affective, psychomotor) and incorporate both the intrinsic (ends) and instrumental (means) values of cultural competence. These goals fall into several clusters—self-exploration, personal development, attitude and values, ethnic and cultural literacy, empowerment, basic skills proficiency, and social competence (Gay, 1994).

Skills and Characteristics

The range of skills needed for cultural competence is as varied as the range of people in the world (Tables 10 and 11). Common to all these essential skills and characteristics is the requirement to go beyond learning tolerance and tact. Cultural competency addresses more than the problem of assimilating different perspectives and backgrounds and being aware of and sensitive to differences. It speaks to the nature of who people are, to the mainsprings of their energy, and to the issues of motivation and creativity.

Persons who have mastered bridging cultural gaps can weave together tradition and culture. They bring together in a personal way the various influences of their upbringings. Each person brings a unique mixture of cultural influences and ideas. They have respect for the values and approaches to life. They are socially active, critically thinking members of society (Gorski, 1997). In the health care field, culturally competent providers have the ability to articulate problems from clients' perspectives, recognize and reduce resistance and defensiveness, and implement culturally appropriate intervention (Wells, 1994; Kavanagh & Kennedy, 1992).

Table 10. Literature Review of Skills and Characteristics for Cultural Competency

Dillard, Andonian, Flores, Lai, MacRae, and Sharkri (1992): Culturally Competent Occupational Therapy in a Diversely Populated Mental Health Setting

- possesses specific and extensive knowledge of the language, values, and customs of a particular culture;
- acknowledges and is aware of one's own cultural, and is willing to explore one's own beliefs and biases; and
- reinforces the beauty of culture, incorporates it in therapy, and is open to different ways of engaging the client in treatment.

Fitzgerald (1992): Multicultural Clinical Interaction and Approaches

- acknowledges that multiple cultures are involved and that both the care providers and care receivers are bearers of culture;
- decreases the degree of disparity among the cultures;
- provides people with information about other cultures and medical systems (intercultural sensitivity training);
- avoids a cookbook approach, that is, avoids compiling a list of information on the beliefs, values, attitudes, and behaviors characteristic of a society or population and then assuming this information applies to all persons associated with that society or population, ignoring all the diversity within a population;
- provides access to some basic information and then helps people develop strategies for acquiring the necessary additional information; and
- decreases the number of cultures involved (trains persons in the community, providing them with the necessary technical knowledge and skills, and then allowing them to provide care in the most culturally acceptable manner).

Sue, Arredondo, and McDavis (1992): Proposed Multicultural Counseling Competencies and Standards for the American Association for Counseling and Development

- is aware of one's own assumptions, values, and biases;
- understands the worldview of the culturally different client; and
- develops appropriate intervention strategies and techniques.

(Continued)

The exploration of different cultures helps people learn about new ways of interpreting reality and increases their understanding of other persons, their experiences, and the world they live in. The demonstration of respect and interest in the cultural perspectives of others also serves as a foundation for developing supportive and cooperative relationships

Table 10. *(Continued)*

Wells (1991): Occupational Therapy Intervention Strategies for Treating Ethnic Minority Women with Disabilities

- has basic knowledge of human development as it relates to ethnicity and race,
- understands the disabling conditions and the stigmas related to them,
- is self-aware or knowledgeable about one's own ethnicity and values and their influence on practice,
- is knowledgeable and respectful of the client's culture,
- can modify and adapt occupational therapy techniques in response to the client's culture, and
- incorporates beliefs and values of the ethnic client into the evaluation process and treatment plan.

Sayles-Folks and People (1990): Skills Needed to Interact with the Diverse Consumer Population

Cognitive domain.
- understands sociopolitical systems operating in the United States with respect to treatment of minorities;
- has specific knowledge about the similarities and differences among Whites, African Americans, Hispanics, Native Americans, and other racial and ethnic groups; and
- is aware of the institutional barriers that prevent or discourage members of minority groups from using rehabilitation services.

Affective domain.
- is aware of and sensitive to one's own cultural heritage and sensitive to the need to value and respect diversity,
- is aware of one's own values and biases and how they may affect the therapeutic relationship with minority consumers, and
- is sensitive to circumstances (e.g., socioeconomic factors, political factors, racism) that may dictate referral of the minority consumer to a minority therapist.

Psychomotor domain.
- can generate a wide variety of verbal and nonverbal responses that will facilitate the consumer's involvement, and
- can send and receive both verbal and nonverbal messages accurately and appropriately.

(Continued)

with persons from different cultures. Cultural exploration can teach us a great deal and help us appreciate the great beauty in the different ways that cultures frame reality, establish social organization, and accomplish different goals (Kreps & Kunimoto, 1994).

Table 10. *(Continued)*

Diversity Forum of the 1996 AOTA Annual Conference

Clinicians, educators, and students outlined the following skills and characteristics that they thought were necessary for a culturally competent occupational therapy practitioner.

- Respectfullness
- Willingness to share
- Willingness to risk
- Willingness to change
- Willingness to explore
- Understanding the power of action

- Ability to recognize learning opportunities
- Possessing knowledge of one's self
- Being aware of ignorance
- Having the attitude that *Different is okay; not good or bad*
- Understanding the power of words

Note. The author created this table referencing nine useful cultural competency resources: "Culturally competent occupational therapy in a diversely populated mental health setting," by M. Dillard, L. Andonian, O. Flores, L. Lai, A. MacRae, and M. Sharkri, 1992, *American Journal of Occupational Therapy, 46,* pp. 721–726. © AOTA, Inc. Adapted with permission. "Multicultural clinical interaction and approaches," by M. H. Fitzgerald, 1992, *Journal of Rehabilitation, 58,* pp. 38–42. © National Rehabilitation Association. Adapted with permission. "Proposed multicultural counseling competencies and standards for the American Association for Counseling and Development," by D. Sue, P. Arredondo, and R. McDavis, 1992, *Journal of Counseling and Development, 70,* pp. 477–486. © ACA. Adapted with permission. No further reproduction authorized without written permission of the American Counseling Association. "Clinical considerations in treating minority women who are disabled," by S. A. Wells, 1991, *Occupational Therapy Practice, 2,* pp. 13–22. © AOTA, Inc. Adapted with permission. "Skills needed to interact with the diverse consumer population," by S. Sayles-Folks and L. People, 1990, *AOTA Physical Disabilities Special Interest Section Newsletter, 13,* pp. 4–5. © AOTA, Inc. Adapted with permission. *Cultural awareness in the human services,* by J. W. Green, 1982, Englewood Cliffs, NJ: Prentice Hall. © 1994. Multicultural competency: Preparing for the next millennium, moderated by S. A. Wells, Diversity Forum of the 1996 AOTA Annual Conference. Information used with permission.
Table by Shirley A. Wells

Learning Models of Becoming Culturally Competent

Dealing with persons whose cultures are different from your own can be very pleasant or very painful. One of the major sources of cultural misunderstanding and conflict lies in the clash of deeply rooted conditioned perceptions of reality.

> As long as our way of perceiving the world—on which our communication styles and behavior patterns are based—is *out of awareness*, it is not accessible to being deliberately changed, managed, understood, or influenced (Pusch, 1979, p. 16).

This condition changes only as one becomes more aware and has more knowledge of the degree to which his or her perceptions and behaviors are culturally conditioned. So how does one become culturally aware and competent?

Table 11. Competency Guidelines for Occupational Therapy

The culturally competent therapist

- is aware of and sensitive to his or her own culture,
- is aware of and willing to explore one's own biases and values,
- is respectful of and sensitive to diversity among individuals,
- is knowledgeable about another's culture, and
- is skilled in selecting and using culturally sensitive intervention strategies.

Characteristics of a culturally competent therapist

- has a willingness to learn about another's culture;
- acknowledges and values cultural diversity;
- has specific and extensive knowledge of the language, values, and customs of a particular culture;
- has a basic knowledge of human development as it relates to race, ethnicity, gender, disability, religion, sexual orientation, and lifestyle;
- understands the interaction of culture, gender, race, ethnicity, religion, disabling condition, and sexual orientation on behaviors and needs;
- understands that socioeconomic and political factors greatly affect the psychosocial, political, and economic development of ethnic and culturally diverse groups;
- understands the effect of institutional and individual racism on the use of the health care system by ethnic and culturally diverse groups;
- understands the effect of institutional and individual racism on the therapist–client relationships and interactions;
- understands professional values and codes of conduct as they relate to cultural interaction;
- understands health-related values, perspectives, and behavioral patterns of diverse populations;
- has the ability to decrease the degree of disparity among the cultures in clinical interaction;
- has the ability to avoid applying a *cookbook approach* to all persons associated with a population or diverse group;
- has the ability to generate, modify, and adapt a variety of intervention strategies to accommodate the particular culture of the client;
- has the ability to use, send, and interpret a variety of communication—verbal and nonverbal—skills to facilitate the therapist–client interaction;
- is creative and resourceful in identifying and using cultural value systems on the behalf of the client; and
- helps the clients to understand, maintain, or resolve their own sociocultural identification.

Achieving cultural competence is not a simple process. Hoopes (1979, p. 16) states there is a natural inclination to resist being culturally competent for the following reasons:

• We are all vulnerable. Anything that probes the nature of our identities is threatening.

• We like to think of ourselves as autonomous and not subject, against will, to forces buried within us by our cultural heritage.

• Awareness is an emotional event derived from experience rather than an idea attained through an intellectual process.

The resistance to self-learning lies at an emotional, unconscious level. If we are going to come to grips with cultural relativity and take important steps toward cultural competence, as individuals and systems, we have to become fully engaged with our own perceptions, behaviors, and communication patterns. Several frameworks, learning models, and approaches have been developed to show the possible stages that an individual or system may go through to become culturally competent.

Intercultural Learning Process

The *Intercultural Learning Process* focuses on learning another culture so as to be able to experience what it is like to be a part of it and to view the world from its point of view; learning it so as to be able to function effectively and comfortably within it. This learning process takes place along a continuum, running from ethnocentrism at one end to some form of adaptation or integration at the other end (Hoops, 1979).

The Cultural Competence Continuum

The *Cultural Competence Continuum* focuses on systems, agencies, and practitioners. To better understand where one is in the process of becoming culturally competent, this model uses a continuum that ranges from cultural destructive to cultural proficiency. There are a variety of possibilities between these two extremes. At best, most human service agencies fall between the cultural incapacity and cultural blindness spectrum of the continuum. The authors suggest that agencies as well as individuals should evaluate where they fall along the continuum before any effective planning for achieving higher levels of cultural competence can occur.

The Seven-Step Process (TSSP) of Cross-Cultural Understanding

The TSSP model emphasizes basic rules about understanding persons of a different culture. This process moves the person from the start of a cultural encounter, to a getting acquainted stage, and to the final stage of establishing trust and cooperation. The inner circle shows that the process of cross-cultural understanding is not simple or clear cut. Very often individuals will go back and forth between the different stages and at times will start the whole process over again (Kabagarama, 1993).

Multicultural Education

Multicultural education is a philosophy that stresses the importance, legitimacy, and vitality of ethnic and cultural diversity in shaping the lives of individuals, groups, and nations. It focuses on institutionalizing a philosophy of cultural pluralism within the educational system—policies and practices that show respect for cultural diversity through educational philosophy, staffing composition and hierarchy, instructional materials, curricula, and evaluation procedures (Burnett, 1994).

Summary

The degree of cultural competence an individual, agency, or system achieves is not dependent on any one factor or method. Self-exploration, knowledge, and skills are three major areas where development and intervention can and must occur if a person is to move toward cultural competence. Attitudes change to become less ethnocentric and biased. Behaviors change to become more open, spontaneous, and flexible. Perceptions change to become more neutral and appreciative of the inner beauty of all persons.

Policies change to become more flexible and culturally impartial. Practices become more congruent with the culture of the client from initial contact through termination. Valuing differences, engaging in self-evaluation, understanding dynamics of relationship and communication, building cultural knowledge, and adapting are musts to becoming culturally competent. Chapter eleven will address the Cultural Competency Education Model, which was developed with the health professional and system in mind to assist providers and students in becoming culturally competent.

References

AOTA Multicultural Task Force. (1995). *Definition and terms.* Bethesda, MD: American Occupational Therapy Association.

Burnett, G. (1994). *Varieties of multicultural education: An introduction.* ERIC Digest. [Online]. Retrieved from: http://www.eric-web.tc.columbia.edu/digests/dig.98.html.

Cross, T. L., Bazron, B. J., Dennis, K. W., & Isaacs, M. R. (1989). *Towards a culturally competent system of care: A monograph on effective services for minority children who are severely emotionally disturbed.* Washington, DC: CASSP Technical Assistance Center, Georgetown University Child Development Center.

Cultural Diversity in Rehabilitation. (1992). *Cultural diversity in rehabilitation: Nineteenth institute on rehabilitation issues.* Hot Springs, AR: Department of Rehabilitation Education and Research, Arkansas Research and Training Center in Vocational Rehabilitation.

Dillard, M., Andonian, L., Flores, O., Lai, L., MacRae, A., & Shakir, M. (1992). Culturally competent occupational therapy in a diversely populated mental health setting. *American Journal of Occupational Therapy, 46,* 721–726.

Editors of Webster's II Dictionaries (Eds.). (1996). *Webster's II New College Dictionary.* Boston: Houghton Mifflin.

Fitzgerald, M. H. (1992). Multicultural clinical interaction. *Journal of Rehabilitation, 58,* 38–42.

Gay, G. (1994). A synthesis of scholarship in multicultural education. *NCREL's urban education monograph series.* Oak Brook, IL: North Central Regional Education Laboratory.

Gorski, P. (1997). *A working definition. Initial thoughts on multicultural education.* [Online] Retrieved from: http://www.curry.edschool.virginia.edu/go/multicultural/activityarch.html.

Hecht, M. L., Collier, M .J., & Ribeau, S. A. (1993). *African American communication: Ethnic identity and cultural interpretation.* Newbury Park, CA: Sage.

Hoops, D. (1979). Intercultural communication concepts and the psychology of intercultural experiences. In M. Pusch (Ed.), *Multicultural education: A cross cultural training approach* (pp. 9–38). Yarmouth, ME: Intercultural Press.

Kabagarama, D. (1993). *Breaking the ice: A guide to understanding people from other cultures.* Newton, MA: Allyn & Bacon.

Kavangh, K. H., & Kennedy, P. H. (1992). *Promoting cultural diversity: Strategies for health care professionals.* Newbury Park, CA: Sage.

Kreps, G. L., & Kunimoto, E. N. (1994). *Effective communication in multicultural health care settings.* Newbury Park, CA: Sage.

Linton, R. (1945). *The science of man in world crisis.* New York: Columbia University Press.

London, H., & Devore, W. (1988). Layers of understanding: Counseling ethnic minority families. *Family Relations, 37,* 310–314.

Pusch, M. D. (1979). *Multicultural education: A cross cultural approach.* Yarmouth, ME: Intercultural Press.

Randall, D. E. (1989). *Strategies for working with culturally diverse communities and clients.* Washington, DC: The Association for the Care of Children's Health.

Roberts, R. (Ed.). (1990). *Workbook series for providing services to children with handicaps and their families. Workbook for: Developing culturally competent programs for families of children with special needs* (2nd ed.). Washington, DC: Georgetown University Child Development Center.

Sayles-Folks, S., & People, L. (1990). Cultural sensitivity training for occupational therapists. *Physical Disabilities SIS Newsletter, 13*(3), 4–5.

Seely, H. N., & Wasilewski, J. H. (1996). *Between cultures: Developing self-identity in a world of diversity.* Lincolnwood, IL: NTC Publishing Group.

Sue, D., Arrendondo, P., & McDavis, R. (1992). Multicultural counseling competencies and standards: A call to the profession. *Journal of Counseling & Development, 70,* 477–486.

Sue, D., Bernier, J., Durran, A., Feinberg, L., Pederson, P., Smith, E., & Vasquez, E. (1982). Crosscultural counseling competencies. *The Counseling Psychologist, 10,* 49–51.

Walker, M. L. (1991). Rehabilitation service delivery to individuals with disabilities . . . a question of cultural competence. *OSERS News in Print IV* (2).

Wells, S. A. (1991). Clinical considerations in treating minority women who are disabled. *Occupational Therapy Practice, 2,* 13–22.

Wells, S. A. (1994). *A multicultural education and resource guide for occupational therapy educators and practitioners.* Bethesda, MD: American Occupational Therapy Association.

Wells, S. A. (1996, April). Multicultural competency: Preparing for the next millennium. In Shirley A. Wells (Moderator), *Diversity forum.* Forum conducted at the American Occupational Therapy Association's Annual Conference and Exposition, Chicago, Illinois.

CHAPTER TEN

Approaches to Multicultural Education

Key Points

- Multicultural education challenges and rejects racism and other forms of discrimination in schools and society.

- Multicultural education uses critical pedagogy to promote the democratic principles of social justice.

- Goals of multicultural education include

  - helping students develop empathy and caring;

  - eliminating stereotypes;

  - fostering the intellectual, social, and personal development of each student;

  - promoting human rights and respect for those who are different from oneself; and

  - promoting social justice and equality for all people.

- There are multiple approaches to multicultural education.

- According to a study by Sleeter and Grant (1987), the most common approaches to multicultural education include

  - teaching the culturally different,

  - the human relations approach,

  - single group studies,

  - "multicultural education," and

  - education that is multicultural and social reconstructionist.

ultural competence can be facilitated through a variety of
methods: by total immersion in a group or culture different
from one's own; by involving oneself with others who are different from oneself; by reading, exploring, or other means of
self-education; or through more formal means of education. Most, if not
all health professional education programs, have been mandated by
their accrediting agencies to include multicultural content as part of the
professional, entry-level program of study. Even if this were not the case,
the previous chapters have offered a compelling argument for the need
for the inclusion of multicultural material in health professions education. However, questions remain. *How? What model(s) do I use? What
kinds of exercises and content should I present? How do I recognize my
own biases or blind spots? Are there videos or speakers that will support
what is taught? What are my goals?* The answers to many of these questions depend somewhat on the context of the teaching situation. The
educational model of the health profession program, the curricular *fit* of
the multicultural content, the interest and knowledge of the faculty, and
the demographics of the student population (e.g., age, gender, ethnicity,
race, nationality, and sexual orientation) may be considered when determining the approach to multicultural education within the professional
program.

The multicultural literature identifies multiple models of multicultural education. Diaz (1992, p. 24) states that in a 1987 survey conducted by Sleeter and Grant of the multiple definitions of multicultural
education, the only commonality was the *view that multicultural education is a reform movement designed to improve schooling for students of
color.* This seems far too simplistic, however, given the plethora of definitions in the literature.

Parekh (1986) set the overall tone of multicultural education in
his judgment that multicultural education is good education for all children. He defines multicultural education (in Banks,1994) as "an education for freedom." Hernandez (1989) also asserted that multicultural
education is for all students and is synonymous with effective teaching.
Banks clarifies this concept when he states, "Multicultural education
should help students to develop the knowledge, attitudes and skills to
participate in a democratic and free society. . . . (It) promotes freedom,
ability and skills to cross ethnic and cultural boundaries to participate in
other cultures and groups" (Banks, 1994, p. 81). Christine Bennett
(1995, p. 14) is more thorough when she states, "A comprehensive definition includes the following four dimensions of multicultural education:

the movement toward equity, the multicultural curriculum approach, the process of becoming multicultural and the commitment to combat prejudice and discrimination." Perhaps the most comprehensive definition of multicultural education is found in the sociocultural context of Nieto's (1996, p. 307) work:

> Multicultural education is a process of comprehensive school reform and basic education for all students. It challenges and rejects racism and other forms of discrimination in schools and society and accepts and affirms the pluralism (e.g., ethnic, racial, linguistic, religious, economic, and gender, among others) that students, their communities, and teachers represent. Multicultural education permeates the curriculum and instructional strategies used in schools, as well as the interactions among teachers, students, and parents, and the very way that schools conceptualize the underlying nature of teaching and learning. Because it uses critical pedagogy as its underlying philosophy and focuses on knowledge, reflection, and action (praxis) as the basis for social change, multicultural education promotes the democratic principles of social justice.

First, one must have an understanding of what multicultural education is. Multicultural education is not a narrow concept, but rather it is broadly conceptualized and comprehensive. It is an interdisciplinary process that fosters understanding, acceptance, empathy, and constructive and harmonious relations among persons of diverse cultures. It encourages learners of all ages to view different cultures as a source of learning and enrichment. It is a transformative movement in education that produces critically thinking, socially active members of society.

Characteristics of multicultural education include the following:

- Allows all persons to reach their potential as learners

- Respects diversity

- Respects individuality and promotes respect for others

- Encourages critical analysis of all material

- Emphasizes the contributions of the various groups (e.g., ethnic, gender, religious, gays, lesbians, and bisexuals) that make up the population of the world

- Emphasizes the importance of people sharing their stories and learning from others' stories

- Takes into account the learner, his or her learning style, and the extent to which the learner has changed relative to the material

- Facilitates effective communication

- Recognizes the power relationship between different groups and critically analyzes the presence of power and privilege inherent within them

- Provides decision-making and critical analysis skills so that each person can make choices in his or her everyday life

Later in this chapter we will further explore the various dimensions of multicultural education. Before that, however, perhaps the definition would be clarified if the goals of multicultural education were outlined.

Goals of Multicultural Education

As health professionals, we are aware of and embrace the importance of writing goals to direct our actions. Clinical goals direct our practice whereas educational goals frame our teaching and learning. Similarly, when considering where multicultural content fits within our curricula, we must explicitly define the reasons or goals for its inclusion.

The goals or aims of multicultural education are many and varied. Banks (1994, p. 16) believes that there is a beginning consensus among scholars that one important goal is *to increase educational equality for both gender groups, for students from diverse ethnic and cultural groups, and for exceptional students.* Although this goal seems important, one must consider the demographics of health professional classrooms. In the latest data analysis for occupational therapy (AOTA, 1998) for instance, 90.1% of all members are White, 92.4% are women, and only 5.6% report handicapping conditions. These numbers are reflected in occupational therapy classrooms. Although most educators would agree that there is a need for increased student diversity, and the profession is working diligently to attract diverse groups of people to the profession, the reality of occupational therapy classrooms at the end of the twentieth century is that there is little diversity. These data are similar to those of other health professions. Therefore, Banks' goal as stated above may not address the focus of multicultural content in an occupational therapy or other health profession curriculum.

Other goals found in the literature, however, may be more appropriate. Some of these include

- helping all students, including White mainstream students, to develop the knowledge, skills, and attitudes needed to survive and function effectively in the society of the future within the United States (Banks, 1994);

- helping students develop empathy and caring towards diverse groups of people (Banks, 1994);

- eliminating stereotypes (Bennett, 1995);

- fostering the intellectual, social, and personal development of students to their highest potential and providing each student with an equal opportunity to learn (Bennett, 1995);

- promoting the strength and value of cultural diversity (Gollnick & Chinn, 1990);

- promoting human rights and respect for those who are different from oneself (Gollnick & Chinn, 1990);

- promoting social justice and equality for all persons (Gollnick & Chinn, 1990); and

- promoting equity in the distribution of power and income among groups (Gollnick & Chinn, 1990).

The goals listed above are representative of those found throughout the literature of multicultural education. Analysis indicates that a particular cluster of goals will be found with each disparate approach to or dimension of multicultural education. Interestingly, one goal that the authors of this book find vitally important that is not often identified in the literature is that of *recognizing one's own values, beliefs, and biases as they relate to groups other than one's own.* We believe that culturally competent professionals must begin with the awareness of themselves as a cultural beings and have knowledge of how one's culture influences one's beliefs, attitudes and behaviors. This should be part of any approach to multicultural education, although as the theories are defined in the section that follows, it is apparent that this goal is not the focus of all of the various models.

Approaches to Multicultural Education

As with many educational reform movements, multicultural education has changed and developed over the years. Initially it was designed to examine only ethnic diversity, and now it encompasses other issues of oppression and injustice, including gender, sexual orientation, class, ability, and age. In the early years the questions were *What is multicultural education, and why are we doing it?* Now the question becomes *How are we going to provide a multicultural education to our students?* Multicultural education is an expected and important part of the curriculum in a large number of elementary and secondary schools across the nation. It is also increasing in institutions of higher education. But the actual practice of multicultural education varies. Although several authors have revealed various ways of identifying the multiple approaches to practice, Sleeter and Grant (1987) developed the most comprehensive taxonomy based on a review of the literature at that time. Their research indicates that there are five distinct approaches used in multicultural education: (1) teaching the culturally different, (2) the human relations approach, (3) single group studies, (4) multicultural education, and (5) education that is multicultural and social reconstructionist.

Teaching the Culturally Different

This approach attempts to assimilate students of color into the cultural mainstream by offering transitional bridges within existing school programs. One of the goals of this approach is to help nonmajority students develop cultural and social competence within the dominant group. This approach also emphasizes the importance of maintaining one's own cultural heritage, often trying to establish a positive group identity, but tries to find areas with which to build bridges between the home culture and the dominant culture. The focus here is on the nondominant group and does not attempt to have the majority group examine themselves. Most authors using this approach discuss race and ethnicity without mentioning other forms of human diversity, and examining issues of power and privilege is not a goal. Bilingual education and English as a Second Language programs fit within this structure.

The Human Relations Approach

This approach is used to help students of different backgrounds get along better and appreciate each other. Advocates of this approach emphasize improving communication between persons of different cultural backgrounds with the hope that this will lead to increased cooperation between different ethnic groups and White Americans. Although positive in its ideals, a critique of this approach is that it "has produced almost no literature that links practical application theoretically and conceptually with social psychology and theory on intergroup conflict and prejudice formation. . . . Nor is there conceptual linkage with research on cross-cultural differences" (Sleeter & Grant, 1987, p. 427). Although this approach may result in immediate and short-term benefits, because of its lack of a theoretical base and the lack of development of long-term goals and outcomes, most scholars of multicultural education do not subscribe to its methods as the sole approach to teaching multicultural content.

However, despite the above, there are some very effective programs using this model. One is the National Coalition Building Institute (NCBI), which uses a variety of exercises as part of a four- to eight-hour workshop that encourages participants to recognize and appreciate the various cultural similarities and differences within the group of participants. This workshop also looks at one's own biases and internalized oppression, and goes on to storytelling where selected participants' experiences with being oppressed are shared. The final piece of the NCBI workshop includes an opportunity to learn and practice one method of interrupting biased and oppressive statements or actions. With effective and ongoing follow-up, the author has experienced and observed a positive change in NCBI participants both in attitude and behavior.

Single Group Studies

This approach fosters cultural pluralism by teaching lessons, units, or courses about the experiences, contributions, and concerns of distinct ethnic, gender, and social class groups. The emphasis here is on specific ethnic groups with an attempt to foster appreciation for cultural and linguistic diversity. This approach seems to focus more on prescription and application rather than on goals or theory. Although single group studies often discuss the victimization and accomplishments of each group, they often do not stress social change as a goal. Many of the reference books on the market support this kind of approach (Spector, 1996; Julia, 1996). However, if a faculty member in Minnesota, for instance, incorporated a single group study, such as the examination of a local Native American tribe, to apply the principles of the cultural competency education model described later in this book, this approach might be seen to be quite effective.

Multicultural Education

Although advocates of other approaches use this terminology as well, Sleeter and Grant (1987) selected this title because this approach truly "promotes cultural pluralism and social equality by reforming the school program for all students to make it reflect diversity" (p. 422). "It emphasizes education that is truly multicultural and that focuses on common goals" (p. 429). The five major goals of this approach include: (1) human rights and respect for cultural diversity, (2) promoting strength and value of cultural diversity, (3) alternative life choices for people, (4) social justice and equal opportunity for all, and (5) equity distribution of power among members of all ethnic groups. The main issues addressed in this approach are institutional racism in society and schools, unequal power relationships among racial groups, and economic stratification and social class.

This approach differs from the first three in that it requires a shift in thought and pedagogy, resulting in a critical analysis of the dominant paradigm and curriculum reform. This involves more than just adding a little multicultural content into the curriculum and stirring; it also means including a conscious effort to critically analyze the current power structure of various groups within our culture.

Although Sleeter and Grant (1987, p. 434) identify many positive aspects to this popular approach to multicultural education, they also suggest that *the literature should grapple more with the relationship of social stratification to culture, as well as consider the integration of race, class, and gender factors when examining oppression.* They suggest that *authors should also endeavor to connect the approach more directly with established bodies of inquiry on educational history and social policy, curriculum theory, the hidden curriculum, and the sorting function of schools.* This approach, or one similar to it, is the one favored by the authors of this book; and it will be addressed later in this chapter.

Education That Is Multicultural and Social Reconstructionist

The final approach that Sleeter and Grant identified through their research prepares students to challenge social structural inequality and to promote cultural diversity. The emphasis on social action is what differentiates this approach from that of multicultural education described previously. Suzuki (as quoted by Sleeter & Grant, 1987, p. 435) suggests that with this approach more emphasis be placed on helping students "gain a better understanding of the causes of oppression and inequality and ways in which these social problems might be eliminated." The categories of gender and social class or stratification receive more attention here than in any of the other approaches. However, of all five approaches outlined, this is the least developed and the most controversial in many ways. There is less agreement as to what to name it. It has been called emancipatory education by Gordon, Miller, and Rollock (1990), transformative education by Giroux (1988), and critical teaching by Shor (1992). At this point in its development, it is more theory than practice; Sleeter and Grant (1987, p. 436) warn that *particularly lacking is material on achieving the goals in schools; without this material the approach runs the risk of being passed off as a good, but impractical or unrealistic, idea.* Shor (1992), however, approaches these issues in a more pragmatic manner than many of his colleagues, providing concrete examples of good and effective pedagogical practice.

In summary, multicultural education means different things to different people, and it is practiced in the classroom in a myriad of ways. It is a curricular reform model that is here to stay, given the changing demographics of the United States and the increasing awareness of educators; but continued study and research must be done in the area for it to progress in a viable way. Because we are mandated to include multicultural content in health professional education programs, however, educators must choose an approach to theory and pedagogy that complements their own style, beliefs, values, and goals.

References

American Occupational Therapy Association. (1998, March). "Demographic Information [of] Occupational Therapists and Occupational Therapy Assistants." Unpublished raw data. Bethesda, MD: AOTA, Inc.

Banks, J. A. (1994). *An introduction to multicultural education.* Newton, MA: Allyn & Bacon.

Bennett, C. I. (1995). *Comprehensive multicultural education: Theory and practice* (3rd ed.). Newton, MA: Allyn & Bacon.

Diaz, C. (Ed.). (1992). *Multicultural education for the 21st century.* Washington, DC: National Education Association.

Giroux, H. A. (1988). *Teachers as intellectuals.* Westport, CT: Bergin and Garvey.

Gollnick, D. M., & Chinn, P. C. (1990). *Multicultural education in a pluralistic society* (3rd ed.). New York: MacMillan.

Gordon, E. W., Miller, F., & Rollock, D. (1990). Coping with communicentric bias in knowledge production in the social sciences. *Educational Researcher, 19,* 14–19.

Hernandez, H. (1987). *Multicultural education: A teacher's guide to content and process.* Columbia, OH: Merrill.

Julia, M. C. (1996). *Multicultural awareness in the health care professions.* Boston: Allyn & Bacon.

Nieto, S. (1996). *Affirming diversity: The sociopolitical context of multicultural education* (2nd ed.). White Plains, NY: Longman.

Parekh, B. (1986). The concept of multicultural education. In S. Modgil, G. K. Verma, K. Mallick, & C. Modgil (Eds.), *Multicultural education: The interminable debate* (pp. 19–31). Philadelphia: Falmer.

Shor, I. (1992). *Empowering education: Critical teaching for social change.* Chicago, IL: University of Chicago Press.

Sleeter, C. E. (1995). An analysis of the critiques of multicultural education. In J. A. Banks & C. A. Banks (Eds.), *Handbook of research on multicultural education* (pp. 81–94). New York: MacMillan.

Sleeter, C. E., & Grant, C. A. (1987, November). An analysis of multicultural education in the United States. *Harvard Educational Review, 57*(4), 421–444.

Spector, R. E. (1996). *Cultural diversity in health & illness* (4th ed.). Norwalk, CT: Appleton & Lange.

CHAPTER ELEVEN

Cultural Competency Education Model

Key Points

- A lack of cultural awareness, knowledge, and skills can make it difficult for both the health care provider and client to achieve the best and most appropriate care.

- The Cultural Competency Education Model is a framework for developing and evaluating one's progress toward becoming culturally competent health providers.

- There are three areas in which intervention for becoming culturally competent can occur—self-exploration and awareness, knowledge, and skill.

- Self-exploration and awareness is a process of looking inward. It is not always a risk-free or pleasant process, but it is a necessary process to open avenues of learning and growth.

- Knowledge promotes understanding. It allows the health care provider to modify treatment, adapt the way in which services are delivered, and develop strategies for acquiring additional information.

- Skill is the acquiring and mastering of strategies, techniques, and approaches for communicating and interacting with persons from different cultures, as well as for enhancing the delivery of care.

Culture is a part of everyone's life. It is a part of every personal encounter, every casual or chance meeting, and every lifelong interaction. Every person is composed of a unique combination of different cultural orientations and influences and belongs to many different cultural groups that directs and shapes his or her multicultural identity. We each are the products of multiple cultural memberships. We are multicultural individuals. Whenever people interact and communicate, there are multiple cultural influences on their interaction (Fitzgerald, 1992; Kreps & Kunimoto, 1994).

Culture is a part of every clinical encounter. The modern health care system is a cultural smorgasbord. It is comprised of persons from different combinations of national, regional, ethnic, racial, socioeconomic, occupational, generational, health status, and cultural orientation. As the American population becomes multiracial, multicultural, and multilingual, those seeking and providing health care are increasingly diverse. The modern health care system is also influenced by the differences in the gender, age, educational background, and occupation of both the health care providers and consumers. All these many different cultures influence the delivery of effective and quality health care (Kreps & Kunimoto, 1994; Mead, 1956; Pachter, 1994; Wells, 1994).

Health care consumers and providers approach the health care situation with their own unique communication characteristics, health beliefs, and customs, on the basis of their personal backgrounds. These cultural influences challenge health care providers to perform evaluations and develop treatment plans with clients who may not share a common language with them; who may have a different understanding of the nature of work, leisure, and self-care; and who may have differing beliefs, values, attitudes, and behaviors. Understanding the cultural relations between culturally unique participants in the modern health care system is a prerequisite to effective health care delivery (Howe-Murphy, Ross, Tseng, & Hartwig, 1989; McNeil, 1990). By understanding and accepting the client's values and beliefs, providers have a better chance of evaluating and producing more effective outcomes.

Health care providers have a responsibility to develop an awareness of self, knowledge about other cultures, and skills, not only to effectively accomplish the health care goals of their clients, but also to interact and communicate within multicultural societies. With the need to have culturally competent providers has come the dilemma of not only quantifying competency in multicultural interaction, but also identifying a model for developing this competency and integrating culture into the health care procedures and teaching approaches. This chapter will outline a model and process for becoming a culturally competent health care provider. It will explore a framework that providers and students can use to develop and acquire the knowledge, skills, and awareness needed to increase their ability to function effectively and provide quality care in a multicultural environment.

Importance for Health Professionals

Participants of the health care system must share relevant information and coordinate many different activities to effectively accomplish their health care goals. Providers depend on receiving information from their clients about health histories and symptoms, lifestyles, and concerns to make appropriate medical decisions. Similarly, consumers depend on receiving clear and descriptive information about health care treatment and strategies from their providers. Members of the health care team also depend on sharing pertinent treatment information with one another to provide effective care (Kreps & Thornton, 1992). Yet the client, provider, and team members are all likely to have very different cultural orientations to providing health care, on the basis of their personal multicultural influences as well as their professional training.

These different points of views can generate a broad base of information that encourages a holistic view of the client's condition, needs, and health care treatment. These different cultural perspectives can also complicate health care if there is a lack of respect and understanding for different cultural orientations and influences. Lack of awareness and knowledge about differences can make it difficult for both the providers and clients to achieve the best, most appropriate care (Fitzgerald, 1992; Good, 1996; Pachter, 1994; Wells, 1994). The plethora of different cultural orientations represented in today's health care system can result in an encroachment of consumers', providers', and team members' personally held cultural beliefs about health and life, especially if cultural diversity is not valued (Kreps & Thornton, 1992).

Often in the medical community the lack of awareness of differences results from a combination of factors, according to Diversity Rx (1997), that may include the following:

• *Lack of knowledge*—resulting in inability to recognize the differences

- *Self-protection or denial*—leading to an attitude that these differences are not important or that our common humanity transcends our differences

- *Fear of the unknown or the new*—because it is challenging and perhaps intimidating to get to understand something that is new and that does not fit into one's view

- *Feeling pressured because of time constraints*—which can lead to a rushed feeling and an inability to look in-depth at an individual client's needs

The consequences of lack of cultural competency can multiply. Miscommunication results. The provider may not understand why the client does not comply with the treatment. The client may reject the health care provider even before any one-on-one interaction occurs because of nonverbal cues that do not fit expectations (Diversity Rx, 1997). The development and expression of genuine interest and respect for different cultural orientations is needed to enhance the effectiveness of health care delivery. We must not only be tolerant of different cultural perspectives; we must demonstrate active interest, knowledge, admiration, sensitivity, and awareness of the cultural norms of other cultures.

Given the need for cultural competency in health care practice, a thorough, systemic, and integrated learning process that incorporates self-exploration, knowledge, and skills is needed to address the issue of acquiring cultural competence. Using this premise, along with goals, principles of multicultural education, and several sociological theories, Wells formulated a culturally competent-oriented model that can be used by health care providers and students to develop the skills needed to be effective in health care delivery.

Conceptual Framework

Sociological Perspectives

In sociological investigation three theoretical perspectives have provided a basis and rationale for the Multicultural Competency Education Model. These sociological perspectives have shaped the study of and described the interaction between minority–majority groups in a society: functional theory, conflict theory, and interactionist theory. *Functional theory* provides the theoretical support for maintaining a harmonious society and seeking new and different adjustments to restore equilibrium when dysfunction occurs. Functionalists believe that a stable, cooperative social system is the basis of society. Rapid social changes, such as demographic changes require compensating adjustments. If these adjustments do not occur, tension and conflicts are created between the groups (Parrillo, 1997). "The key factor in this analysis of social disorganization is whether to restore the equilibrium as it was or to seek a new and different equilibrium" (Parrillo, 1997, p. 18).

Conflict theory emphasizes the tension and conflicts that result when different groups compete for limited resources. Conflict theorists see disequilibrium and change as the norm because of societal inequalities. Group cohesiveness and struggle against oppression are necessary to effect social change (Levine & Campbell, 1972; Parrillo, 1997; Solomos & Back, 1995). *Interactionist theory* focuses on the personal interaction patterns in everyday life. Essential to this perspective is the belief that people operate within a socially constructed perception of reality. Interactionists conclude that shared expectations and understanding, or lack of same, explain intergroup relations. And through better communication and intercultural awareness minority–majority interaction patterns can improve (Ballis, 1995; Berger & Luckmann, 1963; Parrillo, 1997).

The type of interaction between minority persons and those of the dominant culture promoted by the Cultural Competency Education Model is based on the views and values expressed in the ideology and theory of *cultural pluralism*. The accommodation or pluralist theory of minority integration has emerged as a school of thought in recognition of the persistence of ethnic and racial diversity in a society with a commonly shared core culture (Baptiste, 1979; Parrillo, 1997). Cultural pluralism has been defined as "two or more culturally distinct groups living in the same society in relative harmony." According to pluralist theorists, minorities can maintain their distinctive subcultures and simultaneously interact with relative equality in the larger society.

Horace Kallen, in 1915, published "Democracy versus the Melting Pot," in which he expounded that each group tends to preserve its own language, institutions, and cultural heritage. He also stated that the very nature of democracy gave each group the right to do so. Kallen believed that cultural pluralism could be the basis for a great democratic commonwealth. According to Milton Gordon (1964), many minority groups lose their visibility because they have acculturated, but many retain identification with and pride in their heritage and maintain primary relationships mostly with members of their ethnic group.

Cultural pluralism was and is a fact of American society. Early settlements were small ethnic enclaves. Chain-migration patterns resulted in immigrants settling in clusters—Irish in New York, Germans and Scandinavians in the Midwest, French in Louisiana, Asians in California, and Cubans in Miami. "Assimilation and pluralism have always existed simultaneously among different group, at different levels. Whether as persistent subcultures or as convergent ones that gradually merge into the dominant culture over several generations, cultural distinct groups have always existed" (Parrillo, 1997, p. 61).

Multicultural Education Perspective

Grounded in the philosophy of cultural pluralism and the principles of equality, mutual respect, acceptance, understanding, and moral commitment to social justice, multicultural education stresses the importance, legitimacy, and vitality of ethnic and cultural diversity in shaping the lives of individuals, groups, and nations (Baptiste, 1979).

> [Multicultural education is] a humanistic concept based on the strength of diversity, human rights, social justice, and alternative lifestyles for all persons. It [multicultural education] views a culturally pluralistic society as a positive force and welcomes differences as vehicles for better understanding the global society (ASCD Multicultural Education Commission, Grant, 1977, p. 3).

The literature on multicultural education views *multiculturalism* as a cultural concept that recognizes the diversity of cultural differences that exist in a pluralistic society (Banks, 1994; Darder, 1995; Grant, 1994; Sleeter & Grant, 1994). It places emphasis on the universal acceptance of differences—a society in which persons of all cultures are accepted and accorded respect (Kanpol & Beady, 1998). Multiculturalists encourage a positive acceptance of races, religions, and cultures; and they recognize such diversity as healthy (Bank, 1994; Gay, 1994; Parrillo, 1997). They describe the role and goal of education in a multicultural society as one that (Burnett, 1994; Gay, 1994; Gorski, 1997; Kanpol & Beady, 1998).

• develops the potential of each person to the fullest extent,

• offers both the knowledge and critical thinking skills to allow learners to become active agents of change in their lives,

- engages the learner as an active participant in the construction of knowledge,

- presents learners with a language of critique and possibility.

Asante (1991) proclaims that the goal of multicultural education is to achieve cultural pluralism without hierarchy. The goals of multicultural education fall into seven general clusters: (1) ethnic and cultural literacy, (2) personal development, (3) attitude and value clarification, (4) multicultural social competence, (5) basic skills proficiency, (6) educational equality and excellence, and (7) empowerment for societal reform (Banks, 1994; Gay, 1994; Gorski, 1997).

Multicultural education offers a variety of opportunities not only to deal directly with cultural diversity, but also to infuse the perspectives of others into the learning process. It encourages learners to view different cultures as a source of learning and enrichment. It focuses on how to learn rather than on specific information; it emphasizes the importance of people sharing their stories and learning from others' stories; and it takes into account the learner, his or her learning style, and the extent to which the learner has changed relative to the material. Multicultural education is an ongoing process that requires long-term investments of time and effort, as well as clearly planned and monitored actions (Banks & Banks, 1993). It means learning about, preparing for, and celebrating cultural diversity (see chapter 10).

Cultural Competency Education Model

The Cultural Competency Education Model refers to a structural process designed to foster understanding, acceptance, knowledge, and constructive relations between persons of various cultures and differences. This culturally competent-oriented model is built on the assumptions that

- all people have experienced a variety of multicultural influences,

- everyone has been affected and molded by more than one culture and therefore is a multicultural being,

- becoming culturally competent is a lifelong process,

- cultural competence is a professional and ethical obligation, and

- cultural competence enhances the quality of health care delivery.

The model is designed as a tool for developing the knowledge and skills that health care providers will need to provide quality care in the new century. It provides a foundation for understanding personal interaction patterns within social and cultural context. It is designed to assist a person in adjusting to our changing society as well as effecting social changes.

The Cultural Competency Education Model groups the seven goals' cluster of multicultural education into three areas of intervention—(1) self-exploration and awareness, (2) knowledge, and (3) skills. Other personal components necessary to be culturally competent, such as attitudes, behaviors, and perceptions, are not directly addressed but are infused during the learning process. This model aims to

- increase the sense of one's own cultural identity,

- heighten the awareness of one's own cultural perspectives and the effect of those perspectives on individuals from other groups as well as their interaction,

- develop knowledge of and practice in using effective strategies for interrupting culturally inappropriate and offensive remarks and behaviors that hinder relationships across cultures, and

- assist the individual in setting a plan with specific ways to acquire knowledge, develop skills, and build alliances with people who are culturally different form one's self.

The Cultural Competency Education Model provides a clear framework for developing and evaluating one's progress toward becoming culturally competent. "To succeed, workers [health care providers] need an awareness and acceptance of cultural differences, an awareness of their own cultural values, an understanding of the *dynamics of differences* in the helping process, a basic knowledge about the client's culture, knowledge of the client's environment, and the ability to adapt practice skills to fit the client's context" (Cross et al., 1989, p. 32) (Figure 1).

Areas of Intervention

As society becomes increasingly more diverse, it is critical that health care providers and students are prepared for delivering health care as well as living in this multicultural environment. A variety of issues ranging from ethnocentrism to unity through acceptance and under-

Figure 1. Cultural Competency Education Model

Figure by Shirley A. Wells

standing, and from discrimination to equality of experience and opportunity, must be addressed. Practitioners must recognize and understand the dynamics of diversity, explore their own diversity, and acquire knowledge about other groups. It is important for providers to recognize and understand their own biases, prejudices, and their effects on others and the clinical interaction. From self-exploration and accumulation of knowledge will come effective and culturally appropriate intervention strategies, as well as improved intercultural communication skills.

There are truly only three areas in which intervention can occur—(1) self-exploration and awareness, (2) knowledge, and (3) skills (Figure 2).

Self-Exploration and Awareness

Self-exploration and awareness are essential requirements to becoming culturally competent. Knowledge of one's self enables health care providers to be aware of and take responsibility for their own emotions and attitudes as they affect their professional function. An understanding

Figure 2. Areas of Intervention

Self-Exploration and Awareness

Goal
To build an awareness of one's own cultural heritage

Objectives
- To expand cultural awareness
- To provide the individual with an understanding of his or her own culture and of the degree to which he or she is conditioned by it
- To increase tolerance and acceptance of different values, attitudes, behaviors, and perceptions

Knowledge

Goal
To understand that no one culture is intrinsically superior to another, and to recognize individual and group differences and similarities

Objectives
- To foster the affirmation of all cultures, especially those that because of minority status have received a disproportionate amount of negative reinforcement from the society as a whole
- To prepare for effective personal adjustment to the stress of intercultural experiences
- To open avenues of learning and growth that multicultural experiences make accessible

Skills

Goal
To master appropriate, relevant, and sensitive strategies and skills in communicating and interacting with persons from different cultures

Objectives
- To develop intercultural communication skills
- To integrate cognitive, affective, and experiential learning
- To develop the ability to seek information about the economic, political, and social stresses, and the aspirations of various cultures or ethnic groups within a society

Figure by Shirley A. Wells

about how differences, oppression, *ism's*, discrimination, and stereotyping affect the clinical interaction, as well as the individual personally, is also a must to becoming culturally competent.

Self-exploration furnishes providers with an understanding of their own culture and of the degree to which they are conditioned by it. Providers must be willing to take risks and to develop an awareness of their own ethnocentrism (Cross et al., 1989; Devore & Schlesinger, 1981). It is an internal, personal experience. It is a process of looking inward, learning to recognize when old information no longer applies, and using this knowledge of self (Pedersen, 1988; Pusch, 1979). Self-exploration is not always a risk-free and pleasant process. It is looking at and recognizing *Me,* who is sometimes judgmental and noncaring. It is having the ability to recognize when the judgmental, noncaring self interferes with the ability to reach out, to explore, and to help others. However, acknowledging vulnerability in self-introspection can encourage direct communication and bolster personal integrity (Devore & Schlesinger, 1981; Kennedy & Kavangh, 1992).

In getting at the *Who* of *Me,* Schulman (1978) posed three questions to answer:

1. Who am I?

2. Who do others think I am?

3. Who would I like to be?

The answers begin to tap the ability to recognize with some accuracy our perceptions of ourselves, the perceptions of others about us, and our dreams of what we might be. The awareness of one's own race, ethnicity, and cultural diversity, as well as the ability to recognize how they affect practice, is also crucial to this process. Consider the following questions:

• Who am I in the racial, ethnic, or cultural diversity sense?

• What does it mean to me?

• How does it shape my perceptions of persons who are my clients?

A heightened self-awareness, as well as a greater awareness of diversity, leads to a realization that for many persons race, ethnicity, gender, religion, sexual orientation, appearance, and disability is a force that shapes movement through the life cycle and determines appropriate marriage partners, language, dietary selections, and the various subtleties of daily life. Self-exploration and awareness open avenues of learning and growth.

Outcome of Self-Exploration and Awareness

Culturally competent health care providers have knowledge

• about their own racial and ethnic cultural heritage, and how it personally and professionally affects their definitions of normality and abnormality and the process of providing services;

- about how oppression, *ism's,* discrimination, and stereotyping affect them personally and professionally; and

- about their social effect on others, including an awareness of their communication style differences.

Knowledge

Knowledge promotes understanding and allows providers to adapt the way in which services are delivered. The greater the shared knowledge, the less likely there are to be misunderstandings. Many of us have often experienced situations in which we are aware of and sensitive to differences; however, we lacked the specific knowledge of the other cultures or systems involved to avert problems, develop solutions, or acknowledge an interplay of cultures. Knowledge provides the framework that would help health care providers understand the experiences of the client and to intervene at an appropriate, cultural, and individual level (Cross et al., 1989; Fitzgerald, 1992; Good, 1996; Kavanagh & Kennedy, 1992). It also allows providers to look at the interaction from multiple perspectives, *multicultural perspectives*, including the culture in which the interaction occurs, cultures of the persons involved, and the culture of the society or system.

According to Kavanagh and Kennedy (1992, p. 41) "patterns of social interaction, social organization, distribution of resources and social changes are directly relevant to social experiences and behaviors." Individual behaviors often reflect the influences of these social factors. For example, communication styles—eye contact, tone of voice, or greetings—may vary with social characteristics, such as age, gender, racial, or ethnic background. A basic understanding and knowledge of the effects of the following are necessary:

- Social organization, interaction, and processes in the United States

- Sociopolitical systems operating within the United States with respect to treatment of minorities

- Cultural characteristics and life experiences of racial and ethnic populations

- Similarities and differences among racial, ethnic, and culturally diverse groups

- Human development and the life cycle as it relates to ethnicity, race, gender, religion, sexual orientation, disability, and appearance

• Professional behaviors and values in respect to dealing with consumers, clients, and families (Dillard, et al., 1992; London & Devore, 1988; Sayles-Folks & People, 1990; Wells, 1994)

Gaining enough knowledge to know *what, who,* and *how* to ask for information should be a desirable goal for a culturally competent practitioner (Green, 1982). Information that will add to the provider's knowledge is a must because of the diversity within groups. The average provider cannot achieve comprehensive knowledge about any group, population, or culture. More importantly is knowing *where* and *how* to obtain the necessary detailed information for use in specific cases (Cross et al., 1989). Specific knowledge about a client's culture adds a critical dimension to the helping process. It is necessary to know what symbols are meaningful, how health is defined, and how primary support networks are configured. Building a knowledge base is not an end in itself, however (Cross, et al., 1989; Fitzgerald, 1992). The provider must be able to take the knowledge and use it to modify treatment, adapt the way in which services are delivered, or develop strategies for acquiring additional information.

Outcome for Knowledge

A culturally competent health care provider has

• specific and extensive knowledge of the language, values, customs, and beliefs of another culture;

• an understanding about the effects of gender, race, ethnicity, religion, disability, sexual orientation, appearance, nationality, geographic location, and lifestyle on human development;

• a basic knowledge about the effects, real or perceived, of institutional and individual discrimination on interaction and use of services; and

• a knowledge about the influence of culture on behaviors and needs.

Skills

Skill is the last area of intervention. This refers to acquiring as well as mastering strategies, techniques, and approaches for communicating and interacting with persons from different cultures. Multicultural competency skills are based on awareness of attitude and knowledge and dedication to effective communication. This is translating knowledge into "telephone behaviors, receptionist practices, client interactions that build trust, establish credibility, and help create a culture-friendly environment"

(Cultural Diversity in Rehabilitation, 1992, p. 48) for persons from ethnic and diverse backgrounds.

Proficiency in multicultural communication has been described as skills in communicating with members of diverse cultural groups to achieve desired objectives (Kreps & Kunimoto, 1994). Kavanagh & Kennedy (1992, p. 42) state that "effective cross-cultural communication requires awareness that communication is possible and that mistakes will occur, sensitivity to the communication process, knowledge of expectant patterns of communication styles that are appropriate to the client, and a set of practice skills." The development of specific skill areas, such as articulating the problem, managing resistance and defensiveness, and recovering when mistakes are made, are needed to examine communication patterns and their potential for creating barriers or mutual respect. Such skills empower or enable the communicator professionally and personally (Ivey, 1980; Pedersen, 1988). "Intercultural communication proficiency empowers one in the decision-making process of personal health" (Kreps & Kunimoto, 1994, p. 26).

Mutual communication conveys a commitment to involvement in an interactive process that affords respect, recognition and value of human dignity, and a willingness to alter personal behaviors in response to the communication process. Developing the skills to empathize and understand others' beliefs, assumptions, perspectives, and feelings are important communication strategies (Pedersen, 1988). Possessing the willingness to risk and expose oneself as limited and still developing sensitivity, knowledge, and skills are also crucial to the mutual communication process. Mutual and shared communication and understanding, an effective goal of health care professionals, promotes the ability to help clients and others to find and accept appropriate intervention (Kavanagh & Kennedy, 1992).

Through training and experience the health care provider can gain skills to adapt and adjust the helping process to compensate for cultural differences. Styles of interviewing, who is included in *family* intervention, and treatment goals are a few of the things that can be changed to meet cultural needs (Cross et al., 1989). Beyond multicultural communication skills, providers can be taught interviewing skills that are reflective of the person's understanding of culture and diversity; techniques for learning the culture of their client groups; and strategies for managing feelings and attitudes, both of their own and of others. Proficiency in the area of skill enables the provider to communicate effectively with persons of different backgrounds, to learn about others, and to adapt to the constraints of life. It enables one to obtain information from other health care providers and professionals in diverse cultural settings. It enables providers to build supportive environments and to begin institutionalizing cultural interventions as legitimate helpful approaches. It enables providers to continue to acquire skills and behaviors that would enhance the delivery of health care services to all people (Cross et al., 1989; Cultural Diversity in Rehabilitation, 1992; Kavanagh & Kennedy, 1992; Kreps & Kunimoto, 1994).

Outcome for Skills

A culturally competent health care provider has the

- ability to generate, modify, and adapt a variety of intervention strategies to accommodate the particular need of the client and his or her family;

- knowledge to be creative and resourceful in identifying and using cultural value systems on the behalf of the client;

- ability to use, send, and interpret a variety of communication—verbal and nonverbal—skills to bridge the gap between cultures;

- skills and knowledge to learn about cultures; and

- capability to evaluate discriminatory intent and discriminatory effect in their interactions and services.

Summary

The Cultural Competency Education Model is a conceptual model that focuses on the process of developing cultural competency in health care practice. MacDonald (1998) states that this model can be used to structure teaching and learning strategies. "It provides a clear framework for curriculum development and evaluation. It is suggested that educational establishments are the best equipped to assess the knowledge and self-exploration components of the model and that the skills component is best assessed while on fieldwork" (p. 325).

It is critical that educators are prepared to teach, facilitate, promote, and develop cultural competence among students. Educators must take students beyond their own individual experiences. They must encourage active, lifelong learning and positive attitudes about groups of people who are different from themselves. They must model and facilitate ways of evaluating knowledge from different perspectives. More importantly, educators must help students to understand their personal values and beliefs and how they affect the therapeutic relationship and interactions. Lastly, educators must give students the skills and strategies to interact effectively in multicultural environments.

This Cultural Competency Education Model can be used to develop plans for individual as well as systems' multicultural growth. As health care providers examine their practices and articulate effective, culturally appropriate intervention strategies, the delivery of health care will improve. Each person will add to the knowledge base, through both positive and negative experiences, developing his or her expertise over time (Cross et al., 1989). This requires staying abreast of contemporary theories, practice, and research in this area. The next chapter will further outline ways and opportunities to use this model to become a culturally competent practitioner.

References

Arkansas Research & Training Center in Vocational Rehabilitation. (1992). *Cultural diversity in rehabilitation: Nineteenth institute on rehabilitation issues*. Hot Springs, AR: Author.

Asante, M. (1991). Afrocentric curriculum. *Educational Leadership, 49,* 28–39.

Ballis Lal, B. (1995). Symbolic interaction theories. *American Behavioral Scientist, 38,* 421–441.

Banks, J. A. (1994). *An introduction to multicultural education*. Newton, MA: Allyn & Bacon.

Banks, J. A., & Banks, C. A. (1993). *Multicultural education: Theory and practice* (2nd ed.). Newton, MA: Allyn & Bacon.

Baptiste, H. P. (1979). *Multicultural education: A synopsis*. Washington, DC: University Press of America.

Berger, P. L., & Luckman, T. (1963). *The social construction of reality*. New York: Doubleday.

Burnett, G. (1994). *Varieties of multicultural education: An introduction*. ERIC Digest. Retrieved from: http://eric-web.tc.columbia.edu/digests/dig98.html

Cross, T. L., Bazron, B. J., Dennis, K. W., & Isaacs, M. R. (1989). *Towards a culturally competent system of care* (Vol. I). Washington, DC: CASSP Technical Assistance Center, Georgetown University Child Development Center.

Darder, A. (Ed.). (1995). *Culture and difference.* Westport, CT: Bergin & Garvey.

Devore, W., & Schlesinger, E. G. (1981). *Ethnic-sensitive social work practice.* St. Louis, MO: Mosby.

Dillard, M., Andonian, L., Flores, O., Lai, L., MacRae, A., & Shakir, M. (1992). Culturally competent occupational therapy in a diversely populated mental health setting. *American Journal of Occupational Therapy, 46,* 721–726.

Diversity Rx. (1997). *Why is cultural competence important for health professionals?* Retrieved from: http://www.diversity.rx.org

Fitzgerald, M. H. (1992, April/May/June). Multicultural clinical interactions. *Journal of Rehabilitation,* 38–42.

Gay, G. (1994). *A synthesis of scholarship in multicultural education* (NCREL Urban Education Monograph Series). Oak Brook, IL: North Central Regional Educational Laboratory.

Good, D. (1996). Cultural sensitivity: Integrating cultural concepts into clinical practice. *Work, 6,* 61–65.

Gordon, M. (1964). *Assimilation in American life.* New York: Oxford University Press.

Gorski, P. (1997). *A working definition: Initial thoughts on multicultural education.* Retrieved from: http://curry.edschool.virginia.edu/go/multicultural/activityarch.html

Grant, C. (1977). *Multicultural education: Commitments, issues, and applications.* Washington, DC: Association for Supervision and Curriculum Development.

Grant, C. (1994). Best practice in teacher preparation for urban schools: Lessons from the multicultural teacher education literature. *Action in Teacher Education, 16*(3), 1–18.

Green, J. W. (1982). *Cultural awareness in the human services.* Englewood Cliffs, NJ: Prentice Hall.

Hernandez, H. (1987). *Multicultural education: A teacher's guide to content and process.* Columbia, OH: Merrill.

Howe-Murphy, R., Ross, H., Tseng, R., & Hartwig, R. (1989). Effecting change in multicultural health promotion: A systems approach. *Journal of Allied Health, 18,* 291–305.

Ivey, A. (1980*). Counseling and psychotherapy: Skills, theories and practice.* Englewood Cliffs, NJ: Prentice Hall.

Kallen, H. (1915, February 18). Democracy versus the melting pot. *Nations,* 190–194.

Kanpol, B., & Brady, J. (1998). Teacher education and the multicultural dilemma: A "critical" thinking response. *Journal of Critical Pedagogy, 1*(2), 62–66.

Kavangh, K. H., & Kennedy, P. H. (1992). *Promoting cultural diversity: Strategies for health care professionals.* Newbury Park, CA: Sage.

Kreps, G. L., & Kunimoto, E. N. (1994). *Effective communication in multicultural health care settings.* Newbury Park, CA: Sage.

Kreps, G. L., & Thornton, B. C. (1992). *Health communication: Theory and practice* (2nd ed.). Prospect Heights, IL: Waveland.

Levine, R. A., & Campbell, D. T. (1972). *Ethnocentrism theories of conflict, ethnic attitudes, and group behavior.* New York: Wiley.

London, H., & Devore, W. (1988). Layers of understanding. *Family Relations, 37,* 310–314.

MacDonald, R. (1998). What is cultural competency? *British Journal of Occupational Therapy, 61,* 325–328.

McNeil, C. (1990). Culture: The impact on health care. *Journal of Cancer Education, 5,* 13–16.

Mead, M. (1956). Understanding cultural patterns. *Nursing Outlook, 4,* 260–262.

Pachter, L. M. (1994). Culture and clinical care: Folk illness beliefs and behaviors and their implications for health care delivery. *Journal of the American Medical Association, 271,* 690–694.

Parekh, B. (1986). The concept of multicultural education. In S. Modgil, G. K. Verma, K. Mallick, & C. Modgil (Eds.), *Multicultural education: The interminable debate* (pp. 19–31). Philadelphia: Falmer.

Parrillo, V. N. (1997). *Strangers to these shores: Race and ethnic relations in the United States* (5th ed.). Newton, MA: Allyn & Bacon.

Pedersen, P. (1988). The three stages of multicultural development: Awareness, knowledge, and skill. In P. Pedersen (Ed.), *A handbook for developing multicultural awareness* (pp. 3–18). Alexandria, VA: American Association for Counseling and Development.

Pusch, M. D. (1979). *Multicultural education: A cross-cultural approach.* Yarmouth, ME: Intercultural Press.

Sayles-Folks, S., & People, L. (1990, September). Cultural sensitivity training for occupational therapists. *Physical Disabilities Special Interest Section Newsletter, 13,* 4–5.

Schulman, E. D. (1978). *Intervention in human services* (2nd ed.). St. Louis, MO: Mosby.

Sleeter, C. E., & Grant, C. A. (1994). Multicultural education. In C. E. Sleeter & C. A. Grant (Eds.), *Making choices for multicultural education: Five approaches to race, class, and gender* (2nd ed., pp. 136–173). Columbus, OH: Merrill.

Solomos, J., & Back, L. (1995). Marxism, racism, and ethnicity. *American Behavioral Scientist, 38*, 407–420.

Wells, S. A. (1994). *A multicultural education and resource guide for occupational therapy educators and practitioners.* Bethesda, MD: American Occupational Therapy Association.

CHAPTER TWELVE

Plan for Competency

Key Points

• Becoming culturally competent can occur by chance or by design.

• Any plan for competency must include

   – evaluating the person in which the change is desired,

   – building a support system for change, and

   – developing outcomes and concrete action steps.

• The development of cultural competency requires a willingness to learn, risk, explore, and change.

T he overall goal of the Cultural Competency Education Model is to provide a framework within which health care providers can develop skills and acquire knowledge that increase their ability to function effectively in a multicultural environment and to deliver culturally appropriate health care services. The learning tools for this process must encompass a wide variety of dimensions and experiences—cognitive, affective, and experiential. Any basic plan for becoming culturally competent must address three basic components: (1) self-exploration and awareness, (2) knowledge, and (3) skills. Other areas, such as attitude, perception, and behavior, can be integrated into the plan. All these components are related integrally in actual practice.

Formulating the Plan

Change may occur by chance or by design. Changes can occur in large leaps or in incremental steps. Making changes through planned initiatives gives the health care provider steps for implementation. For those who assume the task of becoming culturally competent, a plan for competency can be enhanced through strategic planning (Table 12). First, carefully evaluate the environment—person—in which the change is desired. This will reveal the barriers to and resources for changes. The process of looking inward, reviewing, and examining your values, beliefs, behaviors, roles, biases, perceptions, knowledge, work and personal ethics, health beliefs, orientation to time, family, communication style, and so forth answers the question, *Who am I?* Admit to both the negative and positive aspect of your personality and beliefs. Select the attributes you wish to change and analyze the pros and cons to making these changes.

Second, build a support system to facilitate and assist with making the desired changes. Seek out and select colleagues, advocates, role models, and people who can help in this process. The support system should create a safe environment to discuss issues, conflicts, and feelings without the fear of being judged. It should be a place not only where true self-introspection can occur, but also the opportunity to explore, obtain, and try new behaviors, perceptions, attitudes, skills, and knowledge.

Third, find and develop resources—books, courses, places, people, and information—that will enlighten your knowledge base and aid the implementation of your plan. This will give you the tools with which to work. Finally, the development of outcome goals and concrete action steps will keep your plan realistic and workable (Table 13).

Table 12. Plan for Change

Step I: Evaluating the Personal Context

Evaluate the environment by truly looking at yourself—values, beliefs, behaviors, roles, biases, perceptions, knowledge, work or personal ethics, health beliefs, orientation to time, family, communication style, and so forth. Being honest about your views is necessary for understanding who you are and how you view the world. It is one thing to wish you were bias-free and another to truly live by this principle. Admitting to both the negative and positive aspects of your personality is essential for change and acquiring new knowledge.

Step II: Developing Support

Look for allies, colleagues, advocates, and role models to assist you through this process. A safe environment is needed to discuss issues and concerns openly, freely, and without fear of being judged. A support system will help you deal with the pain that occurs when views and beliefs are challenged.

Step III: Resource Development

Seek out sources of information and tools, including people to enlighten your knowledge base. Locating and securing training materials, advisors, courses, consultants, and mentors are vital functions.

Step IV: Goals and Action

Write a comprehensive plan for becoming culturally competent with concrete action steps and a timeline. Activities addressing the three basic components—(1) self-exploration, (2) knowledge, and (3) skill—must be part of the plan.

Table by Shirley A. Wells

Table 13. Personal Action Plan

Goal	Action Step	Date	Measures
1. I will broaden my reading	Purchase books, magazines, newspapers, and other cultural reading materials	December 1, 2000	Minimum of one per month
2. I will explore belief about others	Create a list of at least 10 stereotypes you think people hold about other populations or groups	March 1, 2001	One list for each diverse population or group
3. I will take a field trip	Attend different religious ceremonies	August 1, 2001	At least three religious groups

Table by Shirley A. Wells

The development of cultural competency requires a willingness to learn, to risk, to explore, and to change. It takes a balance of sensitivity, awareness, knowledge, and skill. It requires building a base of common experiences and understanding.

Recommendations for Action

- Develop a personal action plan with specific goals, steps, a timeline, and measurements.

- Plan regular and interesting diversity discussions and activities.

- Plan educational activities.

- Develop active listening skills.

- Become a student of different cultures.

Suggested Activities and Exercises

Self-Exploration and Awareness

Purpose: Activities to facilitate self-exploration and self-awareness.

Acknowledging your cultural heritage and history.

Procedure: Answer each question. There are no right or wrong answers to these questions. They are intended only to facilitate an acknowledgement of your own cultural heritage.

- What ethnic group, socioeconomic level, religion, age group, and community do you belong to?

- What experiences have you had with persons from ethnic populations, socioeconomic levels, religions, age groups, sexual orientation, disabilities, or communities different from your own?

- What were those experiences like? How did you feel about them?

- When you were growing up what did your parents and significant others say about people who were different from your family?

- How has the cultural setting in which you were brought up influenced your outlook on life?

- What influences in your experiences have led to the development of negative feelings, if any, about your cultural heritage or background?

- What influences in your experiences have led to the development of positive feelings, if any, about your cultural heritage or background?

- What personal qualities do you have that will help you establish interpersonal relationships with other persons from other cultural groups? What personal qualities may be detrimental?

- Complete the following sentences:

  > I like to learn about other cultures because. . . .

  > I do not like to learn about other cultures because. . . .

  > I get along with other persons because. . . .

  > I do not get along with other persons because. . . .

- What changes, if any, would you like to make in your own attitudes or experiences in relation to persons of other ethnic or cultural groups?

- Describe an experience in your own life in which you believe you were discriminated against for any reason, not necessarily because of your culture.

- How do you believe _____ (fill in the blank with the name of an ethnic, racial, or cultural group) should deal with issues of cultural diversity in American life?

(Source: Kabagarama, D., 1993; Ponterotto, J. G., & Pedersen, P. B., 1993; Randall-David, E., 1989)

How do you relate to various groups of people in the society?

Following are different levels of responses you might have toward a person.

Levels of response.

- *Greet:* I think I can *greet* this person warmly and welcome him or her sincerely.

- *Accept:* I think I can honestly *accept* this person as he or she is and be comfortable enough to listen to his or her problems.

- *Help*: I think I would genuinely try to *help* this person with his or her problems as they might relate to or arise from the label-stereotype given to him or her.

- *Background:* I think I have the *background* or knowledge or experience to be able to help this person.

- *Advocate:* I think I could honestly be *an advocate* for this person.

    Table 14 provides a list of individuals. Read down the list and place a check mark by anyone you would *not greet* or would *hesitate to greet.* Then move to response level 2, *accept,* and follow the same procedure. Try to respond honestly, not as you think might be socially or professionally desirable. Your answers are only for your personal use in clarifying your initial reactions to different people.

Knowledge

Purpose: Activities to provide a broad base of knowledge about diverse populations.

- Assume that you have been asked to describe a given diverse population to a class of fifth graders. Prepare a 10-minute presentation you could use to fulfill the request.

- Identify 10 sources of information (e.g., books, articles, journals, or other media material) about a particular diverse population.

- Select a diverse population of interest to you. Create a multiple choice test with factual questions about this group.

- Develop a list of similarities and differences between diverse populations.

- Interview a health care provider from a diverse population. Inquire about the professional problems and issues that he or she most frequently encounters in professional activities and in professional–client interactions.

- Conduct a community evaluation for a particular diverse population. Identify all the institutions the targeted population uses (e.g., schools, churches, hospitals), all the social service agencies that serve the targeted population community, and all community businesses patronized by the targeted population.

- Select a population and interview at least five persons from that group to discover their attitudes about health care system and medical professionals (Wells, 1994).

Table 14. Activity: Level of Response

Individual	Greet	Accept	Help	Back-ground	Advocate
1. Haitian					
2. Child Abuser					
3. Jew					
4. Person With Hemophilia					
5. Neo-Nazi					
6. Mexican American					
7. IV Drug User					
8. Catholic					
9. Senile, Elderly Person					
10. Teamster Union Member					
11. American Indian					
12. Prostitute					
13. Jehovah's Witness					
14. Cerebral Palsied Person					
15. Vietnamese American					
16. Gay or Lesbian					
17. Person With AIDS					
18. African American					
19. Protestant					
20. Ku Klux Klan member					
21. Alcoholic					
22. White American					
23. Amish Person					
24. Nuclear Armament Proponent					
25. Unmarried Expectant Teenager					

Scoring Guide: This activity may help you anticipate difficulty in working with some clients at various levels. If you have a concentration of checks at specific levels, this may indicate a conflict that could hinder you from rendering effective professional help.

Note. The author created this table referencing a useful cultural competency resource: Randall-David, E. (1989). *Strategies for working with culturally diverse communities and clients*. Washington, DC: Association for the Care of Children's Health. Table created by Shirley A. Wells

Skills

Purpose: In the preparation process to work with diverse populations, supervised practice is very important. Activities in this area should help you put into practice all that you have learned about racial, ethnic, and culturally diverse groups.

- Have one person role play the part of a health care provider and another the part of a person from a diverse group. Have a third person serve as an observer. Role play an interview session for about 5 minutes, then stop and critique the activity. Change roles in the activity and repeat two or more times. Offer suggestions for improving the interaction.

- Prepare a critique of an audiotape or videotape of a treatment session between a health care provider and a person from a particular diverse group.

- Solicit volunteers from various diverse populations. Role play the part of a health care provider working with them as part of a health care team or as colleagues. Critique the simulation, offering suggestions on how to improve the interaction.

- Practice carrying on a telephone conversation with someone from a different culture. Allow someone to listen to your conversation and give feedback on your performance.

- List the type of questions that you may want to ask someone [client] from another culture during your first encounter [interview] (Wells, 1994).

References

Kabagarama, D. (1993). *Breaking the ice: A guide to understanding people from other cultures.* Newton, MA: Allyn & Bacon.

Ponterotto, J. G., & Pedersen, P. B. (1993). *Preventing prejudice: A guide for counselors and educators.* Newbury Park, CA: Sage.

Randall-David, E. (1989). *Strategies for working with culturally diverse communities and clients.* Washington, DC: Association for the Care of Children's Health.

Wells, S. A. (1994). *A multicultural education and resource guide for occupational therapy educators and practitioners.* Bethesda, MD: American Occupational Therapy Association.

Integrating Culture  *IV*

*Do not follow the path. Go where there
is no path and begin the trail.*

—Ashanti Proverb

Objectives

The information in this section is intended to help the reader

- understand how culture is a part of the clinical reasoning process and
  can be integrated into daily practice;

- identify cultural issues and create solutions through case studies;

- understand how culture can be blended into a variety of educational
  opportunities, such as the classroom setting, academic curriculum,
  continuing education workshop, and clinical inservice; and

- understand the multiple avenues of presenting multicultural content
  in an educational program.

CHAPTER THIRTEEN

Blending Culture Into Educational Experiences

Key Points

- The classroom or programmatic climate must be an important consideration when teaching about diversity. Aspects of climate include
  - emotional safety,
  - confidentiality,
  - an open and accepting atmosphere, and
  - respect for each person.

- Pedagogical assumptions necessary for the learners' success include
  - multicultural content can and should empower and transform students;
  - each student has a unique, individual, and equal capacity to learn;
  - students must be active participants in the learning process;
  - effective teaching or learning is dialogic;
  - learning is facilitated in an affective environment; and
  - teachers must be excited about multicultural content and open to new learning.

- The model of multicultural education chosen must fit the existing curriculum or program.

- Curricular approaches might include
  - separate courses that emphasize and focus on diversity content;
  - a multicultural or diversity module within a course or program;
  - an individual class, lecture, or short workshop;
  - the integration or infusion of multicultural content throughout several courses within the curriculum; or
  - a combination of two or more of the previous approaches.

Cultural, multicultural, or diversity content is an important addition to health professions curricula. The previous chapters in this book have established that fact. But the question still remains, How? What is the best approach and model in presenting this information? This chapter will focus on some of the more effective models and strategies used today in multicultural pedagogy.

Pedagogy is not just limited to the teaching methods a teacher selects. Pedagogy refers to the integration in practice of particular curriculum content and design, classroom strategies and techniques, and evaluation, purpose, and methods. All of these aspects of educational practice come together in the realities of what happens in classrooms. "Together they organize a view of how teachers work within an institutional context which specifies a particular version of what knowledge is of most worth, what it means to know something, and how we might construct representations of ourselves, others, and our physical and social environment" (Simon, 1987, p. 370).

As was stated earlier in this book, the authors support and promote a model of multicultural education that promotes empowerment and transformation. The philosophy of this model supports a broad approach to equality and social justice, where power relationships are highlighted and examined; and concepts, events, and issues taught are viewed from the perspectives and experiences of a range of groups, including men and women from different social, ethnic, and racial groups (Banks, 1996, p. 339). A transformative curriculum cannot be constructed merely by adding content about ethnic groups and women to the existing Eurocentric curriculum, or by integrating or infusing ethnic content or content about women into the mainstream curriculum (Banks, 1991, p. 130). Using an additive approach, such as this, does not challenge nor substantially change the basic assumptions, perspectives, and values of the dominant culture or curriculum. LaBelle and Ward (1994) list several principles and practices for bringing an empowerment and transformative model of multicultural education to the classroom. Many of these are included in the following examination of classroom climate, assumptions of the teacher, and the teaching strategies employed.

Classroom Climate

The tone or climate of the classroom is the first important consideration when teaching about diversity. Because the issues presented and discussed often elicit strong emotions, a climate of *emotional safety* is vital. Students must be told and must believe that their ideas and comments will be heard and respected, even if they do not match the prevailing attitude of the rest of the class. Challenging and discussing ideas are allowed; but personal attacks, humiliating remarks, or ridicule are never appropriate. Neither is name-calling or accusations. An aspect of class safety is *confidentiality*. Students must believe that whatever is said or disclosed will not be spoken of outside the classroom. If reaction papers are required on classroom discussions, students must be reminded not to share the contents of their papers with friends, or leave them lying around so that others could inadvertently read them. To further assure confidentiality in written work, classmates' full names should never be used. Initials are better. It is often important to discuss climate issues at the beginning of the course and to elicit consensual agreement about classroom safety from each class member.

Classroom climate is strongly influenced by the *teacher's attitude*. There must be an *open and accepting atmosphere* that encourages a willingness to share ideas and beliefs; to explore one's values; and to confront and grapple with concepts that are new, uncomfortable, and possibly frightening. When a student is compelled to examine ideas that conflict with lifelong family and personal values, it may cause anxiety and discomfort. The manner in which the teacher responds to each student provides a model of behavior for all students to emulate. Educators establish this open and accepting climate by treating each student and her or his ideas and beliefs with *respect*. Foss (1991, p. 2) defines a safe classroom as a place where everyone experiences equality in terms of personal value, where students and the professor have equal respect for each other as persons, and where this respect affects all aspects of the interaction and learning in the class.

Not only does the classroom climate influence the teaching or learning process; the assumptions held by the teacher of diversity play an important role in the student's success. Many scholars believe that in order for the educational process to be empowering or transformative for the student, the teacher must hold the following pedagogical assumptions.

Pedagogical Assumptions

Assumption #1

Each student has a unique, individual, and equal capacity to learn. Teacher's expectations influence a student's academic performance. Nieto (1996) summarizes some of the numerous research studies that illustrate that teachers' low expectations of students on the basis of gender, race, or class factors result in lower academic performance. This phenomenon exemplifies the self-fulfilling prophecy concept identified by Merton in 1948. If a teacher believes that a student does not have the capacity to learn because of some inherent quality, he or she will not expect that student to perform at the same level as other students. The teacher then (often unconsciously) treats the student differently than other students, which causes the first student to believe that he or she cannot learn as well as others (internalized oppression), resulting in loss of esteem and diminished academic performance. The student's less than stellar performance affirms to the teacher that her initial assumption of the student's abilities was correct and justifies her lowered expectations. And the cycle continues.

Conversely, having high expectations for each student regardless of such factors as gender, race, and class contributes to an attitude of positive potential, resulting in overall increased academic performance, increased success, and a perceived and real sense of empowerment for students. Attention to increasing student achievement including enhancement of basic skills is a vital component of an empowerment curriculum model according to LaBelle and Ward (1994, p. 170). Open, accepting, and positive teacher attitudes, coupled with a commitment to facilitating success for all students, are necessary for a climate of learning.

Assumption #2

Students must be active participants in the learning process. The traditional approach to teaching incorporates the almost exclusive use of the lecture method, where the all-knowing professor fills the minds of students with knowledge as though they were empty vessels. Students are passive recipients of this wisdom, taking in information and regurgitating it on the exam in a process that Shor labels *endullment*—the dulling of students' minds as a result of their nonparticipation (1992, p. 20). Paulo Freire (1970, p. 58) has called this process the banking method of education, where instead of "communicating the teacher issues communiques and makes deposits that the students patiently receive, memorize, and repeat. . . . The scope of action allowed to the students extends only as far as receiving, filing, and storing the deposits." Freire sees this approach to education as oppressive to students, establishing the teacher as the knowledgeable authority and keeper of wisdom, whereas the students know nothing except what the teacher chooses to impart to them.

In contradiction to the previously described model, a more empowering approach to education is a student-centered classroom where students are active participants in the learning process. Participation is the most important place to begin because student involvement is low in traditional classrooms and because action is essential to gain knowledge and develop intelligence (Shor, 1992). Piaget and Dewey each supported the importance of action for learning. "Knowledge is derived from actiont. . . . To know an object is to act upon it and to transform it" (Piaget, 1979, p. 28). Dewey (1963) argued that participation in school is crucial to learning. He is often credited with the idea that learning is doing.

Experiential education is an important part of the health professional's academic curriculum. Learning labs where specific skills are taught and practiced are both a standard and expected part of the learning process. In addition to participating in lab situations, students engage in active learning in discussion groups, role play experiences, case study applications, problem-based learning experiences, simulated and real client–therapist interactions within the classroom, and field-based internships. All of these activities allow and encourage active student participation from which students can construct meaning.

Having a student-centered philosophy and participatory classroom does not mean that lecture is never employed, however. A fact of health professions curricula is that there are often courses (particularly the sciences) that lend themselves more to the lecture method because of the content needing to be taught. In a human anatomy course, for example, a student must memorize the origins and insertions of each muscle to know their location and function. Having to learn facts and data, such as these, does not naturally lend itself to more active approaches to inquiry, such as discussion groups or reflection papers. Shor (1992) suggests, however, that even a course such as this can be taught in an empowering manner if the information is offered in a context that is functional to the students' lives and work and that reveals critical problems in society (p. 36). An assignment to analyze one's work site for stress on the human musculoskeletal system provides an effective, experiential method to apply the knowledge gained in a human anatomy course. Because it personalizes the information, bringing it to the context of the students' lives, interest in the topic is increased, new meaning is constructed and remembered, and an improved quality of learning occurs.

Assumption #3

Effective teaching or learning is dialogic. Students learn best when teachers talk *with* them rather than *at* them. Mutual discussion is the heart of the dialogic classroom. Shared interaction between students and teachers result in mutual learning, where students and teachers reflect together on the meaning of their experience and their knowledge (Shor 1992, p. 86). In order for dialogue to be effective, each person must enter the conversation with an attitude of openness and a willingness to learn. In his last book, published shortly after his death, Freire (1998, p. 121) discusses the condition of openness in this way:

> To live in openness toward others and to have an open-ended curiosity toward life and its challenges is essential to educational practice. To live this openness toward others respectfully and, from time to time, when opportune, critically reflect on this openness, ought to be an essential part of the adventure of teaching.

This openness and willingness to learn from the students may be seen by some as diminishing the authority of the teacher, placing him or her in a more horizontal (Freire, 1960) rather than hierarchical position with the student. Dialogue transforms the teacher's unilateral authority to a shared authority that calls on faculty to relinquish some of their authority and requires students to codevelop a joint learning process.

Dialogue by definition is a conversation between two or more people (Merriam-Webster, 1995). A conversation implies that two or more voices will be heard. A dialogic classroom, therefore, is one where students are encouraged to have a voice, a say, and an opinion. Within the context of a climate of safety, students who are often silent and silenced in traditional classrooms gain the courage and are empowered to present their ideas and questions, actively entering the conversation in a dialogic classroom. For the very shy and introverted students, small group discussions or conversations in dyads provide the forum for their voices to be heard and included. A dialogic classroom, therefore, results in an increased sharing of diverse ideas and facilitates learning.

Although others might identify additional pedagogical assumptions that lead to an empowering education (Shor, 1992), only one more will be mentioned here.

Assumption #4

Learning is facilitated in an affective classroom. Many authors believe that cognitive learning should be integrated with affective learning to ensure engagement of the students in the learning process (Shor, 1992; Hooks, 1994). Shor discriminates between empowering and traditional pedagogies by the resultant emotions that are elicited. He states, "In traditional classrooms, negative emotions are provoked in students by teacher-centered politics. Unilateral teacher authority in a passive curriculum arouses in many students a variety of negative emotions: self-doubt, hostility, resentment, boredom, indignation, cynicism, disrespect, frustration, [and] the desire to escape" (p. 23). Shor believes that these negative emotions interfere with learning. In contrast, "In a participatory class where authority is mutual, some of the positive affects which support student learning include cooperativeness, curiosity, humor, hope, responsibility, respect, attentiveness, openness, and concern about society" (p. 24). Learning should be fun! There can and should be joy in the discovery and mutual construction of knowledge. Freire (1998) discusses the importance of joy in the classroom and its relationship with hope. "Hope is something shared between teachers and students. The hope that we can learn together, teach together, be curiously impatient together, produce something together, and resist together the obstacles that prevent the flowering of our joy" (p. 69).

In classrooms where emotions are expressed and accepted, the passion of learning is patently evident. Hooks (1994) strongly supports the notion of a passionate and emotional learning environment but believes that little passionate teaching and learning takes place in contemporary classrooms. "Even when students are desperately yearning to be touched by knowledge, professors still fear the challenge, [and] allow their worries about losing control to override their desires to teach" (p. 199).

Multicultural education evokes strong emotions because it often challenges a student's personal values and beliefs. It is important to allow the expression of feelings, even though passionately debating the issues may be uncomfortable for both students and teachers alike, as most of us have been taught that a dispassionate objective stance is the appropriate and rational way to examine ideas. Multicultural education strongly refutes that philosophy. Multicultural content is inherently emotive, personal, conflictual, and involving. Consequently, it is essential that students be given ample opportunities to express their beliefs and emotions, to interact with their peers and classmates, and to express rage or pride when multicultural issues are discussed (Banks, 1994, p. 96).

Affective learning, employing the emotions in the process of constructing knowledge, involves engaging the self in learning. One cannot remain aloof and objective when emotions are involved. By engaging the self in learning, students become the subjects rather than the objects of the learning experience. The focus of the teaching or learning experience is on the student rather than on the teacher, and the student has more control and agency in her own learning and construction of knowledge.

Teachers of diversity must, therefore, take the experiences and voices of students themselves as a starting point. We must confirm and legitimatize the knowledge and experiences through which students give meaning to their everyday lives (McLaren, 1998, p. 225). Knowledge must be made meaningful to students before it can be critically analyzed. By starting with the students' experiences framed within the context of their lives, students comprehend the information first from their own personal and subjective point-of-view, to which they can continue to add new information to construct new knowledge. Learning then becomes personal, meaningful, critical, and often useful.

Within a health profession curriculum, students can be given facts about the changing sensory processing that occurs as a person ages; they can be taught the theories of social disengagement and the isolation of elders; and they can be taught the resultant diminishing of purposeful and productive activities. Students can even be examined on how well they have learned these facts. Yet, for many, these facts and theories will soon be forgotten if they have no experience with elders. But if, in addition to the previous factual information, the teacher requires these students to visit the nursing home where their grandparents or neighbors now reside and asks them to engage the elders in activities that are limited by sensory deficiencies and diminished social interaction skills, the theories and facts will take on new meaning. Personal experiences, imbued with the feelings and emotions that accompany any action and interaction, brighten and highlight the interpretation of the knowledge and make meaning in a way that is often remembered and available for future use. Banks (1991, p. 131) states that "A curriculum designed to empower students must be transformative in nature and help students to develop the knowledge, skills, and values needed to become social critics who can make reflective decisions and implement their decisions in effective personal, social, political, and economic action." A traditional curriculum often disempowers students by not considering the context of the students' lives nor allowing them to have a voice within the classroom.

Curricular Fit and Classroom Strategies

Once the classroom climate has been established and the pedagogical assumptions identified, the teacher must determine which model(s) of multicultural education he or she will be using, how this model will fit into the curriculum, and which classroom strategies will be the most effective.

Assuming that the teachers choose Sleeter and Grant's (1987) conceptual model of multicultural education, the curriculum would be transformed so that students will view concepts, events, issues, and problems from different ethnic perspectives and points of view. Reconceptualizing the curriculum and making ethnic content an integral part of a transformed curriculum should be distinguished from merely adding ethnic content (Banks, 1994, p. 95). No matter how and where the multicultural content fits within the curriculum, and whatever educational strategies are chosen, this transformative model would be presented. For example, if one were to choose to look at the history of African American leaders in the profession of nursing, identifying and listing African American nurses and comparing their achievements to those of White American leaders would just be adding ethnic content. However, if contemporary African American nurse leaders were interviewed and subsequently gave their interpretation of the achievements of African American leaders from their own perspective, or if the thoughts and ideas of deceased African American nurse leaders could be gathered from papers, journals, or letters, a more transformed and balanced curriculum would be achieved.

Beyond the theoretical approach and model chosen, curricular fit and integration of multicultural content will be determined by the philosophy of the institution in which the health profession program is housed, the requirements of the academic accrediting agency, the model and structure of the programs curriculum, the interests and desires of the program director and the faculty, and the demographics of the student body. Curricular fit will determine whether one chooses to teach *a separate course* focusing on multicultural content; include a *multicultural module within a course*; provide an *individual class, presentation, or workshop* devoted to diversity issues; *integrate or infuse multicultural content throughout several or all courses;* or do a combination of these approaches.

     Separate courses might be represented by a course on social issues and ethics, where critical multicultural theory is presented, discussed, grappled with, and applied in the context of an analysis of the ethical issues involved. An examination of poverty might be part of this course with readings that included the most current governmental statistics on the subject, chapters from Sidel's book *Women and Children Last,* and a journal from a homeless White American man. As part of this course, the instructor might also include an opportunity for class discussion with a woman on welfare, and a short field experience in a homeless shelter for destitute families. Analysis of these experiences might include an examination and comparison of the varied perceptions of poverty from each person's point of view; identification of the access to health care and the barriers to access for this population; and a discussion of the ethical principles of beneficence, maleficence, and distributive justice. Institutionalized oppression would be examined, especially at the intersection of gender, race, and class, and evaluated for its effect on persons who fall below the poverty guidelines. Students would be asked to relate and reflect upon their own experiences with poverty and issues of class in both professional and personal settings, and how those experiences influenced or were influenced by their personal values. A comprehensive examination of poverty in this manner is reflective of a transformational curriculum.

     The positive aspects of teaching a course with a multicultural focus include

- an opportunity to examine multicultural issues in depth;

- more time to allow a wider breadth of information about the issues;

- time and opportunity for community and field-based application and experiences;

- a semester-long (or quarter-long) opportunity for personal reflection on a topic that may result in personal growth, increased sensitivity to class issues and people caught within the class power struggle, and positive movement towards cultural competence.

     There are also negative implications for this approach as well.

- It may require more time than is available in an already-packed curriculum.

- If this is the only treatment of multicultural and diversity issues in the curriculum, the course and its information might be ghettoized or marginalized and discounted or devalued by students.

- Students may view a course like this as too liberal or not technical enough to warrant the attention paid to other professional courses.

- There must be a faculty member with enough interest and knowledge in a transformative multicultural approach to coordinate, plan, and deliver this course.

- There may be a need for fairly extensive faculty development.

A *multicultural module within a course* is another way to present multicultural content. A faculty member might choose to examine one ethnic group, such as Native Americans (Sleeter & Grant, 1987), in a course on clinical conditions or etiology of disease. A transformational examination of this group would not only look at the experiences, contributions, and concerns of Native Americans. It would also study their view of health and wellness with resources, such as Spector's *Cultural Diversity in Health and Illness* (1996) or Silko's *Ceremony* (1986), or by bringing a native healer to class to present his or her concept of health through ritual. The module might also have an assignment that requires students to examine the power structure of the Indian Bureau of Affairs within the context of the delivery of and access to adequate health services both on and off reservations. Students might also examine the incidence of certain medical diagnoses (e.g., coronary heart disease, diabetes, alcoholism) within the Native American population and the sociocultural factors that contribute to these.

The benefits of presenting a multicultural module within a class include the following:

- This is a cost-effective, resource-saving way to present multicultural content in an important manner.

- A module allows some depth of a single topic.

- It is easier to find adjunct teachers to present a limited portion of the curriculum such as this.

- This approach provides an opportunity for a beginning understanding of and increased sensitivity to the group or issue presented. It may spark an interest in a student who would continue his or her independent research on this topic or in other courses and assignments where appropriate.

- It provides an affirmation and opportunity for sharing one's culture for any Native American students in the class.

  Negative implications for this approach include the following:

- There is less opportunity for depth of study because of a limited time-frame.

- Without any follow-up or experiential application of the material, the information will be seen as only theoretical, lessening the value and meaning to any student who is not Native American or has had no interaction with native people.

- If examined in a superficial way, the information presented risks increasing stereotypes and prejudicial thoughts rather than increasing awareness and cultural competence.

  An *individual class, lecture, or short workshop* is another way that health professional academic programs may present multicultural content. This might include a guest lecture by a person who will talk about his or her experiences with racism as an African American person in a small, rural community. Another example would be a presentation or discussion with a lesbian couple about the discrimination they have experienced with medical insurers. It might also include a 3-hour workshop on prejudice reduction strategies, or a lecture on bilingualism in a communications for health professionals course. This approach is favored by many programs for the following positive reasons:

- It provides an introduction to a possible variety of diversity issues that may spark an interest for students.

- It can be included in the curriculum without much course revision or extra planning.

- Because these lessons can be presented by a guest speaker, it does not require any program faculty to have special knowledge of diversity or multicultural theory.

- It allows for numerous effective and informational diversity spots in a variety of classes throughout the curriculum.

- It meets any accreditation or institutional requirements for diversity content without a great expense of resources.

  Negative effects of this approach include the following:

- There is a lack of depth of any topic.

- There is a lack of opportunity for extended personal reflection about the topic.

- It may elicit disregard and devaluation by students of information presented because of the lack of opportunity to apply the concepts in a meaningful way.

- There is a limited movement towards cultural competence.

      The *integration or infusion of multicultural content throughout several courses within the curriculum* is an effective way to present this content (Bailey, 2000). By consciously including culture as a factor of analysis in multiple arenas, it lessens the marginalization of the content, increases the visibility and awareness of diversity, and facilitates ongoing, critical awareness and analysis by students. Some strategies involve

- providing opportunities and experiences for students to examine their own values and belief system and recognize how this flows from their culture and social location; increasing self-knowledge is the first step in developing cultural competency;

- modeling inclusive language for students—teaching them to use accepted terms for all groups—to use the word *partner* rather than *spouse* when speaking of committed relationships, to use person-first language with persons with disabilities, and to use *White* as an identifying racial and cultural designation;

- using a variety of cultural groups when developing case studies and making them realistic rather than contrived; learning about aspects of a particular culture before developing a culture-specific case; and being aware of and careful of stereotyping in these cases;

- when performing evaluations on clients, teaching students to include questions about the client's culture and cultural perspectives on health, wellness, independence, family relationships, and other important concepts;

- teaching students to be sensitive to subtle cultural cues during treatment; these are often expressed in body language, such as the interpretation of and comfort with personal space, the use of eye contact, the comfort with touch, the response to someone of the opposite gender, the tone of voice, and the use of smiling or silence rather than saying "no" to the practitioner;

- teaching students not to make assumptions based on White American, middle-class, heterosexual standards; not assuming that all partnered people are married or that all families reflect the traditional family; not expecting that all White Americans have attended college or that non-White Americans are less educated; not assuming that all people hold the same values that you do regarding health and hygiene, work and play, or education and money;

- modeling for and teaching students how to take risks; there is much to learn about people who are different from oneself; to be culturally competent we must be willing to make mistakes, to admit we do not know or are unsure, and to be willing to ask questions; humility is an important characteristic to maintain when engaged in this process;

- teaching students to be critical, sociopolitical analysts; when studying about third-party payers and HMOs, examining the power of those groups when admitting access to persons from a variety of sociocultural categories of class, race, sexuality, gender, age, and ability; using classroom interactions as opportunities to examine power differentials between and among students and between students and teacher(s); encouraging them to ask the question about why societal standards exclude and oppress certain groups; the transformative curriculum teaches students to think and reflect critically on the materials they read and the voices they hear (Banks, 1991, p. 131); and

- modeling respect for each person in the classroom, and their ideas and feelings; being open to and accepting of differences in opinion and perspective; modeling good listening skills and encouraging the development of each student's voice and sense of power in the learning community.

Although the previous list is by no means exhaustive, it does present some approaches to facilitate and develop empowered classrooms. The benefits of this inclusive or integrative approach to multicultural education are as follows:

- It makes sociocultural and sociopolitical issues more apparent, removing the shroud of invisibility, and it increases the awareness of and possibly the sensitivity of students to these issues.

- It recognizes White privilege as an important issue in the examination of sociopolitical power, making students more aware of their own place within this society's power structure.

- It sensitizes students to the oppression of people who are members of nondominant groups.

- It encourages critical analysis and underscores the need for social justice.

- It does not require the addition of extra courses within an already-packed curriculum.

A few of the negative effects of this approach include the following:

- There is a need for all faculty to be knowledgeable of critical multicultural issues, and skilled enough to present these issues in the classroom through planned and spontaneous activities and lessons. Banks (1991, p. 139) writes, "An effective transformative and empowerment curriculum must be implemented by teachers who have the knowledge, skills, and attitudes needed to help students to understand the ways in which knowledge is constructed and used to support power-group relations in society." Supporting faculty in acquiring this knowledge and skill may require increased faculty development that demands the use of time, money, and personal commitment.

- There is lessened opportunity for formal presentation of the theoretical constructs that support analysis of multicultural issues.

- There is a lack of a more unstructured, sequential, and formal approach to gaining knowledge of this content. It may result in fragmented learning and lack of depth.

Applying the Cultural Competency Education Model in an Academic Setting

This chapter has suggested multiple ways to incorporate diversity and multicultural issues into an academic curriculum. This is most effective, however, when one of the goals is the development of cultural competency for health profession students. Using the information in this chapter, combined with the Cultural Competency Education Model outlined in chapter eleven, the educator can begin to plan an effective curriculum.

As one examines the three areas of intervention in the Cultural Competency Education Model, (1) self-awareness and exploration, (2) knowledge, and (3) skills, the educator must be intentional in his or her ability to incorporate these into the content of the course or through various teaching and learning strategies.

Self-Exploration and Awareness

There are multiple avenues that can encourage students to examine themselves and their sociocultural standing within their environments. Some educators (through the use of inclusive texts, provocative articles, videos, reflective journaling, and diversity games) encourage students to examine their own values and beliefs in a private manner. Others, within a context of classroom safety, encourage students to work in small groups to discuss particular beliefs, examine how and from where they develop, and project and predict how they might affect client–therapist interactions. One of the first steps of diversity work should be self-exploration and awareness. Therefore, this area of concentration should occur early in the curriculum so that the skills learned provide the foundation for the next steps in the development of cultural competency.

Knowledge

There are numerous things that a person must know in order to become culturally competent. Knowledge of self, knowledge of groups different from oneself, knowledge of past and current sociopolitical systems that sustain dominant and nondominant status, knowledge of language and behavior that oppresses and discriminates, and knowledge of ways to end discriminatory patterns are only a sample of the things to learn. Any of the curricular approaches previously discussed (e.g., separate courses, multicultural modules within a course, individual classes, presentations and workshops, curricular infusion) lend themselves to the presentation and exploration of this type of information. Multiple teaching and learning strategies can be employed, including discussions of selected articles, books, videos, and movies; guest speakers and panel discussions; independent reading; and other favorite approaches to learning. In many ways this is the easiest part of the model to satisfy because this is what has been traditionally taught.

Skills

Learning the skills of cultural competency is often the piece that is missing in diversity training. Developing skills in communication may include an ability to constantly self-monitor one's language, feelings, attitudes, and behavior when interacting with others who are different. A skilled communicator will also empathize with others, develop rapport through honest and open dialogue, and be willing to risk exposing his or her own developing knowledge and sensitivity (refer to chapter 11). Culturally competent skills also include using inclusive language as well as asking appropriate culturally sensitive questions during interviews and assessments. One must become culturally inquisitive in an inoffensive manner. Another skill that is necessary in diversity work is the ability to recover quickly when a mistake is made, not blaming oneself or others when there is discomfort in the interaction.

Although some of the previous material can be introduced in the classroom with simulations, role plays, and games, much of the skill will actually be learned in the clinic and workplace or during field-based experiences (MacDonald, 1998). Because of this, it is important for the academic and fieldwork programs to work together in the effort of developing culturally competent practitioners.

Summary

There are multiple models of multicultural education and numerous approaches and strategies used to effectively teach and present these. The most effective way to incorporate multicultural content within health professional education is to simultaneously employ all of the approaches delineated in this chapter. Each model and strategy complements, supports, and enhances the knowledge gained from any other method and increases knowledge. A curricular model that incorporates the goal of facilitating the development of cultural competence in its students and faculty will be most successful in meeting this goal if there are resources to provide multiple learning strategies and approaches.

The reality of institutions of higher education, however, is that most are resource-deficient. With limited resources, therefore, an educational program for health professionals must present multicultural content in the best way possible that meets the needs of both the students and the program. As was stated earlier, any approach that increases multicultural content and the awareness of sociocultural inequities in this society is positive. What is important is that we continue to educate students to not only actively and effectively participate in the health care arenas of tomorrow, but also to be culturally competent practitioners who are active agents in the fight for equality and social justice.

References

Bailey, D. (2000). Introducing an awareness of cultural diversity into an established curriculum. In P. A. Crist (Ed.), *Innovations in occupational therapy education 2000.* Bethesda, MD: American Occupational Therapy Association.

Banks, J. A. (1991). A curriculum for empowerment, action, and change. In C. E. Sleeter (Ed.), *Empowerment through multicultural education.* Albany, NY: State University of New York Press.

Banks, J. A. (1994). *An introduction to multicultural education.* Newton, MA: Allyn & Bacon.

Banks, J. A. (Ed.). (1996). *Multicultural education, transformative knowledge, & action: Historical and contemporary perspectives.* New York: Teachers College Press.

Dewey, J. (1963). *Experience and education.* New York: Collier. (Original work published 1938.)

Foss, S. K. (1991). What is feminist pedagogy? Paper presented at the Annual Meeting of the Organization for Research in Gender and Communication, San Antonio, TX.

Freire, P. (1986). *Pedagogy of the oppressed.* New York: Continuum Publishing. (Original work published 1970.)

Freire, P. (1998). *Pedagogy of freedom: Ethics, democracy, and civic courage.* Lanham, MD: Rowman & Littlefield.

Hooks, B. (1994). *Teaching to transgress.* New York: Routledge & Kegan Paul.

LaBelle, T. J., & Ward, C. R. (1994). *Multiculturalism and education: Diversity and its impact on schools and society.* Albany, NY: State University of New York Press.

MacDonald, R. (1998). What is cultural competency? *British Journal of Occupational Therapy, 61,* 325–328.

Merriam-Webster dictionary: Home and office edition. (1995). Springfield, MA: Merriam-Webster.

Merton, R. (1948). The self-fulfilling prophecy. *Antioch Review, 8,* 193–210.

Nieto, S. (1996). *Affirming diversity: The sociopolitical context of multicultural education* (2nd ed.). White Plains, NY: Longman.

Piaget, J. (1979). *Science of education and the psychology of the child.* New York: Penguin. (Original work published 1969.)

Shor, I. (1992). *Empowering education.* Chicago: University of Chicago Press.

Sidel, R. (1992). *Women and children last: The plight of poor women in affluent America.* New York: Penguin.

Silko, L. M. (1986). *Ceremony.* New York: Penguin.

Simon, R. (1987). Empowerment as a pedagogy of possibility. *Language Arts, 64*(4), 370.

Sleeter, C. E., & Grant, C. A. (1987). An analysis of multicultural education in the United States. *Harvard Educational Review, 57*, 421–444.

Spector, R. E. (1996). *Cultural diversity in health and illness* (4th ed.). Norwalk, CT: Appleton & Lange.

CHAPTER FOURTEEN

Culture and Clinical Practice

Key Points

- Culture is an important component of human performance.

- In every clinical interaction there are at least three cultures involved: (1) the personal or familial culture of the provider, (2) the culture of the client and his or her family, and (3) the culture of the primary medical system. There may be a fourth culture—the traditional medical culture of the client.

- The relationship between culture, clinical reasoning, and practice equals a "culturally holistic approach" to health care.

- Standardized evaluation and tests, which are based largely on the sociocultural norms of the White, middle-class population, when used on culturally, racially, or ethnically different populations, should be interpreted within the context of the client's culture.

Culture has been acknowledged as an important component of human performance (Barney, 1991; Dillard, Andonian, Flores, Lai, MacRae, & Shakir, 1992; Kielhofner, 1995; Krefting & Krefting, 1991; Mosey, 1986). According to Krefting and Krefting (1991), in occupational therapy this acknowledgment has occurred primarily on a theoretical and philosophical level. It has seldom been considered in relation to the making of decisions, evaluations, and interventions on a daily basis. A review of the literature shows that it is one of the least developed aspects of knowledge on a practical level. It has not been developed to the point that providers have a clear understanding of how to integrate culture into their daily practice.

The literature has begun to focus on the influence of culture on health and health care, the therapeutic relationship, the outcome of treatment, and the need for training and education of providers (Dresser, 1996; Good, 1996; Jang, 1995; Kavanagh & Kennedy, 1992; Kelly, 1995; Kreps & Kunimoto, 1994; Levine, 1984; McCormack, 1987; Pope-Davis, Prietor, Whitaker, & Pope-Davis, 1993). Cultural clashes among participants in a well elderly program were an unexpected outcome in a study by Jackson et al. (1998). This led to "an attempt to open new doors of understanding about other cultures within the context of occupations" (p. 331) within the treatment program. Lawlor and Mattingly (1998) discovered the difficulties in bridging cultural boundaries between professionals and between practitioners and families on a practical level in their study of family-centered models of services.

Neglecting or taking a noncultural approach in the delivery of health care can result in a sense of dissatisfaction and disharmony for both the provider and consumer. Providers may feel inadequate in their treatment; it can lead to inappropriate treatment models; and it can affect the communication between the consumer and provider (Fitzgerald, 1992; Wells, 1994). Being unknowledgeable about other cultures, unaware of differences, and exclusive in thinking can lead to erroneous assumptions, interpretations, and clinical judgments (Wells, 1995). Culturally congruent care involves decisions and actions that are acceptable and reasonable to the consumer. This care must take into account the consumer's cultural foundation, worldview, systems of values and norms, and orientation to health and illness.

Clinical reasoning and thinking allows the outcome of intervention to be acceptable, meaningful, and satisfying to the client. Clinical reasoning provides a framework within which intervention and care may preserve or maintain the client's original cultural perspective, accommodate and negotiate some change, and yet still preserve other parts of the original view, or result in new patterns of beliefs and behaviors (Leininger, 1988; Kavanagh, 1991). Using the Cultural Competency Education Model, this chapter will present practical ways to integrate culture into daily clinical reasoning process and practice. It will focus on incorporating culture into evaluations, and using cultural knowledge and skills to design intervention strategies.

Clinical Interaction

The first step in establishing a satisfying and productive relationship is the acknowledgement that multiple cultures are involved in the therapeutic relationship. According to Fitzerald (1992), in clinical interactions there are at least three cultures involved: (1) the personal or familial culture of the provider, (2) the culture of the client and his or her family, and (3) the cultural of the primary medical system. In some cases, especially when the individual comes from a nonwestern background, there is a fourth culture—the traditional medical culture. The first step in establishing a satisfying and productive relationship is the acknowledgment that multiple cultures are involved in the therapeutic relationship. This is fairly easy to do when the participants in the interaction come from obviously different cultural backgrounds. It is difficult to do when the participants have grown up in seemingly similar environments and appear similar.

Because we are each a product of our multiple cultures, they provide the filters through which we each interpret reality. Barney (1991, p. 590) states that, because of our individual cultural filters, "we may be ignorant of the customs, language, social relationship patterns, religion, and other practices of various ethnic and minority groups. In other words, we often do not know what we don't know." And with the increasing tension surrounding race relationships and *political correctness* in the United States, it is not surprising that many health care providers are unsure of how to approach their clients regarding cultural beliefs and practices.

According to Fitzgerald, in this multicultural health care environment, providers must act as *cultural brokers*. Their role is to help decrease the degree of disparity between the variety of cultures. Providers are the links between these cultures. They provide information about one another's culture and the medical system. Therefore, health care providers must be comfortable, skilled, and experienced in integrating culture into all aspects and procedures of the health care system.

Clinical Reasoning

Clinical reasoning is the perfect process to use for infusing culture into daily practice. It is the thought process used in practice that enables practitioners to individualize treatment, facilitate functional performance, and create positive outcomes for the clients (Fleming, 1991a; Parham, 1987; Rogers, 1983; Slater & Cohn, 1991). Neistadt (1998b) states that it can be used as a guide to organize and articulate thinking in clinical practice.

Thinking Strategies

Clinical reasoning is an umbrella term to include all the complex processes that health care providers use when thinking about the client, the disability, the situation, and the personal and cultural meanings that the client gives to the disability, the situation, and the self (Flemming, 1991b). It is the process practitioners should use to integrate the client's history, evaluation information, and cultural context into an individualized intervention plan. Health care providers work with people who have serious and often permanent injuries. In these situations, the provider works on reconstruction of the person's ability to function and perform daily life tasks within his or her cultural context. The provider and client, together, work on reconstructing the person's sense of self, ways of accomplishing tasks and engaging in activities, and ways of viewing themselves and their lives. The practitioner, to accomplish this reconstruction, must use many thinking strategies.

The occupational therapy literature has identified several types of reasoning or thinking strategies used by health care practitioners to accomplish their outcomes. According to Fleming (1991b, p. 870), for therapists the term *clinical reasoning* refers to the "many types of inquiry that an occupational therapist uses to understand clients and their difficulties." The types of clinical reasoning used by therapists have been described as follows:

- *Narrative reasoning:* This focuses on the client's occupational story, life history, cultural background, and the activities and roles that he or she values (Clark, 1993; Neistadt, 1996).

- *Interactive reasoning:* This looks for the meaning of the disease or disability to the client (Crepeau, 1991). It also encompasses the interpersonal interaction between the therapist and the client (Fleming, 1991a; Mattingly & Fleming, 1994).

- *Procedural reasoning:* This reasoning identifies problems and treatment on the basis of the client's disease or disability. The practitioner's general knowledge and understanding about a specific disease or disability are called upon (Fleming, 1991a; Mattingly & Fleming, 1994).

- *Pragmatic reasoning:* This considers the treatment environment and possibilities of treatment within a given environment. The therapist's values, knowledge, abilities, and experience, as well as the client's social and financial resources, are also considered (Schell & Cervero, 1993).

- *Conditional reasoning:* This is used to provide a continuous modification of treatment to enable the person to function in the future (Fleming, 1991a; Mattingly & Fleming, 1994).

Cultural Connection

A basic premise of clinical reasoning is that people have reasons for their decisions and behaviors, whether or not they can articulate those reasons or the health care worker recognizes what they are. Culture plays an important role in the decisions and behaviors of not only the client, but also the providers. Using a set of behavioral standards developed according to the norms of the health care provider or medical system to evaluate a client from another culture is a cultural imposition based on ethnocentricity. Neistadt et al. (1998a) found in her study on using case studies to teach clinical reasoning that the use of clinical reasoning resulted in intervention plans that placed the client into a social as well as cultural context. "It allows practitioners to view the client as a *real human being* and integrated the *whole-person* picture into all aspects of the intervention plan" (p. 129). For example, the fact that a traditional form of health care is an important part of a client's cultural and social context would only be revealed through the use of the clinical reasoning process.

Clinical reasoning demands an understanding of the client from his or her own points of view, to see the clients as they see themselves. Narrative and interactive reasoning attempt to understand the meanings people make of themselves, their lives, families, environment, and culture. A lack of cultural inclusion in the clinical reasoning process can prevent practitioners from establishing a therapeutic relationship based on equality and mutual respect. It prevents the practitioner from perceiving clearly the feelings and needs of the client and it may create a reluctance to participate in the treatment program (Wells, 1991). Understanding that we are all products of our own culture, being knowledgeable about other cultures, and having the ability to bridge other cultures, can only lead to a positive and rewarding clinical interaction.

The relationship between culture, clinical reasoning, and practice equals a *culturally holistic approach* (Barney, 1991, p. 592) to health care. It leads to culturally sensitive and appropriate treatment strategies. Explicit details and in-depth information allow the clinical image of clients to be realistic. It paints a picture of the client as a person with unique interests, values, culture, goals, abilities, and priorities. Clinical reasoning helps the practitioner to center on the particulars of the person and not his or her general condition or limiting factors (Fleming, 1991b). Each client is an individual with his or her own identity, culture, background, and lifestyle. Clinical intervention moves from a diagnostic to a more holistic and client-centered approach.

Culture and Evaluations

Many evaluations and assessment tools used in today's health care are based largely on the sociocultural norms of the White, middle-class population (Skawski, 1987). These tools have overwhelmingly incorporated Western values, ethics, theories, and standards. These evaluation norms, however, are not always true for ethnic and culturally diverse populations (Hinkle, 1994). Their use will have a profound effect on the treatment approach based on such interpretation. It is argued that standardized tests and assessment tools are used to evaluate performance skills and not behaviors. Yet, these tools can produce inaccurate data regarding performance skills. For example, the Denver Developmental Test, which has been standardized on a North American sample, may not hold true for an East Asian immigrant child. These children may be labeled as *developmentally delayed* on the basis of this test. Because of differences in child rearing practices and cultural behaviors, the attainment of developmental milestones is not necessarily the same for all populations.

Behaviors, whether typical of a bicultural encounter or not, affect the results of standardized assessment tools. Behaviors, such as eye contact, tone of voice, or greetings, are culturally dependent and varied. Providers run the risk of an incorrect evaluation if they interpret the behavior only on the basis of what it means in the mainstream culture (Cross, Bazron, Dennis, & Isaacs, 1989; Gaw, 1993). For example, when persons encounter a system or provider who is different from them, they will exhibit an adjustment in behavior. They are likely to be more reserved than usual; they may be apprehensive or fearful that the evaluator will judge them negatively; or they may try to fit in by displaying behaviors commonly attached to the mainstream culture. If the provider judges these persons on the basis of these behaviors, the results may be a mislabeling or misdiagnosis. Standardized tests and evaluations can be biased by misinterpretation of behaviors, language usage, and emotional expressiveness. This in turn may lead to inappropriate treatment strategies and an unsatisfactory therapeutic relationship.

Tests should be used as an aid to understanding the client. Using only the results of standardized tests and evaluations based on the dominant culture can create differences or mixed-matched outcome expectations between the client and provider. "Providers choosing to use a standard evaluation tool on a different population need to take an individual's sociocultural background into consideration in interpreting its score" (Paul, 1995, p. 158). Standardized tests and evaluations need to be interpreted in the context of the client's culture. Other forms of evaluation should be used in addition to standardized tools with ethnic and diverse populations.

Accurate evaluation is the first step to effective and culturally appropriate treatment delivery. This can lead to incompatibility between the client and health care provider in goal setting and treatment intervention. Since there is a paucity of culturally fair and culture-specific tests and evaluations, health care providers should continue to use standardized evaluations with culturally distinct clients, at the same time taking their sociocultural backgrounds and cultural foundations into consideration (Cross et al., 1989; Paul, 1995).

General Cultural Information

The need for general knowledge about other cultures fits into the reasoning processes the same way as the need for general medical knowledge. Cultural knowledge promotes understanding, sensitivity, and empathy. It is needed to recognize individual differences and similarities, affirm the culture of the person, and open the avenues of learning and growth for the provider. Information regarding the general characteristics and life experiences of different racial, ethnic, and cultural groups should *never* be used as a *cookbook* approach to treatment or clients. General cultural knowledge provides a starting point for gathering information, asking questions, and establishing a rapport with the client (Table 15). A general overview of basic cultural values, family roles and structures, re-

Table 15. Comparison of Cultural Foundations

Mainstream America	Ethnocultural Groups
Mastery over nature	Harmony with nature
Personal control over the environment	Fate
Doing—active	Being or being-in-becoming
Time dominates	Personal interaction dominates
Human equality	Hierarchy or rank or status
Individualism or privacy	Group welfare
Youth	Elders
Self-help	Birthright inheritance
Competition	Cooperation
Future orientation	Past or present orientation
Informality	Formality
Directness or openness or honesty	Indirectness or ritual or *face*
Practicality or efficiency	Idealism
Materialism	Spiritualism
Nature of man is good and bad	Nature of man is good

Note. The author created this table referencing two useful cultural competency resources: Randall-David, E. (1989). *Strategies for working with culturally diverse communities and clients*. Washington, DC: Association for the Care of Children's Health and Ho, M. K. (1987). *Family therapy with ethnic minorities*. Newbury Park, CA: Sage.
Table by Shirley A. Wells

ligious practices, time perceptions, communication styles, support networks, health practices and uses, and beliefs are helpful in

- interpreting evaluations and assessment tools,

- determining whether standard treatment methods and approaches need to be modified, and

- determining whether the use of Western standards, ethics, and ideas may negatively affect clients and their families.

Clinical Reasoning Process

Using the clinical reasoning process (Opacich, 1991) for clinical decision making, cultural queries can be easily incorporated (Table 16).

Table 16. Culture and the Clinical Reasoning Process

Phase I: Problem Setting

Client's Referral Information + General Cultural Knowledge = Initial Response

Initiate information about the client:

- Racial or ethnic identifier
- Age
- Gender
- Diagnosis or disability
- Medical history
- Family or social history (limited)

Provide clues to (narrative reasoning):

- What culturally sensitive approaches to take
- What additional information is needed regarding the client's occupational history, cultural background, life history, and values
- What potential cultural and performance problem(s) exist

Phase II: Framing and Delineating Problem

General Cultural Knowledge + Professional Knowledge = Preliminary Evaluation

Gather additional information about the client:

- Performance level
- Goals and concerns
- More family or social history
- Life experiences
- Present life situation
- Health beliefs
- Values

Provide clues to (interactive & procedural reasoning):

- The meaning of disease or disability to the client
- The interaction between the client and provider
- The provider's professional knowledge and understanding about the disease or disability

(Continued)

Phase I: Problem Setting

This is the initial evaluation phase. It is the "process by which data are gather, hypotheses formulated, and decisions are made for further action" (Opacich, 1991, p. 356). The information that is gathered during this phase guides the establishment of treatment goals and intervention. A general knowledge of the culture of the client regarding basic beliefs, values, and behaviors can determine whether standard treatment approaches should be modified at the onset. For example:

- In most ethnic cultures the elderly are addressed more formally than are younger persons.

Table 16. *(Continued)*

Phase III: Forming Hypotheses and Developing Intervention Plans

Client's Information + General Cultural Knowledge + Professional Knowledge = Cultural Treatment Strategies

Provide clues to (pragmatic reasoning):
- The health care provider's values, knowledge, abilities, and experiences
- The client's social functioning and financial resources
- The treatment environment and possibilities of treatment within a given environment

Phase IV: Implementing Treatment

Client's Information + General Cultural Knowledge + Professional Knowledge + Cultural Treatment Strategies = Beneficial Outcome

Gather information about the client's:
- Performance changes
- Personal cultural and lifestyle situation

Provide clues to (conditioning reasoning):
- The continuation or modification of treatment
- The future functioning of the client

Table by Shirley A. Wells

- African Americans tend to look at someone when they are talking and look away when listening.

- A highly casual manner should be avoided with Asian American clients.

- Conduct the interaction in the preferred language of the client if possible.

How you approach the person sets the stage for all therapeutic interactions as well as establishes the trust factor between the provider, client, and health system. Having a basic knowledge concerning cultural and ethnic groups and an awareness of your own values and biases creates a wide range of appropriate responses to the needs of the client. Culturally skilled and competent providers are aware of and comfortable with differences that exist between themselves and their clients. They are sensitive to circumstances that may suggest referral of clients to others for delivery of services.

Phase II: Framing and Delineating the Problem

This is the process of illuminating the problem(s) of the client. It entails the selection of assessment tools and instruments. In this phase the provider combines general cultural knowledge with his or her professional and technical knowledge. For example, in the Hispanic culture there is no differentiation between physical and emotional illness. The client may express physical complaints when, in fact, the cause is an emotional problem. The health care provider should not only look for physical causes, but also encourage the client to talk about why he or she is ill.

When selecting an evaluation strategy, the provider should be aware of the validity, reliability, and the test construction process of the instrument or tool. Many test instruments have not been standardized for ethnic populations. Therefore, caution should be used in the interpretation of their results. If cultural differences are not taken into account, inappropriate treatment strategies can be selected. Inquiring about the use of traditional *healing practices and healers* should also be done; otherwise they can alter the results of some standard tests and evaluations.

Constructing a narrative and life history of the client, whether formal or informal, allows the provider to frame the problems and limitations in a cultural context. This gives the provider a way to share his or her ideas about what is going on with a particular client with colleagues, to discuss specific client-centered issues with the family, and to plan culturally appropriate strategies with the treatment team members and other professionals. A working knowledge of sociocultural questions to ask is an essential skill for health care providers. One mechanism for learning about a client's life history, cultural beliefs, and attitudes toward illness and health is to use an opening statement and series of questions (Table 17).

Phase III: Forming Hypotheses and Developing Intervention Plans

This phase allows the provider to articulate and apply theoretical reasoning and understanding of the client's problem(s) from a contextual and cultural perspective. The provider should examine the specific client's known facts, general cultural information, and professional or technical data to develop goals and treatment strategies. This process will result in a better match with the client's expectations, which are grounded in cultural values and behaviors; and the health care provider's treatment expectations, which are grounded in his or her professional orientation. This type of integration increases the likelihood of accomplishing therapeutic goals, compliance with treatment requests,

Table 17. Eliciting Cultural Information in Clinical Interaction

Proposed Opening Statement

Mr. or Mrs. or Ms. _____, sometimes clients and health care providers have different ideas about health and diseases as well as outcome expectations. To design and provide individualized care, it is important for me to have a clear picture and understanding of your thoughts and concerns about this illness. I would like to ask you some questions about your culture, values, and beliefs. This way we can work together to improve your health or function and address your concerns.

Questions Regarding Current Illness

- What is your general understanding about your illness?
- What do you think caused your problem?
- Why do you think it started?
- How severe is your illness? How long do you think it will last?
- What are the main problems your illness has caused for you?
- Have you tried any home remedies, medicines, folk or traditional treatment for your illness? Did it help? Are you still using it or them?
- What type of treatment do you think you should receive?
- What results do you hope to receive from the treatment?
- Is there any other information that would be helpful in designing a workable treatment plan?

Questions Regarding Health Beliefs and Practices

- Do you adhere to a religious healing system (e.g., Seventh Day Adventist, West African voodoo, Fundamentalist sect, Pentecostal)?
- Do you adhere to a cultural healing system (e.g., Asian healing system, Raza or Latina curanderismo)?
- How is illness explained in your culture (e.g., germ theory, presence of evil spirits, imbalance between *hot* and *cold,* yin and yang, disequilibrium between nature and man)?
- Do you rely on cultural healers (e.g., medicine men, shaman, curandero, Chinese herbalist, spiritualist, minister, hougan [voodoo priest])?
- What types of cultural healing practices or remedies do you [family] practice? (e.g., massage to cure empacho, coining, wearing of talismans or charms for protection against illness)
- How would you describe a state of *wellness or good health?* A state of *poor health or illness?*

Questions Regarding Cultural Beliefs and Values

- Are there any taboos or restrictions on who can see a woman or man's body?
- Are there any taboos or other beliefs connected with mental illness?
- Describe your spirituality or religious practice or belief.
- What cultural, racial, or ethnic group do you identify with?
- How would you describe your family structure?
- What type of support system or network is available to you?
- Who is the primary decision maker in your family?

Table by Shirley A. Wells

and satisfaction with the treatment outcome for both the client and provider. This integration results in culturally appropriate strategies and intervention.

Phase IV: Implementing Treatment

During this phase the provider must monitor, reevaluate, and modify the treatment strategies. The provider continually and systemically collects specific information about not only performance changes but also cultural values, beliefs, and behaviors. If the treatment is not beneficial or in-line with the client's cultural expectations, the provider can alter or terminate the therapy.

Case Example

Phase I: Problem Setting

Client's Referral Information + General Cultural Knowledge = Initial Response

- Single, 29-year-old male
- Traumatic brain injury and right hemiparesis
- Asian American
- Lived alone; worked as a laborer

What do you know about the Asian American or Pacific Islander culture?

- The family system is extremely important. Various levels of acculturation. Generational diversity.
- Communication style—touching of strangers is inappropriate; eye-to-eye contact with a stranger is considered shameful; high value on emotional restraint; nonconfrontational; noncommunicative of personal feelings.
- Time perception—belief that time is flexible so there is no need to hurry
- Health practices—concept of yin–yang, meditation, healers, hot or cold theory, Western medicine
- Health beliefs—illness may result from bad conduct by an individual or family member

What initial approach should be used?

- Should avoid a highly casual manner. Be cautious about touching.

- Small talk at the beginning of a session will be considered good manners and keeps from appearing too rushed.

- Client may be hesitant to admit health problems. Encourage client to share his or her thoughts about illness.

- Client may think he or she is personally responsible for the illness. Careful explanation of the etiology of illness may be necessary.

What additional questions should be explored?

- What specific Asian group is the client a member of (e.g., Korean, Japanese, Vietnamese)?

Phase II: Framing and Delineating Problems

Client's Information + General Cultural Knowledge + Professional Knowledge = Preliminary Evaluation

Client's information.

- Motorcycle accident; did not wear helmet

- Second generation Cambodian American; demonstrates assimilative patterns

- Contributed much of his time to working in the family store

- Has completed high school, however, has expressed little interest in higher education

Professional knowledge.

- 2 months post injury; impaired gross and fine motor coordination

- Unable to perform some self-care activities

- Problems with memory, organization, and judgment

- Standard treatment approach emphasizes individual's independence and self-help

Cultural knowledge.

Khmer is the official language of Cambodia. Many speak this language at home. Children are fluent in speaking and writing English.

When interpreters are required for communication, most prefer same-gender interpreters.

When Cambodians greet each other, they will place their hands together and near their faces, and often state the greeting *chum reap sur.* They appreciate such a greeting from persons other than Cambodians as well.

Cambodian Americans value interdependency among family members, as members of an extended family are expected to share or pool resources to meet the needs of the family and its members. The family takes basic responsibility for the care of its members. The role of the sick person is viewed as dependent and passive, even to the extent of discouraging the sick person from physical self-help. It is believed that a person is ill because of the sins committed by the family members. The family is responsible for all decisions. The senior man is the head of the household. Relationships between the father and sons are especially emphasized. This relationship can be both a strength and source of conflict.

Most Cambodians are Buddhist and attend temple regularly. Rice is typically the base of each meal and is accompanied by a clear or vegetable soup, fish, or meat and vegetables (i.e., fresh and dried). Most families eat all three meals together.

It is very insulting to touch a person's head. This is considered the most important part of the body and the place where the spirit is found. Feet are considered the lowest in value of the body parts and it is insulting to point them at someone. While lying down, it is impolite to step over the feet and legs. When walking, it is impolite to walk in front of someone except children. It is impolite to have eye contact with someone who is older or someone who is considered a superior.

Cambodians have traditionally dealt with illness through self-care and self-medication. The assistance of a health practitioner is sought if his or her own remedies do not work. Traditional healers (i.e., a Khru Khmer) or spiritual healers may be sought for illness thought to be caused by spirits. Spirit possession or sickness may be the result of evil spells cast by another, mistakes made in various rituals through the life cycle, or neglect of rituals. Cupping, pinching, or rubbing are the most commonly used treatment strategies and are thought to restore balance by releasing excessive *air.* Western medicine is generally considered hot, and herbal remedies have cooling properties.

Western health care is confusing and overwhelming for many Cambodians. Language and cultural barriers, crowded waiting rooms, multiple interviews, mysterious procedures, and the somewhat abrupt behavior of personnel combine to make obtaining health care an unpleas-ant experience. Cambodians expect to receive medications for every ill-ness because it makes them feel like something is being done. Many Cambodians are hesitant to share the fact that they are using other forms of health care because they believe the person providing Western medical care will think it is wrong to use alternatives.

Some principle stressors are language barriers, limited education, fear of children becoming involved in gangs, and economic difficulties (Wetzel, 1995).

What are the preliminary problems?

• Motor functioning

• Impaired self-care skills

• Cognitive impairments

• Intrapersonal or interpersonal difficulties

• Productivity or return-to-work issues

• Cultural and ethical conflicts

Phase III: Forming Hypotheses and Developing Intervention Plans

Client's Information + General Cultural Knowledge + Professional Knowledge = Cultural Treatment Strategies

Cultural treatment strategies.

• Involve the family in the treatment process. Use them as aides.

• Teach the family members why independence in function is important and good for the client and family.

• Ascertain the family's perception of the cause(s) of the client's illness.

• Ascertain the family's practice of cultural traditional medicine. Work with traditional healers or diviners.

• Use a directive rather than a nondirective approach.

Phase IV: Implementing Treatment

Client's Information + General Cultural Knowledge + Professional Knowledge + Cultural Treatment Strategies = Beneficial Outcome

• Reevaluate and modify as needed

Cultural Approach to Healthy Delivery

In creating a multicultural approach to the delivery of care, three strategies should guide your action (Leininger, 1991):

1. Cultural Preservation or Maintenance

2. Cultural Negotiation or Accommodation

3. Cultural Repatterning or Restructuring

The client's beliefs, values, and practices should be preserved and incorporated into the intervention process as much as possible. This allows the person to be a partner in his or her health care, as well as encourages the ability to select the method(s) that work within their cultural context. Negotiation and accommodation should be used when there is a conflict between Western medical practice and the traditional health practice of the client. Both the provider and client should develop a plan that incorporates both approaches. This may mean modifying what is perceived as *best* practice or *optimal* treatment. Cultural repatterning and restructuring is used when a shift or change is needed for a client's overall health or safety. Why and how a certain cultural practice is detrimental to the health and safety of the client must be explained in terms that they understand. Discuss with the client how potential treatment outcomes may alter typical cultural roles and practices. Let the client decide when and to what extent he or she wishes to engage in the new behaviors (Wells, 1991).

In providing culturally sensitive intervention it is also important to become aware of the individual's inclination on issues of privacy, self-disclosure, familial power and distribution, and discussion of intimate matters with persons outside the family. Use an interpreter if you are not fluent or effective in the preferred language of the client. Avoid using family members as an interpreter if possible, for they are ill-prepared to deal with the complexity of medical terms and information. This situation could also change the role of the involved family member. Developing a wide variety of verbal and nonverbal responses facilitates the involvement of the client and family in the planning and implementation of the treatment program. Lastly, avoid patronizing or condescending approaches (Wells, 1991).

When a diversity or cultural issue interrupts the therapeutic communication, it is time to *LEARN—listen, explain, acknowledge, recommend,* and *negotiate* (Berlin & Fowkes, 1983):

- *Listen.* Learn to listen with sympathy and understanding to the client or family about their perception of the illness and problem. Concentrate on actively listening versus preparing your response. Respond to what is being said, as well as how it is being said. Listen for facts and feelings.

- *Explain.* In clear and everyday terms, explain your perceptions, as a health care provider, of the problem. Openly discuss your personal views and the sources of those views. Communicate the *cultural context,* as well as the *cultural effect,* of your advice and intervention. This type of discussion helps the client to better understand the options and resolve some ethical conflicts.

- *Acknowledge.* Admit and discuss the similarities and differences in the two perceptions. Acknowledge that some health beliefs and practices are derived from basic needs and may have little basis in reality. Some practices, which you may consider to be *primitive,* do serve a purpose for the person within the culture and must be respected.

- *Recommend.* Offer options or alternative treatment interventions. Suggest a number of ways in which the client might view a given treatment approach from your, as well as their, cultural point of view.

- *Negotiate.* Work out treatment options and come to an agreement. Allow the client to choose, as long the choice avoids harm. Go as far as your system will allow to accommodate the client's needs. If necessary, change the system.

For other specific treatment strategies, see Tables 18 and 19.

Summary

In the presence of cultural differences it is important that the health care provider serve as a *cultural broker* between the many cultures in the interaction. Integrating culture into the daily clinical reasoning process and activities allows the providers not only to bridge cultures, but also to use a *culturally holistic approach* to care. This permits each client to be seen as a person with his or her own identity, culture, experiences, background, and lifestyle. This moves the clinical intervention from a diagnostic approach to a client- or family-centered approach.

Accurate evaluation of the client is the first step to culturally appropriate treatment intervention. Review the cultural validity of the

Table 18. Creating a Multicultural Approach: Treatment Implications

African Americans or Blacks

- Involve the extended family in the treatment process.
- Identify the important decision maker and involve him or her in the treatment process.
- Address the elderly by their last name and title.
- Work within the religious belief system of the client. Involve the minister in the treatment process.
- Help the client identify the cause(s) of illness and the specific actions he or she can take.
- Focus on the immediate situation rather than future plans.
- Be aware that guilt may influence the client's perception of the illness.
- Give the client permission to have problems.
- Focus on survival issues.
- Use action- and task-oriented activities.
- Some clients may be reluctant to discuss family problems and personal relationships with outsiders.

Hispanic or Latino Americans

- Allow the client to define body space parameters.
- Address the elderly more formally than younger clients.
- Focus on the immediate solution rather than long-term goals.
- Be aware of the role(s) each family member plays.
- Encourage the client to talk about why he or she feels ill or depressed.
- Probe for the cause(s) of physical complaints.
- Conduct the session in the preferred language of the client.
- Use an interpreter.

Asian Americans or Pacific Islanders

- The family system is extremely important.
- Involve the family members in the treatment process. Use them as aides.
- Teach the family members why independence in function is important and good for the client and family.
- Avoid a highly casual manner. Be cautious about touching.
- Encourage clients to express their thoughts and to see themselves as equal partners with the practitioner.
- Small talk at the beginning of a session will be considered good manners and keeps from appearing too rushed.
- Females may experience conflictual thoughts between traditional roles and mainstream American women's roles.
- Ascertain the client's perception of the cause(s) of his or her illness.
- A directive rather than a nondirective approach should be taken.
- Encourage the client to begin to take initiative in making changes.

Native Americans or Alaska Natives

- Involve the extended family in the treatment process.
- Address the elderly in a formal way.
- Acknowledge and work with traditional *healers.*
- Focus on the immediate situation rather than future plans.

Table by Shirley A. Wells

Table 19. General Guidelines for Creating a Multicultural Approach and Environment

- Expect every client, family, colleague, or person to be different. *(A client is not just a client.)* Each person has his or her own identity, culture, ethnicity, background, experiences, and lifestyle.
- The culture and lifestyle of people do matter. Being *aware of* or *respecting* differences is not enough. Knowledge about and the effect of these differences must be integrated into all your interactions.
- Take into account the client's culture and how it affects and shapes the individual.
- Acknowledge that some health beliefs and practices are derived from basic needs and may have little basis in reality. Additionally, be aware that some practices you may consider to be *primitive* do serve a purpose for the person within the culture and must be respected.
- Be cognizant of gender and age. These characteristics do affect the clinician approach used, as well as the perceptions held by the client, family, or caregiver about the practitioner.
- Use good basic health care practices, such as completing a thorough evaluation with the client and the family, checking diet restrictions before planning or initiating a cooking activity, involving the client and the family in the program, and doing an evaluation of the home environment.
- Look for cues, both verbal and nonverbal, that will help you involve the client in the treatment session.
- Be flexible and adaptable in your treatment of the client and, by all means, avoid a *cookbook approach*.
- Be aware of your personal biases and how they may affect the therapeutic relationship.
- Do not misjudge people because of their accents or grammar.
- Avoid being patronizing or condescending. Use language that fosters trust and alliance.
- Use an interpreter if you are not fluent in the client's preferred language. If an interpreter is unavailable, learn basic words, phrases, or sentences in that language. This will show that you are making an effort to identify with the client.
- Be aware of discriminatory *intent* versus discriminatory *effect*.
- Be an agent of change.
- *Listening to* the client and being responsive to his or her needs is a demonstration of cultural competency. It is important to understand the view of the world from the perspective of the client, family, and caregiver.

Note: From *Creating a Multicultural Approach and Environment* video, 1996, Bethesda, MD: American Occupational Therapy Association. © 1996 by the American Occupational Therapy Association. Reprinted with permission.

standard assessment tools used. The result from these tools should be interpreted within the context of the client's culture. If the possibility of bias is present in the tool, acknowledge it in the documentation. It is also important to consider the environment in which the client functions. It may directly influence the client's ability to adhere to an intervention program

(Dyck, 1992). Keep in mind differences of communication style and expressions of emotions. These are directly influenced by culture, age, geography, ethnicity, race, gender, and generational conditioning or acculturation.

Do not be afraid to ask culturally specific questions. The possession of general cultural information and knowledge only provides a starting place for communication and interaction. Exploring the individual's values, beliefs, environment, and life history promotes practitioner–client collaboration and builds a relationship based on mutual respect and equality. Potential cultural issues, concerns, and conflicts must be addressed upfront to ensure that the clinical interaction will be beneficence to all parties—client, health care provider, and medical system—involved.

Culture and Clinical Practice Worksheet

Directions

Using the following case study, place the information in the appropriate clinical reasoning phase. Based on the case study, also include additional information that you may know about the ethnic or racial group.

Case Study

Angie, a 48-year-old Mexican American female, was found by her daughter at home with a broken hip. This is her third bone fracture—right wrist and left humerus—in the past 12 months. She was diagnosed with osteoporosis, a chronic disabling condition.

Social history. Angie is the daughter of migrant farm workers. She has been married for 30 years and is the mother of four daughters and two sons ranging in age from 16 to 25. She has worked as a laborer and store clerk. She is currently not working. She lives with her husband and four of her children in a one level three-bedroom house.

Physical. Angie has a family history of diabetes and high blood pressure. She is alert and oriented. Examination revealed limited active range of motion of the right hip in all planes, increased pain with all movement, decreased right lower extremity weight bearing, and difficulty walking. She also has decreased muscle strength of both upper extremities and limited range of motion of the right wrist. She has been placed on a calci-um-enriched diet and supplement.

Phase I: Problem Setting

[Client's Referral Information + General Cultural Knowledge = Initial Response]

- What culturally sensitive approach should you take?

- What additional information is needed regarding the client's occupational history?

- What potential cultural and performance problem(s) exist?

Phase II: Framing and Delineating the Problem

[General Cultural Knowledge + Professional Knowledge + Preliminary Evaluation]

- What health beliefs may this client have about her disease or illness?

- What type of client–provider interaction can be expected (your beliefs and values versus the client's)?

- What professional knowledge and understanding about the diseases or illness do you bring?

Phase III: Forming Hypotheses and Developing Intervention Plans

[Client's Information + General Cultural Knowledge + Professional Knowledge = Cultural Treatment Strategies]

- What are the client's possible social functioning and financial resources?

- What experiences, knowledge, values, and abilities do you (the provider) bring to the treatment environment?

- What possible treatment or intervention is needed for this client?

Phase IV: Implementing the Treatment or Intervention

[Client's Information + General Cultural Knowledge + Professional Knowledge + Cultural Treatment Strategies = Beneficial Outcome]

- What is the future functioning of this client?

- What cultural issues may affect or change your treatment strategies?

References

American Occupational Therapy Association. (1996). Creating a Multicultural Approach and Environment [Video]. Bethesda, MD: Author.

Barney, K. (1991). From Ellis Island to assisted living: Meeting the needs of older adults from diverse cultures. *American Journal of Occupational Therapy, 45,* 586–593.

Berlin, E. A., & Fowkes, W. C. (1983). A teaching framework for cross-cultural health care—Application in family practice. *Western Journal of Medicine, 12*(139), 93–98.

Christiansen, C., & Baum, C. (1991). *Occupational therapy: Overcoming human performance deficits.* Thorofare, NJ: Slack.

Clark, F. (1993). Occupation embedded in a real-life: Interweaving occupational science and occupational therapy. 1993 Eleanor Clarke Slagle lecture. *American Journal of Occupational Therapy, 47,* 1067–1078.

Crepeau, E. B. (1991). Achieving intersubjective understanding: Examples from an occupational therapy treatment session. *American Journal of Occupational Therapy, 45,* 1016–1025.

Cross, T. L., Bazron, B. J., Dennis, K. W., & Isaacs, M. R. (1989). *Towards a culturally competent system of care, volume I.* Washington, DC: CASSP Technical Assistance Center.

Dillard, M., Andonian, L., Flores, O., Lai, L., MacRae, A., & Shakir, M. (1992). Culturally competent occupational therapy in a diversely populated mental health setting. *American Journal of Occupational Therapy, 46,* 721–726.

Dresser, N. (1996). *Multicultural manners: New rules of etiquette for a changing society.* New York: Wiley.

Dyck, I. (1992). Managing chronic illness: An immigrant woman's acquisition and use of health care knowledge. *American Journal of Occupational Therapy, 46,* 696–704.

Fitzgerald, M. H. (1992). Multicultural clinical interaction. *Journal of Rehabilitation, 58,* 38–42.

Fleming, M. H. (1991a). The therapist with the three-track mind. *American Journal of Occupational Therapy, 45,* 1007–1014.

Fleming, M. H. (1991b). Clinical reasoning in medicine compared to clinical reasoning in occupational therapy. *American Journal of Occupational Therapy, 45,* 1007–1015.

Gaw, A. (1993). *Culture, ethnicity, and mental illness.* Washington, DC: American Psychiatric Press.

Good, D. (1996). Cultural sensitivity: Integrating cultural concepts into clinical practice. *WORK: A Journal of Prevention, Assessment, & Rehabiliation, 6,* 61–65.

Harborview Medical Center, University of Washington. Retrieved from: http://healthlinks.washington.edu/clinical/ethnomed/cambcp.html

Hinkle, J. (1994). Practitioners and cross-cultural assessment: A practical guide to information and training. *Measurement and Evaluation in Counseling and Development, 27,* 103–115.

Ho, M. K. (1987). *Family therapy with ethnic minorities.* Newbury Park, CA: Sage.

Jackson, J., Carlson, M., Mandel, D., Zemke, R., & Clark, F. (1998). Occupation in lifestyle redesign: The well elderly study occupational therapy program. *American Journal of Occupational Therapy, 52,* 326–336.

Jang, Y. (1995). Chinese culture and occupational therapy. *British Journal of Occupational Therapy, 58*(3), 103–106.

Kavanagh, K. H. (1991). Social and cultural influences: Values and beliefs. In J. L. Creasia & B. Parker (Eds.), *Conceptual foundations of professional nursing practice* (pp. 167–210). St. Louis, MO: C. V. Mosby.

Kavanagh, K. H., & Kennedy, P. H. (1992). *Promoting cultural diversity: Strategies for health care professionals.* Newbury Park, CA: Sage.

Kelly, L. (1995). What occupational therapists can learn from traditional healers. *British Journal of Occupational Therapy, 58*(3), 111–114.

Kielhofner, G. (1995). *A model of human occupation: Theory and application* (2nd ed.). Baltimore: Williams & Wilkins.

Krefting, L. H., & Krefting, D. V. (1991). Cultural influences on performance. In C. Christiansen & C. Baum (Eds.), *Occupational therapy: Overcoming human performance deficits.* Thorofare, NJ: Slack.

Kreps, G. L., & Kunimoto, E. N. (1994). *Effective communication in multicultural health care settings.* Newbury Park, CA: Sage.

Lawlor, M. C., & Mattingly, C. F. (1998). The complexities embedded in family-centered care. *American Journal of Occupational Therapy, 52,* 259–267.

Leininger, M. M. (1991). *Culture, care, diversity, and universality: A theory of nursing.* New York: National League of Nursing Press.

Leininger, M. M. (1988). Leininger's theory of nursing: Cultural care diversity and universality. *Nursing Science Quarterly, 1*(4), 152–160.

Levine, R. (1984). The cultural aspects of home care delivery. *American Journal of Occupational Therapy, 38,* 734–738.

Mattingly, C., & Fleming, M. H. (1994). *Clinical reasoning: Forms of inquiry in a therapeutic practice.* Philadelphia: F. A. Davis.

McCormack, G. L. (1987). Culture and communication in the treatment planning for occupational therapy with minority clients. *Occupational Therapy in Health Care, 4,* 17–36.

Mosey, A. C. (1986). *Psychosocial components of occupational therapy.* New York, NY: Raven Publications.

Neistadt, M. E. (1996). Teaching strategies for the development of clinical reasoning. *American Journal of Occupational Therapy, 50,* 676–684.

Neistadt, M. E. (1998a). Teaching clinical reasoning as a thinking frame. *American Journal of Occupational Therapy, 3,* 221–233.

Neistadt, M. E., Wight, J., & Mulligan, S. E. (1998b). Clinical reasoning case studies as teaching tools. *American Journal of Occupational Therapy, 2,* 125–132.

Opacich, K. J. (1991). Assessment and informed decision-making. In C. Christiansen & C. Baum (Eds.), *Occupational therapy: Overcoming human performance deficits.* Thorofare, NJ: Slack.

Parham, D. (1987). Nationally speaking—toward professionalism: The reflective therapist. *American Journal of Occupational Therapy, 41,* 555–561.

Paul, S. (1995). Culture and its influence on occupational therapy evaluation. *Canadian Journal of Occupational Therapy, 62*(3), 154–161.

Pope-Davis, D. B., Prietor, L. R., Whitaker, C. M., & Pope-Davis, S. A. (1993). Exploring multicultural competencies of occupational therapists: Implications for education and training. *American Journal of Occupational Therapy, 47,* 838–844.

Randall-David, E. (1989). *Strategies for working with culturally diverse communities and clients.* Washington, DC: Association for the Care of Children's Health.

Rogers, J. C. (1983). Clinical reasoning: The ethics, science, and art. 1983 Eleanor Clarke Slagle lecture. *American Journal of Occupational Therapy, 37,* 601–616.

Schell, B. A., & Cervero, R. M. (1993). Clinical reasoning in occupational therapy: An integrative review. *American Journal of Occupational Therapy, 47,* 1033–1037.

Skawski, K. A. (1987). Ethnic/racial considerations in occupational therapy: A survey of attitudes. *Occupational Therapy in Health Care, 4,* 37–46.

Slater, D. Y., & Cohn, E. S. (1991). Staff development through analysis of practice. *American Journal of Occupational Therapy, 45,* 1038–1044.

Wells, S. A. (1991). Clinical considerations in treating minority women who are disabled. *Occupational Therapy Practice, 2*(4), 13–22. Gaithersburg, MD: Aspen Publishers.

Wells, S. A. (1994). *A multicultural education and resource guide for occupational therapy educators and practitioners.* Bethesda, MD: American Occupational Therapy Association.

Wells, S. A. (1995, December). Creating a culturally competent workforce. *Caring Magazine,* 44–48.

Wetzel, L. (1995). *Cambodian cultural profile.* Ethnic medicine guide. Harborview Medical Center, University of Washington. Retrieved from: http://healthlinks.washington.edu/clinical/ethnomed/cambcp.html

CHAPTER FIFTEEN

Clinical Applications and Case Studies

Read each case and answer the questions. In a small group or with your cultural mentor, discuss the questions and your responses and reactions. Identify those areas where you need to seek more information, develop skills, or perform a self-evaluation to act in a culturally competent manner.

Case A: Description

Jim Crowfeet, a 25-year-old Creek Indian man, sustained an internal head injury in a motorcycle accident. A 1973 graduate of a Georgia high school, Jim continued his education at a Georgia vocational technical college. He graduated in June 1975 with an Associate of Arts Degree (AA) in occupational therapy. During high school and technical college he worked part-time (20 to 30 hours per week) for a sporting equipment manufacturer. Upon obtaining his AA degree and certification for occupational therapy, he was employed full-time as an occupational therapy assistant in a work-hardening facility.

Before the accident, Jim had his own apartment. He is the second oldest in a five-child family with an older brother, three younger sisters, and his mother. His father died when he was five years old.

After stabilization at an Atlanta medical center, Jim was transferred to the Roosevelt Warm Springs Rehabilitation Center. Total family support services were provided, and *cautiously received*, as Jim's mother was skeptical of the rehabilitation system, overall. To further compound the family's distrust issue, the center has documented difficulties in relating to Native Americans.

Source for case studies H, I, J, and K: From *Multicultural manners: New rules of etiquette for a changing society* (pp. 60–61, 80–81) by N. Dresser, 1996, New York: John Wiley & Sons. © 1996 by John Wiley & Sons. Reprinted with permission of John Wiley & Sons, Inc. Additional case studies courtesy of Roxie M. Black.

Some results of the closed head injury that Jim sustained include the following:

• Denial of permanence of injury

• Undue optimism

• Impairment in expressive dimension of communication or memory

• Frustration and confusion

• Time, relationship, and trust issues compounded

His pre-injury personality was friendly, outgoing, self-motivating, and determined.

Questions

• What are the general cultural values, attitudes, and behaviors of this ethnic group?

• What are the potential cultural barriers to care?

• What are the potential ethical and moral conflicts?

• What are some potential cultural treatment strategies?

• What additional information is needed?

Case B: Description

Maria Elena, a 52-year-old Mexican American woman, was recently hospitalized with slurred speech and weakness of the left side of her body. She has a long history of hypertension and myocarditis.

Maria Elena had worked as a migrant field hand from the age of 12 through 25, but she had trouble doing this work because it required prolonged standing and walking (one leg is 3 inches shorter than the other). After leaving her job as a field hand, she moved to Brownsville, Texas, in the Rio Grande Valley and worked as a part-time maid averaging 2 to 3 days a week.

At the age of 27, she married and moved to Houston, Texas. She had three children—two sons and one daughter. Spanish was the primary language spoken in her house. Her daughter usually acted as the go-between for communication outside the home.

Questions

- What are the general cultural values, attitudes, and behaviors of this ethnic group?
- What are the potential cultural barriers to care?
- What are the potential ethical and moral conflicts?
- What are some potential cultural treatment strategies?
- What additional information is needed?

Case C: Description

Wind-Wolf, a 5-year-old Creek Indian boy, was born and raised on the reservation. He has black hair, dark brown eyes, and an olive complexion. And like many Indian children his age, he is shy and quiet in the classroom. He is in kindergarten and has already been labeled a *slow learner.*

If you ask him how many months there are in a year, he says *13.* He has trouble writing his name on a piece of paper. He does not engage in conversation with the other children or do class activities. He responds only when called upon. When you speak to him, Wind-Wolf does not maintain eye contact. Instead he looks down at the floor. He has difficulty grasping the English language. And he is not as fluent in English as the teacher thinks he should be at this age.

Questions

- What are some generally held cultural values and beliefs about children for this ethnic group?
- What are the potential cultural barriers to services?
- What are the developmental issues?
- What are the potential ethical and moral conflicts?
- What are some potential cultural treatment strategies?
- What additional information is needed?

Case D: Description

Mary Malone, a 73-year-old White American woman, was brought to Three Rivers Community Mental Health Clinic by her friend,

Jane Houston. Mary has become more and more despondent since the death of Lucy Stephenson, her companion of 18 years. Mary and Lucy had shared the maintenance of a small house, which Jane reports is now dirty and unkempt. It appears that Mary also has not been taking care of herself or the five cats that live with her.

Mary's only child is a married son who lives three hours away and does not seem interested in helping his mother. Jane pulls you aside to tell you that he is "very religious" and did not approve of his mother's relationship with Lucy. When you ask if it was a lesbian relationship, Jane appears uncomfortable, turns red, and does not really answer.

After another half hour of interviewing Mary with Jane's help, you realize that the advice most people have been giving Mary is that she just has to "get over" Lucy's death and get on with her life.

Questions

- What are the potential cultural barriers to services for Mary?

- What are the general cultural values, attitudes, and behaviors of and for the homosexual community?

- Are there additional cultural and moral barriers or expectations regarding Mary's sexuality given her age?

- Are you comfortable talking openly with Mary about her relationship with Lucy? Why or why not?

- What is the best treatment approach to follow with Mary?

- Will you try to influence Mary's son to help support her? How?

Case E: Description

Mr. Yeaton, a 54-year-old Nigerian man, has an aggressive T-cell lymphoma and underwent emergency for acute cholecystitis; during the surgery he was placed on a respirator. The physician had difficulty weaning the ventilator, and it became apparent that the client has extensive lung involvement with the lymphoma.

After several days, the physician informed the son and daughter that the client's survival and chance of getting off the ventilator might be improved if he underwent chemotherapy. Given the son and daughter's opposition to any direct communication with the client regarding his condition, the oncologist was unwilling to initiate chemotherapy. However, the oncologist firmly stated that the client must know the diagnosis, as well as the risks and benefits of the proposed treatment, so that treatment could be initiated in an ethical way. The son and daughter refused the request to reveal the diagnosis and prognosis to their father.

After several extended consultations with the son and daughter and health care team regarding cultural views and beliefs, the oncologists agreed that the son and daughter could act as proxy decision makers in signing the consent agreement for chemotherapy. After the treatment, the client came off the ventilator, went into remission, and was able to return to his native home of Nigeria.

Questions

• What are some potential cultural barriers to services?

• What ethical or moral conflict does the health care professional face?

• Whose cultural values would you follow? Why?

Case F: Description

Chi-Kwan, a 38-year-old Chinese American woman, has been admitted to the hospital for surgery the next day. Upon entering her room she noticed that the foot of the bed is facing the doorway. She asks, "Can this bed be turned to face south or can I be placed in another room that does face south?" The nurse tries to explain that all the rooms on the floor are set-up the same way, and it would be impossible to rearrange the bed. Chi-Kwan insists that the bed is changed or she could not stay at the hospital.

Questions

• What possible cultural practices or issues are at play here (i.e., principles of feng shui)?

• How would you handle the situation?

• What intervention option is available to you?

Case G: Description

Abdul is a 37-year-old Northern African immigrant who was admitted to the hospital two weeks ago as the result of a hit-and-run accident. He sustained multiple fractures of arm, hand, ribs, and hips on his left side and a mild concussion. He is presently in the New England Rehabilitation Center receiving occupational and physical therapy, and nursing care.

Abdul is single and educated, and had been working as a night clerk in a local hotel when the accident occurred. He had been living in a boarding home near his work. Social services has been working with him regarding placement following his hospital stay.

A new therapist, Milly Tidwell, has just been assigned to Abdul's case. While reading his records she learns that he is HIV positive. There is no mention of his sexual orientation in the chart. Milly is from a small conservative New England town and harbors strong moral convictions about issues of homosexuality. She assumes that Abdul is gay, and tells her supervisor that morally she cannot work with him and that ethically it would not be right to not offer him equal and unbiased care.

Questions

• What are the cultural beliefs that are influencing Milly?

• Are there additional questions she should ask about Abdul's culture?

• What are the ethical principles that are affected by Milly's decision?

• Is Milly correct to ask to be withdrawn from this case?

• What would you do in this case? Why?

Case H: Description

The new emergency room intern, Dr. Jones, is frantically trying to save the life of 75-year-old Mr. Cohen, an Orthodox Jew. Seriously injured in an auto accident, the elderly man is bleeding profusely. In spite of Dr. Jones' efforts, the old man dies.

When the physician steps into the waiting room to notify the family, they ask him to remove his bloodstained trousers. Shocked by such a request, he refuses. This agitates the grieving family. His coworkers beseech him to comply with the family's demand. This astounds Dr. Jones. He sees no sense in changing his clothes in the middle of his shift.

Questions

• What cultural beliefs or practices are at play here?

- What cultural knowledge and skills do you need to resolve this situation?

- How would you handle this situation?

Case I: Description

Nurse Jackson, a 48-year-old Southern, White American man, is in charge in the hospital emergency room, and phones are ringing off the hook. A teenager is now on the line panicked about her father. He has just cut himself with an electric garden edger and is bleeding profusely.

Jackson questions the girl about how the injury is being treated. Jackson is astounded when he hears that the grandmother has put honey on the wound. Jackson urges the girl to have someone drive the father to the hospital at once. He needs *real* medical care.

When the family arrives, Jackson expects that the father will need stitches, but he is amazed when he sees his hand. The bleeding has stopped, and the wound has already begun to close—no stitches are necessary.

Questions

- What cultural practices or home remedies are at play here?

- What other ailments are often treated with food?

- Should you as a health care provider dissuade clients from using folk remedies?

- What folk remedies do you use for treating hiccups, a bee sting, or a fever?

Case J: Description

You are a health care provider of African descent who has been assigned a client on the rehabilitation unit of a rural hospital. You know from the physician's order that the client's name is John Weston. He is 35 years old and has kidney diseases with dialysis. He has just been transferred to the rehabilitation unit from a major urban hospital. You have been asked to complete an evaluation of the client and evaluate his or her potential for home health care.

On your way to the client's room you run into one of the therapists who will be working with John. "Did you know that John is an active member of the Ku Klux Klan?" he says. "He is very vocal about his beliefs. I would not go into his room if I were of your ethnic background."

Questions

- What might be your first reaction to discovering that the client is a Klansman?

- What fears or concerns might you have about treating this person?

- How does the comment from the therapist make you feel? How would you handle your feeling when working with this client?

- What is your ethical responsibility to providing quality care to this client?

Case K: Description

Judy, a 25-year-old woman, was admitted to the psychiatric unit after being arrested for arson when she set fire to the local soup kitchen. She was diagnosed with schizophrenia. Her chart reveals that she is of biracial heritage; her mother is White, and her father is Haitian. She has lived with her parents off and on in a small midwestern town. Judy frequently traveled to the city and stayed for extended periods of time. She was often picked up by the police for loitering, panhandling, and creating a public disturbance. This is her first serious offense.

The mother reported that Judy had been a happy, caring, and studious person who wanted to be a teacher. She was attending the local college until about five years ago. She began to exhibit a variety of behaviors, such as talking to herself, fascination with fire, and hearing voices. She would have occasional outbursts about her White half abusing the Black half. Upon admission to the unit she exhibited a flat affect, immobility, and difficulty organizing her thoughts.

Her parents often commented that Judy's problems were caused by the stress of being biracial. They had failed her by insisting that she did not identify with any one racial group. They thought that evil spirits possessed their daughter and the only hope was an intervention by a voodoo priest.

Questions

- How does this situation challenge or fit with your values and belief system?

- What cultural biases might interfere with your interaction with the parents? Why or why not?

- How would you advise this family? How would you support the client?

- Whose cultural value system would you use to evaluate the client? Whose system would you promote to the client?

- Would you be willing to work with a voodoo priest? Why or why not?

Case L: Description

Mrs. Garcia, a 32-year-old female recovering from a spinal fusion, tells her morning nurse Shirley how hungry she is. Later when Shirley comes to check on her, she sees that the client has not touched her orange juice, cold cereal, and milk. "I thought you were hungry," says Shirley.

"I am, but the food is cold," says Mrs. Garcia. "Of course it is," says Shirley.

"I can't eat cold food," says Mrs. Garcia. Shirley is baffled.

Questions

- What cultural health belief system does this client subscribe to?

- What questions might the nurse ask to clarify this situation?

- What cultural knowledge does the nurse need to gather? How will she find the information needed?

Reflections of Two Lifelong Learners

V

". . . the key to transforming our hearts and minds is to have an understanding of the way our thoughts and emotions work . . . the way to examine how thoughts and emotions arise in us is through introspection. . . ."

—the Dalai Lama

Objectives

The information in this section is intended to help the reader

• recognize that the development of cultural competence is a lifelong process,

• understand how a personal narrative can reflect the process of cultural competency development, and

• recognize that there are multiple similarities between people of different cultures

CHAPTER SIXTEEN

The Ongoing Journey of a White Woman Truth-Seeker

The answer to the question of how I arrived here, at this place in time with these interests and beliefs, is not always clear to me; but I will try to reconstruct the journey as clearly as possible for you, the reader. I must admit to some trepidation in doing so, however, because it leaves me feeling vulnerable. After all, I am White American and privileged, and my story may offend some. Given that caveat, I will take my courage in hand and begin.

I was born in 1946, the first of the baby-boomer generation, after WWII. My brother was 3 1/2 years older than I, and we were part of a working class, rural family from Northern Maine. Both my parents worked hard for what we had, and although I recognize now how little that actually was, at the time I never felt deprived. Growing up, I was not aware of people who were different from me, with the exception of the numerous Franco Americans in the area who spoke French. I remember my family making fun of the *Frenchies*. Although Loring Air Force Base was not far from where we lived in Presque Isle and Mapleton, and there must have been men and families of color on base and in town, I have no recollection of actually *seeing* or noticing them. Perhaps I was blind to skin tones as a child, or maybe I was taught that persons of color were or should be invisible to me.

When I was 9 years old my parents divorced, which was not the common occurrence that it is today. My brother and I lived with my mother, who as a single parent without help from any child support, worked doubly hard to make ends meet. It must have been very difficult for her, and I was vaguely aware of her struggles then, but her love for us and her determination to give us whatever we needed again kept us from being aware that we had less than our friends. In retrospect, I now recognize that my strong feminist values began to develop as I observed the courage and strength of my mother during those years.

During and after the time of my parents' divorce we moved often, trying to find a locale where my mother could find a good paying job, or a home that we could afford, or to settle in with a new stepfather.

By the time I was 17, I had moved 18 times, all within the state of Maine! I became adept at meeting all sorts of new people, and used humor often to *break into* a new group. Luckily, my brother and I were good students and always were able to excel in whichever school system we found ourselves. Perhaps it was during all this moving that I began to appreciate the differences among people. Or perhaps it happened because when I found myself alone in a new community I would seek out the local library and lose myself in numerous books describing people and places so different from me.

Nevertheless, as I was preparing to apply to colleges, I knew I wanted a large, city university where I could be exposed to all sorts of new places and people. I never considered myself racist nor privileged at that point, and I prided myself on my openness. When I arrived at Boston University (BU), I was as overwhelmed as I was exhilarated! The diversity in the student body thrilled me! I met my first African Americans, Jews, Hispanics, and persons from wealthy families. I tried my first *foreign* foods. My favorite class was cultural anthropology! I was discussing existentialism as the Vietnam War accelerated, and I was feeling quite cosmopolitan! Quite a change for a naive, sheltered young woman from Rockland, Maine!

My interactions with a diverse group of people also forced me to be more introspective. I remember literally bumping into an African American man, a very dark-skinned African American man, in the stacks in the BU library one winter evening. I was not only startled, I became immediately aware of being irrationally afraid, and then felt guilty for thinking that way. I realized that I was afraid simply because of the color of his skin. It was my first awareness of my own racism, and I felt ashamed. I could not understand how this had happened! I had always thought I was so open-minded and welcoming to others. I realize now, of course, that no one can escape having racist and sexist thoughts in this society that is so oppressive to those outside of the dominant group; but at that time, the *library experience* was an epiphany to me. Being raised in a traditional-thinking family, living in many conservative small towns, and attending a fundamentalist church had made an unconscious effect on my beliefs and values. Although I had worked hard to think beyond the narrow boundaries that guarded my beliefs, the conservative, ethnocentric viewpoint of my culture and of our society had provided the foundation for my thinking. And I was not happy with it!

I would like to tell you that I suddenly *saw the light* and was magically transformed into a culturally competent, diversity-embracing, tol-

erant, and pluralistic thinker at that point, but I'm afraid I cannot. Instead, I married a hard-working, extremely conservative, patriotic man,
and spent the next two years in Germany where he was stationed in the
Army. Living and traveling in Europe in 1969 and 1970 was wonderful!
It fed my need for learning about other cultures and people, but it kept
us out of the United States during a period of upheaval. We missed much
of what happened during the Civil Rights and Women's Rights movements, and we missed Woodstock! Any information we received about
the United States was from newspapers where the stories were filtered
through the very conservative viewpoint of the U.S. military system. I
began to mouth the sayings and words espoused by my husband and his
Army buddies, and I did very little thinking for myself at this time.

After returning to the States, and my husband's subsequent dis-
charge from the military, we developed our careers and began our family, and the difference in my attitude and my husband's regarding diverse
people and other important issues became more and more apparent. I realize now that his very conservative viewpoints were the impetus to make
me evaluate my own values. I recognized the need to further my education, and I began a master's degree in adult education in 1984. In a
course on adult development, with a focus on women's development, I
found that the feminist literature *spoke to me* in a way that nothing else
had. The words of Miller, Friedan, Woolf, Gilligan, and others articulated what I had been thinking but had been unable to say. I immersed myself in feminist literature, and I applied it by beginning dialogues and
developing special programs on gender at the Univeristy of New England
(UNE) where I was then employed as a faculty member in the occupational therapy program. In 1992, I and three other feminist colleagues at
UNE co-edited a special issue of the *American Journal of Occupational
Therapy* on *Feminism, an Inclusive Perspective.* Although controversial
at the time, this special issue opened a dialogue about women's issues in
the occupational therapy profession that continues today.

As I furthered my studies in the feminist literature, I realized that
it generally portrayed a very White, middle-class perspective of American
women. I then began to broaden the scope of my reading to authors who
were women of color, and then to a variety of multicultural and critical
pedagogy authors. As I began to more clearly articulate my viewpoint on
gender, diversity, and social justice, the discrepancy between my beliefs
and values and those of my still very conservative husband became too
wide and after 23 years of marriage, we divorced. It was at that time that
I truly felt free to *follow my passion* in my study of multiculturalism and

diversity issues. A frustration for me was living in Maine where there is limited racial diversity. It was sometimes difficult to know about diversity when I experienced only segments of it. To learn, however, I turned to my usual approach to inquiry—reading. Sometimes I accomplished this in a formal manner by taking classes that focused on gender and diversity as a factor of analysis. Most of the time, however, I learned by reading on my own, talking about what I had read with my friends and colleagues, and infusing the content into the classes that I taught. I learned a tremendous amount about diversity and White racism from my students, the majority of whom are White American, and continued to develop skills when I also made mistakes as I learned about the best ways to present these issues in class.

I constantly struggle with the fact that I am White American and teaching mostly White American students about diversity. Is this arrogant or presumptuous? After much analysis, supported by my reading, I believe now that it is not. Although I have not experienced the kind of racism that persons of color have, nor the discrimination faced by lesbian women and gay men, I have dealt with other issues of oppression and can begin to understand. I do not try to speak for groups other than my own, but I can bring to class voices of others who can speak for themselves, either in person or in literature and books. And I can present facts and theories for students to grapple with, as I have done.

Additionally, I have sought out other ways to express my new thinking. With encouragement from my colleague Jan Froehlich, I became a member of the National Coalition Building Institute team at UNE. This is an international organization that offers prejudice reduction and embracing diversity workshops. I also was instrumental in infusing issues of gender, race, and class in the revision of the UNE core curriculum.

Seven years after receiving my master's degree, I realized again that I wanted and needed to continue my education. In 1996 I was matriculated at Lesley College in Cambridge, Massachusetts, in a doctoral program where I could more formally study diversity issues. The Ph.D. in Educational Studies is a self-designed (with the exception of four required core courses) program of study where I am focusing on transformative curricula for health professionals.

Along the way I met Shirley Wells, and despite the differences in our backgrounds, we found that we were *kindred spirits*. It has always amazed me how much our values and beliefs coincide. I have learned a lot from Shirley, and I believe this is mutual. This book is the culmination of our joint efforts to share some of what we have lived and learned about diversity and culture.

But the journey does not end here. Studying about diversity, multiculturalism, and cultural competence has made me realize how much there is yet to know and learn. Because diversity is interdisciplinary in nature, it is impossible to begin to keep up with the burgeoning literature of the field. I have found myself reading feminist literature, theory and application of multicultural education, the theory of critical pedagogy, literacy and linguistics, educational theory, and more. As the field grows, more disciplines emerge, such as cultural studies, communication ethics, and liberation theology. It is at the same time exciting and overwhelming, but it is never boring! As I continue to learn about groups other than my own, I continue to learn more about who I am and why I am the person I have become. I have learned no longer to feel guilty about being White American, but continue to try to make a difference as a White American ally to others. Social justice is vital to me and, although I do not see myself as a social activist, I believe that as an occupational therapy educator and administrator I am in a position to develop curricula that shares this knowledge and raises the consciousness of my students.

Am I culturally competent? Probably not fully, but I am becoming. It is a constant challenge, and I expect that I will be forever learning and growing in this area. My invitation to you is that you join me in the journey.

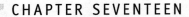

CHAPTER SEVENTEEN

Going Beyond "Awareness of" and "Sensitive to"

"There are two strikes against me when I come up to bat.
One strike for being female. One strike for being Black. So,
I stand up tall, through it all, my head up high, 'cause I
know that I'll be female and Black 'til the day I die."

—*Attala Giles & Gladys Knight*

The commitment to becoming an individual who is culturally adept takes a lifetime. The road is challenging, adventurous, and interesting to say the least. It has no specific beginning and no specific ending. It is a journey of learning, risking, exploring, and changing. It is easy to find comfort in what we know what we believe, and how we think and react. The difficulty is to be knowledgeable about a variety of beliefs. The challenge is to be cognizant of the effects of our interactions and approaches on others. The test is to try on different ideas, perceptions, customs, values, and lifestyles.

For me the journey to become culturally competent spans many years and many miles. It has introduced me to a variety of people and cultures, both here and abroad. It has taken me from the urban inner city of Dallas to the Navajo Indian reservation, the coldness of Minneapolis, to the border towns of El Paso and Brownsville, to rural America, and the streets of England and Germany. It is a journey that I take each day with every encounter or interaction. My journey began in the early 1960s, in an urban city, in an African American community. Within this environment there were plenty of African American role models—teachers, shop owners, media personalities, ministers, and doctors. There was a sense of community, belonging, and fitting in. It was within this setting that the foundation for accepting others originated.

To Learn

A willingness to learn is the first component of becoming culturally competent. We all are cultural beings with our own identities, cultures, lifestyles, and values. These things are learned very early in life. They shape who we are, how we react, and our initial view of the world. For me, this component started with learning that I was part of a family with customs, rituals, and values. I was part of an extended family that included sisters, brothers, aunts, uncles, cousins, and friends. And they all had "a say" about everyone's life. Education, hard work, and perseverance were valued. These values provided mobility to move onward and upward, power to expand and inspire, and information to continue to grow on. Respect, honor, and remembrance of the elders were taught. Through the "Liberation" ritual the elders are recognized for their contributions, endurance, and wisdom. For without their struggles and shoulders, where will we stand, or our children and their children?

It was here that I learned what it was like to be different and accepted at the same time. At an early age I begin listening to classical music, reading books, and visiting museums. These were not common activities that children in my neighborhood engaged in. Although I had to endure the teasing of others, they also totally accepted me along with my differences into the group. They often said, "Oh, Shirley likes those strange activities but she's really ok." My mother continually reinforced the view that each and every one of her children were different and should not, could not, and would not be compared to one another or to others.

During this time I discovered that gender and race did matter. It influenced the advice given, expectations held, and choices available to me. Growing up there were places that I could not go to or games that I could not play, just because I was a girl. I remember having to sit in the balcony of the movie theater because I was African American. Yet, my mother and brothers not only advocated but also encouraged me to defy the expected. It is because of this solid and stable upbringing that I am able to risk and explore. I am able to move around, travel, and try new things because I know where home is. I know where my support is. It does not matter if I fail or succeed, my family will be there. They are my strength. They have allowed me to defy the expected.

To Risk

A willingness to risk is another component to being culturally competent. We go through our lives constantly calculating risks. It may seem unwise or scary but, if we are to make progress and to change, it entails risks. I have taken many risks along this journey. The two biggest risks have centered on career choice and being the only one, the only

African American. These two issues somehow went hand in hand. This challenge first appeared during my last year in high school. I was selected to participate in a citywide, advanced science class offered by the Museum of Natural History. Top students were selected from the district high schools. These students would spend the mornings at their regular school and the afternoons at the museum. They would work and study with curators and participate in all of the activities of the museum, including expeditions for animals to display.

I was very excited about this opportunity. When my mother and I, along with an aunt, attended the orientation for the program, I realized that I would be the only African American student out of the 21 students in the class. Naturally my mother was concerned. This was expressed and discussed at a family gathering on whether or not I would participate in the class. The prevailing voice came from my aunt who said, "I know that she will be the only African American in the program, but think about the educational opportunity. We can't deny her this because of our fears. If she really wants to do this we must let her. Besides, we will always be here to support her."

This challenge presented itself again in the selection of a college, "Do I attend an Historically Black College/University or a predominately White American College/University?" I selected a predominately White American University. It was strange being the only African American in a class of 100 students and one of six African Americans in the freshman dorm of over 300 girls. Most of my schooling as well as professional career has been spent "being the only one."

The actual preparation and pursuit of a health care career also created another point of risk. This integration process became a source of conflict, confusion, and discord. It created an internal battle on how to preserve my ethnic and cultural traditions, roles, values, and lifestyle while tapping into the American dream of success. It was during this process that the term "bicultural" became real. With increased exposure to knowledge, ideas, and differences, I was no longer a true part of my traditional culture, nor was I a part of the White American group either. There were limited topics or issues that I could talk about with my old neighborhood friends. At the same time, I could not talk about cultural issues that were important to me with my White American friends. I truly became bicultural, functioning in both worlds without really belonging to either.

Yet, we must follow our own paths. No one can forcefully point you in one direction or another. We pick and discard among the influences that are presented to us. Many people are afraid of taking even the smallest chances. They cling to routines as if they are life rafts. Taking risks allows you to truly feel alive.

To Explore

Most of us are eager to determine our own political, philosophical, and temperamental style—to define who we are, what we believe, and how we think and react to things. In order to find this personal style, we try on a lot of different attitudes, organizations, and philosophies (or "hats"). To be culturally skilled you must explore and experiment, try on different ideas, customs, and lifestyles. A career in occupational therapy has provided me with the means and mechanisms to explore a variety of cultures and to learn about people. To continue my journey to be culturally competent, I sought out experiences and employment opportunities in places whose cultures were different from my own—north to Minnesota, the Navajo Reservation, the border towns of Mexico, the rural areas of Texas, and the East Coast life of Maryland and Washington, DC. I have also experienced traveling through England and Germany, meeting people, learning about their culture, and discovering our similarities and differences.

Life is not designed to stay the same. It is constantly changing. We have permission to try new things and new hats all the time. Exploring provides knowledge of the values, customs, language, and interaction with people. It gives an understanding about the influences on our behaviors, lifestyle, and beliefs. It encourages questioning the stereotypes we hold about others as well as ourselves. Talk with your clients, colleagues, and friends. Exchange stories. Share your culture.

To Change

When we allow ourselves to change, we become pioneers and explorers. We push our limits, expand our boundaries, and take control. Paving the way for others and changing negative attitudes and assumptions about persons of colors and women become a responsibility to change. I remember a job interview process for the director of an occupational therapy department. The hospital was located in an area known for its *red neck* attitude. The first interview went according to traditional interview procedures. I was asked back for a second interview even though no other candidate was asked for a second interview. This time the group included the two rehabilitation physicians—a cardiologist and an orthopedist—and a hospital administrator. As we sat around the conference room table, no one spoke, and heads were held down. Finally one of the physicians said, "Shirley, we are impressed with your credentials and experiences. We feel that you are the most qualified person for the job. [Silence.] I'm just going to put this on the table—I have a problem with the fact that you are Black." This statement did not surprise me. I was glad that the topic had finally been addressed openly. I simply asked, "Why do you have a problem with my racial identity?" He stated, "I had a bad experience working with a Black physician in the past." He continued to explain his experience and concerns.

To say the least, after some lengthy and frank discussions, the job was offered to me. My initial reaction was not to accept it. Yet, I did accept the job. Providing a positive interaction and encounter for those with racist and sexist prejudices may lead them to at least doubt or acknowledge that people should be judged for who they are and not what they look like. My working relationship had a positive outcome on the physicians. They both apologized to me for their fears and beliefs within the first year.

The reality is that change is inevitable. We must learn to trust our intuition and instincts for what is right. Every small positive change we can make in ourselves and others repays us in confidence in the future. Every day is a new experience for me. Despite all the roles—student, teacher, friend, colleague, and explorer—that I have had, the journey to being a culturally competent individual is not completed. I am always evolving, changing, and reevaluating. All of my experiences—good and bad—were part of the process of going beyond awareness. They have not only enriched my life, but also the lives of those around me. My circle of friends is a rainbow of people—educators, laborers, African American, White American, Hispanic, Jewish, disabled, male, female, and a host of others. This circle of friends is forever changing in variety, perspectives, and philosophies.

Principles in Being Culturally Competent

Through my experiences, I have learned several principles that guide my interaction with others, including the following:

• Expect every person to be unique and different.

• The culture and lifestyle of people do matter.

• Every individual is shaped and affected by his or her culture.

• Be cognizant of gender and age.

- Be flexible and adaptable in your approach.

- Know yourself. Be aware of your own values, culture, and biases.

- Be aware of discriminatory intent versus discriminatory effect.

- Listen and view the world from the perspective of the others.

- Be an agent of change.

Conclusion

Going beyond "awareness" means taking responsibility for your own learning and growth. It opens you up to the adventures of life. It demands looking for the commonality among us; it demands direct as well as indirect contact with different groups of people; and it demands working through the doubts and questioning of beliefs that occur as a result of cultural conflicts and education. Being culturally skilled insists on tolerance, openness, and a sense of inquiry regarding human variety and ambiguities. It means balancing sensitivity, awareness, knowledge, and skills.

We are who we are. We must build from that point. Being culturally competent requires a lifetime of learning, risking, exploring, and changing. It requires balancing self-exploration with attitude, knowledge, perception, skill, and behavior. We can go beyond "awareness of" and "sensitive to" differences.

 *Appendix*

Attitudes, Beliefs, and Practices
Related to Health and Illness Across Cultures

Views of the Body

The concept of appropriate shape and size as well as decoration of the body varies from culture to culture.

Size: What is considered an acceptable or desirable body size varies. In the U.S., there is a tendency to encourage a thin body to the point of anorexia in women. In parts of Western Africa, artificial fattening of girls is practiced to make them more appealing for marriage (Helman, 1990).

Shape and Appearance: The manipulation of body shape may be partly cultural. Scarring of chest and limbs is seen in Central Africa; tattooing in Tahiti and the U.S.; female circumcision in Africa; male in the United States. Self-mutilation is common in Western societies as noted by orthodontics, plastic surgery, dieting to produce a thin body, etc. (Helman, 1990).

Body Parts: In some cultures, the soul is believed to be attached to parts of the body. Thus surgery may be perceived as a threat to life if parts are removed or the body is cut open, allowing the soul to escape (Dinh, Ganesan, & Waxler-Morrison, 1990, p. 202). Hindus may consider the loss of a limb a sign that one has done something wrong in a previous life. Orthodox Jews and Roman Catholics may require burial of the amputated limb. Many Jehovah's Witnesses do not condone organ transplants (Pumphrey, 1977).

Blood: Blood may be seen as finite in amount in many cultures across the world. Any blood loss may be seen as permanent, causing the individual

Source: Schulz, M. (1999). *Respectful Practice Manual.* Published by Respectful Practice Workshops, 1616 Utica Street, Denver, CO, 80204. © 1999 Monica Schulz. Reprinted with permission.

prolonged weakness (Helman, 1990). Among Cambodians and Laotians, blood tests may not be considered acceptable due to the belief that a person who is already physically compromised should not be weakened further by the removal of blood (Richardson, 1990, p. 26). Blood transfusions are forbidden for most Jehovah's Witnesses because they are conceived to be a form of "eating blood", which is forbidden in the text of their Bible (Watch Tower, 1989).

Views of Illness

Germ Theory (Biomedical model): A belief system based on the idea that illness is caused by exposure to viral, bacterial and parasitic organisms. There are rational, scientific explanations for the presence of illness (Chrisman, 1986).

Equilibrium Theory: Illness is believed to be caused by an imbalance within the body. How this imbalance is understood and balance restored depends on the belief system. The concept of equilibrium may be expanded to include the idea that health is dependent on harmonious relationships among elements of the universe: humans, environment and the supernatural world (Native American, Chinese) (Chrisman, 1986).

Body As A Machine Theory: Descartes, in the 17th century, introduced his "man-as-a-machine" model, separating the body and the mind. The body is seen as an organism that is run by an engine dependent on certain fuels. Parts may fail or wear out and need to be replaced. The mind is seen as a computer; mental illness seen as faulty "wiring" within the brain. Statements such as, "Your heart isn't pumping well", "I've got my wires crossed" and "your batteries needs recharging" reflect the Body As A Machine theory (Helman, 1990).

Intermediary Theory: Belief that sickness and other misfortunes are caused by the malevolent action of supernaturally powerful human beings and require the intervention of intermediary healers in order to regain health. This view of illness is found among Southern Europeans, African Americans, Native Americans, Latin Americans and Filipinos (Chrisman, 1986). "Hexes" or spells arise when spirits or demons cause illness on their own or on behalf of another person (conjuration). Hexes may be placed on a person because of resentment, jealousy, love or envy (Ness & Wintrob, 1981). The belief that someone can cast the "evil eye" and therefore cause illness is an example (Chrisman, 1986). Healing is administered through the interventions of shamans, voodoo priests and other healers.

G-d and Spirit Theory: Explains illness as being caused by actions of supernatural beings (Chrisman, 1986).

Among Puerto Ricans and some Latin Americans, spirits are believed to be present in all aspects of everyday life and subsequently, to influence health and illness.

For Asian Americans, traditional beliefs support the idea that ancestral spirits may send physical or mental illness as punishment when family obligations are not tended to (Lin & Lin, 1981).

Violation of taboos among Native Americans may mean supernatural punishment to the individual and family (Chrisman, 1986, p. 66).

In Christian belief systems, G-d may be involved in illness in the following ways: "the illness may be a test of faith, a punishment for sin, or simply as an unknowable part of G-d's plan" (Chrisman, 1986, p. 67).

Holistic Theory: Holistic theory is based on the belief that natural healing can occur through self-regenerative processes that influence the mind, body, emotions and spirit. This healing is achieved through methods that open the client to spiritual healing forces. The client is perceived to be responsible for her/his own well being and is assisted in accessing inner resources that will bring about wellness (Fuller, 1989).

Exploring a Patient's Understanding of Their Illness and Expectations for Treatment

Kleinman, Eisenberg and Good (1978) suggest using an explanatory model to determine how a client conceptualizes her/his illness. The following questions may assist you with this process:

• What do you think caused your illness?

• Why do you think it started when it did?

• What do you fear most about your illness?

• What are the main problems your illness has caused?

• How severe is it?

• What kind of treatment do you think you should receive?

Culture and Health Care

General Approaches

Dual use: The practice of consulting medical practitioners simultaneously who have different beliefs and approaches related to health. This is seen commonly among people in the United States who utilize naturopathic medicine and alternative healing methods while continuing to use Western medicine as their primary method for restoring health (Chrisman, 1983).
Note: See Dyck's article for case study of client who employed "dual use".

Hierarchy of resort: This refers to the practice of consulting with a series of more specialized or powerful practitioners when previous healing methods have failed. An example is a patient who has cancer and seeks natural healing after traditional medicine has proved unsuccessful (Chrisman, 1983).

Exclusive use: The practice of selecting one approach to healing and not varying from it (Chrisman, 1986).

Specific Approaches to Treatment According to View of Illness

The following section explores Non-Western and Western approaches to treating physical ailments. It is quite probable that patients will use a variety of methods that may or may not originate from their culture. Therefore, none of the information provided below is definitive for any cultural group. For example, North American culture has traditionally valued Western or scientific medical approaches. Yet, many Americans are beginning to use other healing methods, such as acupuncture or herbal remedies, as methods to regain health.

Some of the healing approaches listed are administered by lay practitioners and folk healers. Folk or non-traditional healers may provide treatment that benefit the client in several ways:

- Folk services are readily available and considered reliable by people in the area

- Folk remedies and treatments may be less expensive

- Folk practitioners use healing methods that are culturally relevant and familiar to the client

- Folk healers are easily accessed if further assistance is needed (Leninger, 1978)

Germ Theory:

Pharmaceuticals: Pharmaceuticals, derived from organic and synthetic chemicals, are used to counteract illness caused by viruses and bacteria in the body. A typical example is the use of antibiotics to combat the flu.

Herbs: Herbal remedies may be used to combat illness caused by exposure to viruses, parasites and bacteria. An example is the use of echinachea to ward off viruses and prevent colds.

Equilibrium Theory:

Traditional Chinese Medicine (TCM): Within Traditional Chinese Medicine, disease is perceived to be caused by an imbalance of Yin and Yang and Zheng Qi (Vachon, 1991). Treatment focuses on re-establishing this balance throughout the system. In TCM, evaluation of patients is done by looking, listening and smelling, asking and palpating (Ke, 1991).

* *Looking:* The practitioner examines posture, complexion, eyes and tongue.

* *Listening/Smelling:* Tone of voice, manner of speaking, and smell is taken into account. Certain body odors, according to ancient teaching, are indicative of specific illnesses.

* *Asking:* The practitioner seeks information on the patient's symptoms.

* *Palpation:* The condition of the skin (hot/cold moist/dry) is examined; areas of pain are noted and six pulses are taken which are "read" in terms of rhythm.

Treatment is prescribed, depending on the composite picture that results from the evaluation. Treatment may consist of herbs, acupuncture, massage, and/or meditation in order to regain balance and health in the body (Ke, 1991). Some families may send their loved one's to their homeland in order to seek traditional Chinese healing (Lai & Yue, 1990, p. 77).

Acupuncture: A system of healing that relieves pain, works as an anaesthetic and can resuscitate coma victims. Balance in energy flow promotes health and is achieved through the placement of needles in the skin. Needles are arranged in relation to twelve major meridians along which the qi (life force) flows. Evidence points to the fact that acupuncture stimulates endorphins in the brain and is effective 60–75% of the time (Ke, 1991).

Coin Rubbing: A practice used by Cambodians and other Southeast Asian cultures in which an area of the body is rubbed with a metal object to relieve headaches, colds, fever and fatigue. The rubbing helps to relieve the body of toxins. This treatment method can cause bruising which may be misperceived as signs of abuse (Richardson, 1990, p. 23).

Cupping: An ailment known by the Vietnamese as bad wind (indicated by high fever, convulsion, and even sudden death) is treated with a method called cupping. Cupping is done by placing a hot cup on the skin until the skin draws upward. When a bruise appears, it indicates that the bad wind or toxins have come to the surface and left the body. This approach attempts to achieve balance by removing toxins from the body (Dihn, Ganeson, & Waxler-Morrison, 1990, p. 194).

Hot and Cold Foods/Substances: Asian, as well as, Latin cultures may use hot and cold foods as well as diet to influence health. Health is believed to be restored through the effect of heat or cold on the body. Hot or cold temperatures are delegated to certain substances including foods, herbs and medicines. Balance is restored in the system by exposure or ingestion of items of the opposite nature to the problem (Helman, 1990).

Native American: Balance is achieved through internal harmony of the physical, mental, and spiritual. These components must also be in balance with one's family and one's environment. To help someone gain balance and harmony, a Medicine Man must "look at what someone is doing wrong vs. what is wrong with someone" (Amoneeta Sequoyah, Eastern Band of Cherokees). Wisdom from the Four Directions guides practices for health and healing (Garrett, 1990).

Body As A Machine Theory:

Western Medicine: Treatment approaches arise mainly from the Western medical model. Examples include surgical correction or removal of deformed, malfunctioning or diseased body parts, and physical treatment such as traction and exercise. Machinery, such as a respirator or insulin pump, may be used to sustain life.

Intermediary Theory:

Voodoo/Root Work: According to Jordan (1990), the terms "voodoos, root work, and roots" all refer to folk medicine practices that originate from Africa and Haiti. A voodoo priest is able to cast out evil spirits and perform healing rituals. The work of the priest/priestess is to maintain harmony with the spirits that serve as intermediaries between G-d and human beings. The spirits control such forces as water, fire, love and death (Camphina-Bacote, 1992). Training includes learning techniques of healing, the functions and remedies of different herbs, and the reading of bones (Jordan, 1990).

Curanderos: Curanderos are Latin/Latino American healers who are able to cast out evil spirits. Illnesses treated include *susto* (soul loss) and *mal puesto* (hex placed by a *bruja* or witch in which the hexed individual experiences auditory and visual hallucinations and agitation). It is estimated that 10% of Mexican Americans use curanderos for healing (Gaw, 1993, p. 450).

G-d and Spirit Healing Theory:

The Spiritualist: The spiritualist is someone who feels called into healing work. Their ability to heal is derived spiritually and is considered a gift from G-d. The Spiritualist's healing is based on Christianity and in the healing power of G-d.

Espiritistas: Espiritismo (spiritism) was originated in 1869 by Alan Kardec, who taught that every human soul is in the process of evolution. During one's lifetime, this evolution may be challenged by hardships and difficulties. One evolves when one is able to move through and overcome these trials. Espiritistas heal through prayer, laying on of hands, and the use of herbs and potions which help to create harmony with the spirit world and move one from a place of discord to a place of peace (Gaw, 1993, p. 485).

Alternative Healers: Psychic healers, channelers and healers who use "laying on of hands" most often indicate that the source of their healing is spiritual in nature.

Holistic Theory:

Reiki: An ancient Buddhist practice, Reiki is as a "laying on of hands" technique that heals by transferring energy to the sick, painful or weak part of the body in an effort to strengthen, balance and promote health (Sell, 1996) (Baginski, 1988).

Trager: Trager therapy is a combination of manual therapy, exercises and a mindful approach on the part of the practitioner in order to produce relief of pain, reintegration of the body and deep relaxation (Ramsey, 1997). The manual therapy is administered through light, non-intrusive movements that work to release physical and mental patterns that develop as a result of injuries, emotional trauma, poor posture and movement patterns (Juhan, 1993).

Therapeutic Touch: Therapeutic touch is a technique developed by Delores Kreiger and Dora Kuntz (Ramsey, 1997). It is effective in producing relaxation, pain reduction and accelerated healing responses (Kreiger, 1975). These responses are elicited through transference of energy from the practitioner to the patient. This is done by holding the hands 3–6 inches away from the body, using the senses to identify areas that have sluggish or excessive energy and balancing that energy through brushing movements in the patient's energy field (Ramsey, 1997).

References

Baginski, B. (1988). *Reiki: The Universal life energy.* Mendocino, Ca.: Life Rhythm Press.

Campinha-Bacote, J. (1992). Voodoo illness. *Perspectives in Psychiatric Care, 28*(1), 11–17.

Chrisman, N. (1986). Transcultural care. In Donna A. Zschoche (Ed.), *Mosby's Comprehensive Review of Critical Care* (3rd ed.) (pp. 58–69). St. Louis: Mosby.

Dihn, D., Ganeson, S., Waxler-Morrison, N. (1990). The Vietnamese. In J. Anderson, E. Richardson, & N. Waxler-Morrison (Eds.), *Cross-cultural caring: A handbook for health professionals.* Vancouver: UBC Press.

Dyck, I. (1992). Managing chronic illness: An immigrant woman's acquisition and use of health care knowledge, *American Journal of Occupational Therapy, 46,* 696–704.

Fuller, R. (1989). *Alternative medicine and American religious life.* New York: Oxford Press.

Garrett, J. (1990). Indian health: Values, beliefs and practices. In M. Harper (Ed.), *Minority aging: Essential curricula content for selected health and allied health professions.* Health Resources Administration, Department of Health and Human Services (DHHS Publication Number HRS P-dv-90-4). Washington, DC: US Government Printing Office.

Gaw, A. (Ed.). (1993). *Culture, ethnicity and mental illness.* Washington, DC: American Psychiatric Press.

Helman, C. (1990). *Culture, health and illness.* Boston: Butterworth-Heinemann.

Jordan, W. (1990). Black American folk medicine. In M. Harper (Ed.), *Minority Aging: Essential curricula content for selected health and allied health professions*. Health Resources Administration, Department of Health and Human Services (DHHS Publication Number HRS P-dv-90-4). Washington, DC: US Government Printing Office.

Juhan, D. (1993). *Multiple Sclerosis: The Trager Approach*. Mill Valley: Trager Institute.

Ke, S. (1991). The point of the cure. *The Observer*, 50–51.

Kleinman, A., Eisenberg, L. & Good, B. (1978). Culture, illness and care: Clinical lessons from anthropologic and cross cultural research. *Annals of Internal Medicine, 88*, 251–258.

Kreiger, D. (1975). Therapeutic touch: The imprimatur of nursing. *American Journal of Nursing, 75*, 784–787.

Lai, M., & Yue, K. (1990). The Chinese. In J. Anderson, E. Richardson & N. Waxler-Morrison (Eds.), *Cross-cultural caring: A handbook for health professionals*. Vancouver: UBC Press.

Leininger, M. (1978). *Transcultural Nursing: Concepts, Theories, and Practices*. New York: John Wiley and Sons.

Lin, T. and Lin, M. (1981). Love, denial and rejection: Responses of Chinese families to mental illness. In A. Kleinman, Netherlands, D. & T. Lin (Eds.), *Normal and abnormal behavior in Chinese culture*, pp. 387–401.

Ness, R. & Wintrob, R. (1981). Folk healing: A description of synthesis. *American Journal of Psychiatry, 138*, 1477–1481.

Pumphrey, J. (1977). Recognizing your patient's spiritual needs. *Nursing, 7*(12), 64–70.

Ramsey, S. (1997). Holistic manual therapy techniques. *Primary Care, 24*(4), 759–785.

Richardson, E. (1990). The Cambodians and Laotians. In J. Anderson, E. Richardson, & N. Waxler-Morrison (Eds.), *Cross-cultural caring: A handbook for health professionals*. Vancouver: UBC Press.

Sell, S. (1996). Reiki: An ancient touch therapy. *RN*, February, 57–59.

Vachon, D. (1991). West meets East: The art of subconscious healing in traditional Chinese medicine and acupuncture. *American Journal of Acupuncture, 19*(1), 37–57.

Watch Tower Bible and Tract Society of Pennsylvania (1989). *Reasoning from the Scriptures: 1989*. Brooklyn, NY: Watch Tower Bible and Tract Society of Pennsylvania.

 *Glossary*

—A—

Ableism: Discriminatory beliefs and behaviors directed against persons with disabilities.

Acculturation: A term used to describe the degree to which people from a particular cultural group display behaviors that are like the more pervasive American norms of behavior.

African or Black American: A generic term that applies to persons who are Americans of African ancestry. However, in recent years there has been notable immigration of Blacks from several Caribbean countries. Because of their shared African roots, many of these people—whether native or foreign born—share common beliefs, practices, attitudes, and values. There is much diversity within this population.

Africentric Orientation: The belief and orientation to African values and form manifested in contemporary African American culture in spirituality, harmony, movement, verve affect communalism, expressive individualism, and social time perspective.

Ageism: Discriminatory beliefs and behaviors directed against people because of their age.

Antilogy: A contradiction in terms or ideas.

Asian American or Pacific Islander: This generic term describes persons whose ethnic heritage is identified with China, Japan, Korea, Southeast Asia, and other Pacific Islands such as Samoa, Guam, and the Philippines. There is great ethnic diversity within the Asian American and Pacific Islander subculture.

Assimilation: The merging of cultural traits; the process of becoming identical or similar to a dominant culture.

—B—

Bias: A tendency or inclination of outlook reflecting a subjective point of view. A strong inclination of the mind. To influence, bend, slant, or lean opinion or feeling, either favorable or unfavorable. To cause prejudice.

Bicultural: Implies the presence and manipulation of two different cultures by one person.

Bigot: Anyone who is obstinately devoted to his or her own opinions, based more on stereotypes and biased sources than on evidence, and intolerant of others and their views.

Biracial: Being of, combining, or representing two different races.

Bisexual: A person who finds sexual pleasure and interest with persons of either gender.

Black English Vernacular: Also called African American language, Black English, African American English, and Ebonics, refers to the language system characteristically spoken in the African American community. It has its own sociolinguistic rules that differ from the standard language used by White Americans and is generally devalued by White Americans.

—C—

Classism: Discriminatory beliefs and behaviors based on differences in social class, generally directed against those from poor or working-class backgrounds.

Clinical Reasoning: The process of integrating the client's history, evaluation, medical information, and cultural context into the individual intervention's plan.

Cultural Capital: Refers to Pierre Bourdieu's concept that different forms of cultural knowledge, such as language, modes of social interaction, and meaning, are valued hierarchically in our society.

Cultural Competence: Refers to the process of actively developing and practicing appropriate, relevant, and sensitive strategies and skills in interacting with culturally different people. The capacity to respond to the needs of populations whose cultures are different from what might be called *dominant* or *mainstream*.

Cultural Group: Persons with common origins, customs, and styles of living.

Cultural Pluralism: An ideal state of societal conditions characterized by equity and mutual respect among existing cultural groups.

Cultural Relativity: The idea that any behavior must be judged first in relation to the context of the culture in which it occurs.

Cultural Values: The standards that people within a cultural group use to evaluate themselves and others. A widely held belief about what is worthwhile, desirable, or important for well-being.

Culture: Refers a set of values, beliefs, traditions, norms, artifacts, and customs. The sum total of a way of living, including values, beliefs, standards, linguistic expression, patterns of thinking, behavioral norms, and styles of communication that influence the behavior(s) of a group of people that is transmitted from generation to generation. It includes demographic variables such as age, gender, and place of residence; status variables such as social, educational, and economic levels; and affiliation variables.

—D—

Discourse: Represents the ways in which reality is perceived through and shaped by historically and socially constructed ways of making sense, that is, language, complex signs, and practices that order and sustain particular forms of social existence.

Discrimination: The overt actions one engages in to exclude, avoid, or distance oneself from another.

   Individual Discrimination: Overt discriminatory acts that one person performs against another.

   Institutional (Organizational) Discrimination: The institution of rules, policies, and practices of the organization that have an adverse effect on nondominant groups of people.

   Structural Discrimination: Discrimination that is found between the fields of employment, education, housing, and government.

Discriminatory Effect: An attitude, policy, or practice that, while not intentional and exclusionary, prevents a person or group of persons from full participation and benefits.

Discriminatory Intent: An attitude, policy, or practice that knowingly excludes a person or group of persons from full participation and benefits.

Diversity: A reference to the varied national, ethnic, and racial backgrounds of U.S. citizens and immigrants; but it also applies to categories of class, gender, age, ability, and sexual orientation.

Dominant Ideologies: Bodies of ideas held by cultural groups that are politically, socially, and economically in positions of power, and are therefore able to impose on the greater society, through various social institutions and practices, particular traditions, bodies of knowledge, discourse styles, language uses, values, norms, and beliefs, often at the expense of others.

—E—

Ethics: The rules of conduct or moral principles recognized in respect to a particular group, culture, or profession.

Ethnic Group: A group of people within a larger society that is socially distinguished or set apart, by others or by itself, primarily on the basis of racial or cultural characteristics, such as religion, language, and tradition.

Ethnicity: A cultural concept in which a large number of people who share the same traits and have a close social interaction regard themselves and are regarded by others as a single group on that basis.

Ethnocentrism: The tendency to view one's own cultural group as the center of everything, the standard against which all others are judged. The belief that one's cultural group is right and must be defended.

Eurocentric Orientation: The belief in the comparative superiority of the Anglo/American culture in particular, and the Euro/American culture in general. It emphasizes Western European values, ethos, and beliefs, valuing mastery over nature, competition, and individuation; and theoretically at least, it emphasizes rigid adherence to time.

—G—

Gay: A generic term for homosexual men and women, and specific to homosexual males. Homosexuals are men and women whose sexual desires or behaviors are directed towards a person of his or her own sex.

—H—

Health Status Data: Describes the well-being or ill health of a population. Data include a variety of measures—mortality, morbidity, and disability rates.

Hegemony: A term used to express how certain groups manage to dominate others. An analysis of hegemony is especially concerned with how the imposition of particular ideologies and forms of authority results in the reproduction of social and institutional practices through which dominant groups maintain not only their positions of privilege and control, but also the consensual support of other members of society.

Heterosexism: Discriminatory beliefs and behaviors directed against gay men, lesbian women, bisexuals, and transgendered persons.

Hispanic: A collective designation (in the United States) for any person of Spanish-speaking background or who has a Spanish surname. Included within this group are persons of Mexican ancestry, Cubans, Puerto Ricans, and people from many Central and South American countries. People within this subculture share many characteristics, values, traditions, and customs; yet there are important differences among and within specific Hispanic groups.

—I—

Inclusion: Refers to the belief that all individuals should be able to participate fully in the activities of life with the same benefits and opportunities.

Individual with a Disabling Condition: A person with a physical or mental impairment that substantially limits at least one of that person's major life activities; an individual with a record of such impairment; and an individual regarded as having such an impairment.

Internalized Oppression: This occurs when a member(s) of an oppressed group comes to believe in the dominant group's description of them as *inferior.* As a result of such oppression, people often attempt to assimilate into the dominant culture.

—J—

Jargon: Specialized or technical language of a profession that may serve to separate professionals from their clients, rather than supporting effective communication and dialogue.

—K—

Knowledge: Refers to the process of acquiring specific and extensive information about the language, values, customs, and beliefs of another culture. It is knowing *what, who, where,* and *how* to ask for and obtain information and to use it to modify, adapt, and develop appropriate cultural interaction.

—L—

Latino(a): A Latin or Hispanic man or woman, someone sometimes broadly designated as an Ibero-American. Some Hispanics prefer the term *Latino(a)* because it takes into consideration not only the language, but also gender, and the country of origin and shared cultural heritage.

Lesbian: A homosexual woman; a woman whose sexual interest and behavior focuses on other women.

Linguistic Style: The manner in which one uses words and language and incorporates features such as pronunciation, intonation, grammatical variants, and choices of vocabulary. Linguistic style is influenced by cultural characteristics.

—M—

Marginalize: To force an individual or a group out of mainstream society, limiting their access to political or economic power, or to push ideas and concepts that conflict with dominant ideologies to the fringes of academic debate, labeling them as important only to special interest groups.

Minority Group (in terms of subordinate position): A group of persons who, because of their physical or cultural characteristics, are singled out from others in the society in which they live for differential and unequal treatment, and who therefore regard themselves as objects of collective discrimination.

Multicultural: Denotes the maintenance of several distinct cultural or subcultural forms.

Multicultural Education: A philosophy of education that challenges and rejects racism and other forms of discrimination in schools and society. It permeates the curriculum and teaching strategies used in schools, promoting the democratic principles of social justice.

Multicultural Perspective: Represents the process of looking at cultural phenomena from multiple perspectives, including the culture in which the interaction occurs, cultures of the individuals involved, and culture of the society.

Multiculturalism: The process in which one has mastered the knowledge and developed the necessary skills to feel comfortable and communicate effectively with people of any culture, as well as being able to bridge differences.

—N—

Native American or American Indian: This is a generic term that applies to persons who are native to the continental United States and Alaska. *First Americans* is another name given to American Indians, and it emphasizes their presence in this hemisphere before Columbus' landing.

—P—

Persons of Color: Denotes non-White American ethnic persons; it is less offensive than racial minority because it does not imply a lesser status than that of White Americans.

Prejudice: An erroneous judgment, usually negative, which is based on incomplete or faulty information. Any preconceived opinion or feeling, either favorable or unfavorable. Unreasonable feelings, opinions, or attitudes, especially of a hostile nature, directed against any group of persons.

Privilege: Freedoms and benefits offered to certain people based on sociocultural power and status.

—R—

Race: An erroneous concept used to divide humankind into broad categories according to physical characteristics, such as size and shape of head, eyes, ears, lips, nose, and the color of skin and eyes. A categorization in which a large number of people sharing visible physical characteristics regard themselves or are regarded by others as a single group on that basis.

Racial Minority: One whose "members are readily identified by distinctly physical characteristics that are perceived as different from those of other members of society, such as skin color, hair type, body structure, shape of head, nose or eyes" (Axelson, 1985, p. 125).

Racism: A system of privilege and penalty based on one's race; a belief in the inherent superiority of some persons and inherent inferiority of others based on race.

> *Cultural Racism:* The use of power by White Americans to perpetuate their cultural heritage and impose it upon others, while at the same time destroying the culture of ethnic minorities.

> *Individual Racism:* The belief that one's own race is superior to another (i.e., racial prejudice) and behavior that suppresses members of the so-called inferior race (i.e., racial discrimination).

Institutional Racism: Consists of established laws, customs, and practices that systematically reflect and produce racial inequalities in American society, whether or not the persons maintaining those practices have racist intentions.

—S—

Self-Exploration: The process of looking inward; being aware of and taking responsibility for one's own emotions, attitudes, behaviors, and perceptions; and using this knowledge of self when interacting with others.

Sexism: Discriminatory beliefs and behaviors based on one's gender, usually directed at women.

Skill: Refers to acquiring as well as mastering strategies, techniques, and approaches for communicating and interacting with persons from different cultures.

Social Location: A person's placement in class, gender, racial, age, geographical, and national groups that shapes that person's identity.

Sociocultural Power: The capacity to produce desired effects on others. It can be perceived as mastery over self as well as over nature and other people.

Stereotype: The well-learned, widely shared, socially validated general beliefs or cognitions about disempowered groups that reinforce or justify prejudice and reduce ambiguity. An exaggerated belief, concept, idea, or image about a person or group of persons that is held and sustained by selective perception and selective forgetting.

—T—

Tolerance: A fair and objective attitude toward those whose opinions, practices, race, religion, nationality, sexual orientation, or the like, differ from one's own. A liberal spirit toward the views and action of others. Celebrating diversity.

Transcultural: Implies a bridging of notable differences in cultural and communication style, beliefs, or practices.

—V—

Voice: Refers to people's authentic self-expression, where one is speaking with integrity and from a position of self-empowerment, or even liberation.

—W—

White Privilege: Unearned freedoms and benefits given to people based on race and ethnicity alone.

Reference

Axelson, J. (1985). *Counseling and development in a multicultural society.* Monterey, CA: Brooks-Cole.

 *Index*

Note: Study data is indexed under the ethnic term used in the study

mastectomy treatment, 34
Medicaid, 32, 38
medical ethics, 51–52
Mexican Americans
    case studies, 238–239, 245–246
    decision-making, attitudes toward,
        58
    poverty rate among children, 23
    primary care access, 31
migrant workers, 38. *see also* farm
        workers
minority groups, term defined, 280
modules, 209–210
morals, 49–53, **51**
mortality rates, 18, **19**
multicultural education, 159–167,
        207–213
multicultural perspective, 280
multiculturalism, 125–127, 148,
        174–175

N
names, as exercise of power, 117, 119
narrative reasoning, 221
National Center for Health Statistics,
        16
National Coalition Building Institute,
        165, 258
Native Americans. *see also* American
        Indians
    case studies, 244–245, 246
    issues in health care, **236**
    negativity, avoidance of, 47
    OMB classification standards, 76
    and use of health care services, 36
Navajos, 27, 58
negativity, 56, 58, 247–248
neoconservative thought, 126–127
newborns, 68
normative ethics, 48

O
obesity prevalence, 27
obligations. *see* ethics
occupational therapy, cultural
        competency in, **154**
Office of Management and Budget,
        U.S., **76**
Oklahoma nations, 27
open-mindedness, in teachers, 142
oppression, internalized, 279

osteoporosis prevalence, 21, 26–27
outsiders' point of view, 68

P
participation, in learning process,
        202–203
pathological model of research, 70
patient disclosure, 56–58
patient evaluation, 223–224, **226**,
        228, **229**
patients. *see* clients
personal development, author's story,
        255–259
personal ethics, 48
persons of color, 281
pesticides, 21
physicians
    cultural differences, 61–62
    visit frequency, 30
points of view, 68
policy bioethics, 54
political correctness, 125–127
population, U.S., 5–8
poverty rates, 23–24
power
    and discrimination, 107, 109–111
    origins and exercise of, 102–107
    in patient-provider relationships, 59
pragmatic reasoning, 222
prejudice, 107, 111–113
prejudices, overcoming, 263–264
primary care access to, 31
principlism, 49
privilege, 281
problem setting, **226**, 226–227
procedural reasoning, 222
professional language. *see* jargon
providers, health care, 11, 61–62
Public Health Service, 16–17
public interest. *see* social good
Puerto Ricans, 23, 27

R
race
    data on, 73–78
    as determinant of health care, 33
    OMB classification standards, **76**
    vs. class, 24
    vs. ethnicity, 74
regulatory bioethics, 54
Reiki, 273